PREPAID ADVERTISEMENTS INSERTED IN THE "LEICESTER DAILY MERCURY."

SITUATIONS WANTED, SITUATIONS VACANT, APARTMENTS WANTED, APARTMENTS TO BE LET, PARTNERSHIPS WANTED, MONEY WANTED, MISCELLANEOUS WANTS, HOUSES AND OTHER PREMISES TO BE LET OR SOLD, SPECIFIC ARTICLES FOR SALE BY PRIVATE CONTRACT.

Advertisements of the above class are now inserted in the *Chronicle and Mercury* at the following charges:—

Words.	One Insertion. s. d.	Three Insertions. s. d.	Six Insertions. s. d.
20	0 6	1 0	2 0
40	1 0	2 0	4 0
50	1 6	3 0	4 6
60	2 0	4 0	5 6

And ½d. per word for every additional word.

This Scale applies *strictly* to the class of advertisements above enumerated, and must be PREPAID, otherwise the ordinary scale charge will be made.

Remittances may be made in Stamps.

The *Leicester Daily Mercury* is published every afternoon (except Friday). Advertisements of the above class ordered six times, will have the advantage of one insertion in the weekly paper.

Wanted.

WANTED a Respectable YOUTH as an Apprentice. Must have had a fair education.—Apply to the OVERSEER at the Office of this Paper.

STOCKINGMAKERS.—Wanted, good hands for broad and narrow frames, by DICKSONS and LAINGS, Hawick. 156

WANTED, an APPRENTICE to a Carpenter and Joiner.—Apply, R. H. G. BARNETT, Builder, Queen-street, Leicester. 175

A PERSON, age 21, requires a situation as FIRST CLERK in a good office. Highest references.—Address, M.H., *Chronicle and Mercury* Office. 346

A GENTLEMAN, as BOARDER, can be received in a quiet family, in the best part of the town.—Apply by letter, W. G. O., Post Office, Leicester. 260

WANTED, a daily GOVERNESS.—Apply by letter to "W.," care of Messrs. Jacobs and Kennard, Atlas House, Leicester. 323

WANTED a respectable YOUTH, as an apprentice to the Grocery Business.—Apply to J. LANDER, High-street, Loughborough. 315

WANTED, by a Gentleman having a private income, any LIGHT OCCUPATION or place of trust, which would occupy him some hours daily.—Apply, G. P. O., Post Office, Leicester. 261

THE Great Seer of England will reveal YOUR FUTURE.—Seven years, six stamps; Life time, twelve; Love Charm, sixteen. State age.—Methratton, 22, Post-office, Daventry. 252

PAVER DRESSERS WANTED.

GOOD HANDS will find constant employment with liberal remuneration on application to Mr. T.P. GOWLAND, the Foreman at the Whinstone Quarries.—Middleton in Teesdale, County of Durham. 23

TO PARENTS AND GUARDIANS.

T. S. HARRIS and SON, Wellington-street, have a vacancy for a respectable YOUTH in their Office. Terms on application. 147

WANTED, immediately, in a Ladies' School, an ARTICLED PUPIL, on most advantageous terms. Instruction given in thorough English, French, music, and class-singing, in return for moderate premium, and some assistance with the junior pupils.—Address H., 16, Spring Hill, Birmingham. 305

A YOUNG MAN, possessing a knowledge of the hosiery trade, is desirous to represent a Leicester HOUSE, in Lancashire and Yorkshire. Either for Salary or on Commission. Good reference.—Apply BETA, Post Office, Halifax. 356

WANTED, a JUNIOR TEACHER (non-resident) in a private Boy's School. Letters stating age, qualifications, salary, &c., to be addressed ALEPH, Post Office, Leicester. 351

TO FARMERS, DEALERS, &c.,

WANTED, at once, a supply of Geese, Ducks, Turkeys Fowls, Rabbits, and Game.—Those having any Poultry fattening for Christmas are also invited to sent particulars. Best prices in the trade given. Bankers or trade references if required.—Apply to W. BARNES, "The Eagle" Provision Stores, Eagle-street, City-road, London, E.C. 3285

To be Sold, or Let.

BEDROOM to be Let, very centrally situated.—Address, 45, *Chronicle and Mercury* Office, Leicester. 314

TO BE DISPOSED OF, An old-established Tobacco Business, with House in a good thoroughfare. The Stock and Fixtures to be taken at a Valuation.—Address, W. G. *Chronicle and Mercury* Office. 324

BLAST FURNACE CINDERS suitable for repairing and making roads, to be had at 1s. per ton, at the Bedworth Coal and Iron Co. limited.—Apply to P. A. …WARD, Secretary. 76

TO PRINTERS, BOOKBINDERS, &c.

TO be Disposed of, the BUSINESS of the late Mr. J. H. Beazeley.—For particulars apply at the Office, 38, Belvoir-street, Leicester. 3580

TO MANUFACTURERS.—To be LET in the centre of Leicester a FACTORY or WAREHOUSE, with 10-horse power STEAM ENGINE; also a House and Shop.—Enquire of W. F. Bramley, 40, Granby-street. 2872

TO BE LET, with immediate possession,

AVENUE HOUSE, Avenue-road, Stoneygate, near Leicester; a detached villa residence, with drawing, dining, breakfast, and five bedrooms, two cellars, kitchen, w.c., washhouse, greenhouse, lawn and garden planted with shrubs, fruit and other trees.—Apply to Mr. THOS. WEBSTER, Avenue-road. 180

TO BE SOLD OR LET,

HAVELOCK-STREET WORKS, late in the occupation of Messrs. John Whitehead and Sons, comprising, Factory, 3-storeys—100ft. by 32ft, with shed attached—75ft. by 16ft.; warehouse, 3-storeys—70ft. by 18ft., with counting house 2-storey building in yard—42ft. by 18ft.; mechanics' shop—28ft. by 16ft.; engine house and two boiler houses with chimney shaft—100ft. high; and large and convenient yard, well secured.—For further particulars, and to view the same, apply THOS. BLAND, Builder, Redcross-street. 242

MOTIVE POWER.—In any case where small power is required, under circumstances in which it is not desirable at great expense to erect a tall chimney, for carrying away smoke; or in concerns where it is found expedient to stop or set on machinery in a minute or so, at meal-hours—the GAS ENGINE proves exceedingly useful and convenient. A three-horse power engine of this kind, in good condition, is TO BE SOLD, at moderate price.—Apply to Mr. EVANS, Manager, *Chronicle and Mercury* Office, Leicester.

TO BE SOLD BY PRIVATE CONTRACT,

EIGHT WELL-BUILT COTTAGES, and likewise a HOUSE, SHOP, and BAKEHOUSE, with Store-room and Dwelling-house adjoining, in Gresham-street, Belgrave-road. The above property is substantially built, and has been recently papered. Will be Sold to pay a good rate of Interest.

Inquire of John White, Church-gate; Messrs. Porter and Taylor; or at

Messrs. STONE and BILLSON.

N.B.—The House, Shop, and Bakehouse, to be Let. 331

Contracts.

TO BUILDERS.

TENDERS are required for the erection of a house-warehouses, stabling, &c., at Hinckley, Leicestershire, for Messrs. Chawner.

Plans and Specifications may be seen, and quantities obtained at our offices, 12, Horsefair-street, Leicester, on and after THURSDAY, the 29th inst.

No pledge given to accept the lowest or any Tender.

BURTON and WILLOUGHBY, Architects.

January 22nd, 1874. 289

WAR OFFICE CONTRACTS.

…ders will be received on or before the 10th …ruary ne… the supply of HOSIERY … to patterns and …ation of the …

THE "DAILY MERCURY" OF MONDAY NEXT, FEB. 2, WILL CONTAIN

Meeting of Mr. Hussey Packe's Supporters at Ashby-de-la-Zouch: Full Report of the Speeches.

Meeting of Liberal Electors at Lee-street School: Addresses by Messrs. Taylor and McArthur.

Meetings of Mr. Warner's Supporters.

FULL RETURN of all the BOROUGH NOMINATIONS throughout England, Ireland, Scotland, and Wales.

Latest Election Movements, Sporting, Markets, and Foreign and Home Intelligence, by Telegraph, &c., &c.

PRICE ONE HALFPENNY.

May be had from

Mr. Hewitt, Granby-street.
Mr. Oldershaw, Granby-street.
Mr. Bent, Town-hall-lane.
Mr. Catlow, Humberstone-gate.
Mrs. Emery, Belgrave-gate.
Mr. Bradley, Welford-road, &c., &c.

First Edition, 3 o'clock; Second Edition, 6 o'clock.

The Leicester Daily Mercury,

SATURDAY, JANUARY 31, 1874.

THE SOUTHERN DIVISION.

"*Alea est jacta.*" The die is cast. The Liberal Party in South Leicestershire has put everything to venture, and must now stand the hazard. Its champion, T. T. Paget, Esq., of Humberstone, who sat once as its representative and who, regardless of temporary defeats, still presses on to ultimate victory, has announced himself its candidate, in response to the invitation of the largest meeting of Liberal electors of the Southern Division ever held in Leicester.

Mr. Paget's connections and sentiments, in relation to national politics, are too well known to need detailed explanation in this place; but we invite attention to his address, which appeared in our late edition of last (Friday) evening. From that it will be seen that Mr. Paget has no scruples about declaring himself a party man: he "knows" too well that Liberals not well organized under a leader whom they can trust are but a "rope of sand," and that to be useful he must serve loyally under a political captain, without menacing desertion or "sulking in a corner." Hence, it will be seen, the Liberal candidate avows himself to be desirous of being returned to Parliament "proud to support Mr. Gladstone's Government," and he tells the constituency it will be for them "to say whether—weary of progress and tired of improvement"—they are prepared to return to a period of Tory Misrule and obstructive policy, or, on the other hand, whether they believe with him "that the chapter of progress is by no means closed, and that the stream of improvement will flow on, year by year, irresistibly strengthening and extending in its salutary course." Mr. Paget further declares himself an advocate of Income Tax Abolition and a Free Breakfast Table.

But the special claims of Mr. Paget on a rural constituency are something in addition to and besides all this: he is himself a considerable landowner who is known to be liberal in his dealings with his own tenants, who does not exact a double rent by game-preserving, who is favourable to the compensation of out-going tenants for unexhausted improvements, and who is prepared to help in rendering the holding and transfer of the soil freer from artificial restrictions than at the present time. He is also friendly to an extension of the suffrage in the counties. We may ask whether Mr. Pell or Mr. Heygate is as Liberal or as progressive as this? Whether as much can with truth be said of either of them as can be said of Mr. Paget? We may assert, without fear of successful contradiction, that the Liberal candidate stands, in all the respects here indicated, far before either of the Tory candidates. Now, this being the case, it is the bounden duty of every Liberal agriculturist—we may say of *every* agriculturist who knows his own interest—to vote for Mr. Paget, and to use his influence with his friends to induce them to do the like, on the day of polling. Fortunately, the Ballot is now an "accomplished fact," and the county elector may, if he will, freely exercise his franchise. Let him show that he appreciates the advantage he now possesses, and that the Ballot is not a failure, by voting for Mr. Paget.

It is incumbent, moreover, on every friend of Progress in the Southern Division to strain every nerve, to exert every effort, to employ every energy in this crisis of the National history, in asserting his principles. The most popular, patriotic, and distinguished of modern statesmen has challenged a conflict with his opponents on this issue—Is the country to be governed for some years to come on the principles of Conservative Reaction or Liberal Progress? It becomes therefore a matter of duty, on the part of every Liberal, to use his utmost exertions to answer the question in the affirmative; to fail in this emergency, to be a recreant in such an hour, would render a man self-abased in his own eyes and those of his fellows. If South Leicestershire does not bestir itself at this time, on behalf of a candidate to whom the Liberals owe so much, for his unflinching courage and unsparing zeal on their behalf, it will virtually disfranchise itself, and sink back into a species of medieval serfdom and political annihilition "Now or never," then, is the party cry. Without extravagance it may be said the Liberal party must "awake, arise, or be for ever fallen."

One word more: the contest for South Leicestershire is no "forlorn hope." We are informed, on the best authority, that as the result of quiet but vigilant attention to the Register, since the last election, the number of Liberals upon it exceeds by a good majority that of the Tories. If, then, they are only true to themselves, their cause, and their country, by polling for the Liberal candidate, they must be triumphant in the pending conflict.

Mr. Paget will be at HINCKLEY on Monday, and at MELTON MOWBRAY on Tuesday evening next, to meet his friends and supporters.

Local Intelligence.

The laying down of the tramway rails have been commenced. The first rail was laid on Tuesday, near the horse-trough, on the Belgrave-road.

At the Town Hall yesterday, an application was made for an extension of time on the occasion of the officers of the Volunteers' dinner last night, but the Bench refused to grant the request.

THE BOROUGH CANDIDATES AND THE PROTESTANT ALLIANCE.—We are informed that a deputation from the Leicester branch of the Protestant Alliance has had an interview with each of the candidates for the borough, and that the deputation received very cordial and satisfactory replies to the questions put; each candidate expressing a full determination to oppose the progress of Romish aggression.

THE SPRING ASSIZES.—The duty for the Norfolk circuit have now been fixed:—(Mr. Justice Blackburn and Mr. Justice Brett.)—Oakham, Monday, March 2; Leicester, Tuesday, March, 3; Northampton, Saturday, March 7; Aylesbury, Thursday, March 12; Bedford, Monday, March 16; Huntington, Thursday, March 19; Cambridge, Saturday, March 21; Norwich, Thursday, March 26; and Ipswich, Wednesday, April 1.

ENTERTAINMENT.—Under arrangements made by Mr. S. Tebbutt, an entertainment consisting of dramatic and pianoforte recitals was given in the New Lecture Hall, Wellington-street, on Thursday evening last. There was a very fair attendance, considering the number of political meetings being held in the town. Mr. Pennington's dramatic recitals were exceedingly well received, and the same may be said with regard to the pianoforte executions … …ored for the brilliant … elf in the rondo … grand valse

THE CANDIDATURE OF MR. E. S. ELLIS.

TO THE EDITOR OF THE LEICESTER DAILY MERCURY.

Sir,—It having been stated at the meeting in the Corn Exchange, and also from the communication I received from the solicitors of Mr. Ellis, that I posted and delivered the bills containing his address recently circulated, I beg to state most emphatically that I was not employed either to post or deliver them; and as there was no printer's name attached, I should have refused to post them under any circumstances. Trusting this explanation will prove satisfactory to all concerned in the above,

I remain,
Yours faithfully,
C. W. ADCOCK, Jun.

16, Clarence-street.

TOWN HALL,

SATURDAY.—*Before W. Bowmar, Esq.*

THEFT.—*Edward Crane* was charged with stealing a quantity of paper from the warehouse of Mr. J. Webster, Bowling-green-street, on Thursday last.—Prisoner went to the Stockdale Arms on Thursday night and saw a person named Charles Harding, and said he had some paper to sell. Harding had been called upon previously by the detectives respecting some paper which had been stolen from Mr. Crofts, and he told prisoner to fetch it. He did not pay prisoner, but told him he would see him again, and afterwards brought the paper to the police station. Prisoner was subsequently arrested.—Remanded for a week.

NEGLECT OF FAMILY.—*Joseph Lines* was charged with neglect of family.—Mr. B. G. Chamberlain appeared for the Board of Guardians.—Mr. Cartwright, relieving officer, said three children belonging to the defendant were now in the Workhouse, and were chargeable to the common fund of the Union Workhouse. Last Tuesday week defendant and his wife were before the Board, and defendant admitted to the Board that he was only able to earn 12s. per week, and that he could not afford to maintain them.—Defendant said he was suffering from diseased heart and defective sight, and he was now able to earn but a few shillings per week.—Remanded till Monday.

SIMILAR CHARGE.—*Joseph Oldershaw* was charged with neglect of family, but the case was adjourned till Monday.

CHARGE AGAINST A BANKRUPT.—*Samuel Beeson*, hosiery and elastic web manufacturer, Leicester, was charged under the Bankruptcy Act, with concealing his property, and his books, and in failing to make a true discovery of his property to the trustee, (the defendant having become a bankrupt in August last), and also with having disposed of his goods within the statutory period of four months.—Mr. Owston appeared for the prosecution, and Mr. Parsons for the defendant.—Mr. Robert Mantle, partner in the firm of Wykes Brothers and Mantle, said he was appointed and confirmed trustee of the estate of the defendant. An investigation was gone into by his partner, Mr. Wykes, in order that they might know the true state of affairs.—Mr. Wykes said he investigated the debtor's affairs. According to the statement given to the meeting of the creditors held in September, 1873, the liabilities of the defendant amounted to £12,000, and the assets between £5,000 and £6,000. Looking over the books, he discovered a "Carrier's Book," and it contained entries of goods sent to a Mr. Swift, Aldermanbury, London. He found a large portion of the goods so entered had not been entered in any account book. He was satisfied there ought to have been a stock book, and that it would contain several entries of goods to Swift. He had not found that book, although he had searched everywhere for it. He applied to Mr. Swift, and went to London to gain full information about the goods. On the 17th November, he applied to the London and North Western Railway Company for an account of all goods consigned to Swift by defendant, and he received it next day. Had an interview with Mr. Swift, and also with Messrs. Cook, in London. Mr. Mantle and witness had an interview with the defendant on the 29th November. They informed him that they had seen Mr. Swift and Messrs. Cook, and that Mr. Swift had paid him on the 10th June £92 13s. for goods supplied on June 6th; and on the 14th July £213 16s., partly in bills and partly in cash, for goods invoiced June 18th and July 2nd; and on August 2nd, £191 13s. These sums, amounting to upwards of £500 had not been accounted for by defendant in any shape or form, and they told him so. Defendant replied that when the books were properly examined, the money would be fully accounted for. He distinctly admitted receiving the money, but said he had paid it away in discharging liabilities. On obtaining the account from the London and North Western Railway Company, he compared it with the books kept by the debtor, and discovered considerable discrepancies from 6th June to 8th August. The result of his investigation showed that the defendant had sent goods to Swift, between these dates, amounting to more than £600. The aggregate weight of the goods was over 3 tons 5 cwt., and the nett weight 6,610 lbs. He found that the defendant only charged £159 against Swift, accounted for as follows:—1st July, £20; an entry in pencil, £46 15s.; 7th Aug., £7 5s. 9d.; another entry in pencil, £85 11s. 9d.; total, £159 12s. 6d.—The case was proceeding when we went to press.

COUNTY PUBLIC OFFICE.

SATURDAY.—*Before the Rev. H. J. Hoskyns (Chairman), Sir A. R. Palmer, Bart., and R. G. Pochin, Esqrs.*

KIRBY MUXLOE.—*William Argyle*, cowman, was charged with leaving the employ of Simeon Stretton.—Complainant claimed £1 as compensation.—Defendant admitted the offence, and promised, if taken back, to conduct himself better in future.—Complainant agreed to take defendant back, and the magistrates then ordered defendant to pay the costs, and to enter into his own recognizances in the sum of £5 to fulfil his contract.

HUMBERSTONE.—*Martha Goodman* was charged with assaulting Adeline Allen, at Humberstone, on the 24th January.—Complainant said on the day in question she was picking up a bucket of soft water, when defendant came out of her house, and told her to get some one to pump it for her. She then asked witness what she had been saying about her. They had some angry words, and bad language was used. Defendant eventually followed her into her own house and assaulted her. Defendant's daughter was there also, and the two got her down, and bumped her head on the floor. After that she got up as well as she could, and went out.—By defendant: She (defendant) struck her first.—Mrs. Boulter said she heard a disturbance on the day named, and went to see what was the matter. Complainant was pumping her bucket full, and defendant and her daughter stood in the yard. They were quarrelling. Shortly afterwards she heard a scream inside complainant's house, and went there and saw Mrs. Goodman with a tea-tray in her hand raised above her head, and trying to get into the living-room, where complainant was at the time. She did not see any blows struck, but Mrs. Allen's hair was about her shoulders, as though she had been knocked about.—Defendant said complainant struck her first, and tried to break her arm. She had been subjected to much annoyance from complainant.—Defendant was fined 15s., with the alternative of ten days' imprisonment.

SYSTON.—*Elizabeth Marshall* was brought up on remand, charged with picking the pocket of Esther Johnson, at Syston railway-station, on the 20th of January.—The evidence was fully gone into on Saturday last, and appears in this week's edition of the *Chronicle and Mercury*.—Prisoner was further charged with picking the pocket of Mrs. Sharp.—Prosecutrix deposed to leaving Syston on the 20th of January, and missing her purse containing 12s. 6d. at Leicester. When the prisoner was taken into custody at the railway-station at Syston on the first charge, P.C. Grundy was sent for, and on searching prisoner he found a purse belonging to Mrs. Sharpe, but not the one belonging to Mrs. Johnson.—Prisoner pleaded guilty to both charges, on each of which she was sentenced to four months' imprisonment.

WANLIP.—*Timothy Furborough*, rivetter, was charged with assaulting Wm. Powell, assistant gamekeeper to Sir A. Palmer, and Charles Blankley, parish constable, at Wanlip, on the 17th January.—Mr. Haxby appeared for the prosecution.—Committed.

TOWN MUSEUM.—Daily number of visitors for the week ending January 24:—Monday 360, Tuesday 280, Evening 30, Wednesday 210, Thursday 270, Friday 170, Saturday 320, Free Lecture 320, total for week 1960.—Wm. J. Harrison, curator.

On Wednesday afternoon a shocking wife murder occurred at Plymouth. The murderer is a young man of that town, named Sylvanus Sweet, of independent means, and the victim, his wife, was the only daughter of the proprietor of the Globe Hotel. It appears that … a violent quarrel about some pomatum, and in the heat of passion the husband seized an old cutlass which was hanging on the wall, and struck his wife several times with it on the head. She was killed instantly, and in his fury the murderer continued … her when she was dead. Immediately after … went in … to the police station, an…

GREAT … OF … ELEC… SOUTHERN …

Last (Friday) night the Corn Exchange was again well filled with an enthusiastic body of Liberal electors, who had attended for the purpose of inviting T. T. Paget, Esq., to come forward as a candidate for the representation of the Southern Division of the County. On the platform were many leading Liberals. From the commencement to the termination of the proceedings the utmost interest was manifested by the electors present.

On the motion of Mr. W. BAINES, seconded by Mr. HALL, Mr. R. HARRIS was voted to the chair.

The CHAIRMAN, in opening the proceedings, said it was with no small pleasure that he met them there that night to announce to them that their friend, Mr. Paget, had intimated his intention if he were invited by a large number of the electors of the Southern Division, to come forward and oppose the Conservative candidates in that division. (Hear, hear, and applause.) He was sure that announcement to them would be satisfactory. They had all proved how staunch Mr. Paget was as a Liberal, and how ready he was to fight the battles of Liberalism. He was ready at all times to come forward and devote not only his time, but his money, to endeavour to break through the monopoly which existed in that division of the county. (Hear, hear, and cheers.) He trusted that by their exertions, and by their faithful adhesion to Mr. Paget as their candidate, that they would be able to return him at the head of the poll. (Cheers.) He was glad to announce to them that day, that Messrs. Bright, Muntz, and Dixon had been returned again for Birmingham. (Cheers.) That was good news, and he hoped it would cheer them, not only in the Borough, but also the County elections. He believed Mr. Packe was the right man to fight their battle in the Northern Division, and he thought they were much indebted to him for coming forward to try to open to the Liberals that division of the county, which had been represented by the Conservatives for more than forty years. (Applause.)

Mr. G. TOLLER said some of them would recollect that about 17 years ago he had the privilege and the honour to nominate his esteemed and able friend, the late Mr. John Biggs, as a member of Parliament for that Borough—a gentleman whose memory was still fragrant in this town; and he recollected being under a disadvantage on that occasion, as he was unable to tell the audience anything with which they were not fully acquainted. He laboured under the same difficulty that night. Mr. Paget was so well-known to them that he hardly knew how to make any further allusion to him. They knew he was a man of singular intelligence, of high speaking powers, and he had hereditary claims on the county in addition, as his father represented the county for some time. Mr. Paget had, as far as he knew, every quality which strongly recommended him to a Liberal constituency. Having said this, he had no doubt they would pass with perfect unanimity the resolution he was about to propose. Mr. Paget had already fought two or three unsuccessful contests in the county, but he was not a man to be borne down by that; and then the circumstances by which they were now surrounded were very different to what they were before. They had not hitherto had the protection of the Ballot, and therefore he congratulated them that they would be able to vote as they thought proper on the present occasion. They would test the efficiency of the Ballot, and with that and the popularity of Mr. Paget, and the determination the Liberal electors would throw into the contest, he thought at the close of the poll they would find that they had achieved a great success. He begged to move, "That Mr. Thomas Tertius Paget be invited to offer himself as the candidate of the Liberal party for the Southern Division of the County of Leicester at the present election."

Mr. JOS. ELLIS (Glenfield) said he should not have felt ill-pleased if, after the abominable way in which Mr. Gladstone had been used, Mr. Disraeli had been allowed to take the reins of power. (No, no.) There was pleasure in variety, and he for one, when looking back into history, could almost wish that Guy Fawkes had succeeded in blowing up Parliament. (Laughter.) He wondered what James would have done if that had been the case. He had almost wished that the Conservatives would have a majority in the House—(no)—just to show for a little time what they would do with it, but when he felt the stir around him he was obliged to stir too. With regard to Mr. Paget, he agreed with what had been said that he ought to be one of the county representatives, but he did not think the people in the county were sufficiently wide-awake at present in regard to what they wanted. (A voice: That's it.) They had been running too much in leading-strings. He was not quite certain as to the result of this election, but he thought pegging away was a step in the right direction to get a footing in the county. Those who had voted openly hitherto would now be protected by the Ballot, but he thought some few men in small villages might still vote as though under influence. There were certain great questions coming on in the future in relation to the land in this country in which they were all deeply interested. A great part of England was exceedingly badly farmed, and he could tell them why. Because it did not pay a man to use his energies on his farm. Supposing a man took some acres of land, and laid out on it £5,000, what did the law of England do with the money he had expended? Handed it over to the landlord. At Michaelmas, if the landlord thought that a profit could be gained by driving the man out, he gave him a bit of paper, and the next Lady-day he had to go; and when the next tenant came in he had to take it at a higher rent. On some estates in all counties they would find the land well farmed, because the landlords would take away only that which he and the tenant had agreed upon. On all estates they wanted security that what a man laid out on the land he or his children should receive. It seemed to him that the man they could best send to carry out that was the man who had already carried it out himself. He knew of no man who had done this but Mr. Thomas Tertius Paget. (Cheers.) He would defy any one to find a man who was more willing to farm under somebody else rather than under Mr. Paget. The law of England said that if a tenant-farmer planted 500 apple trees and he gathered one apple off each of the trees, the trees thereafter were the landlord's. (Laughter.) He maintained that this was not justice. Mr. Pell would tell them that he and his party were the men to alter this state of things, but he advised those present not to trust them. The people to alter that law were Mr. Gladstone and the Liberal party at his back. The landlords had their own interest at heart, and that consisted chiefly in the keeping of game. They had never had a government in office that wished to do greater justice than the one which had been in office during the last five years. The government were blamed by the Conservatives because they entered into arbitration with America, but they ought not to be, although he himself thought they should not have paid so much money. They thought nothing of government spending £3,000,000 on armaments, and why then, he asked, should they not spend £3,000,000 on peace. What did the Conservative government want to get in office for? (A voice: Loaves and fishes.) Some of them he believed to be very good men, but others wished to go and look after themselves. He had felt surprised in looking at the newspapers to find that their opponents' meetings were held at public-houses. He had no feeling of enmity towards the publicans, but he thought public-houses were not the proper places to hold political meetings in. He had pleasure in seconding the resolution. (Applause.)

Mr. D. MERRICK was very glad those present had taken the initiative in calling the meeting to request Mr. Paget again to come forward as a candidate for the southern division of the county of Leicester. Wherever Mr. Paget went he was well-known and much respected. Everyone in that room, who had had any acquaintance with Mr. Paget, well knew that he was a kind, intelligent, and earnest man—one who was prepared to advance the interests of all, rich and poor, on an equal and fair basis. (Hear, hear, and cheers.) These were the kind of men they wanted to represent them in the House of Commons. They did not want the clique to which Mr. Ellis had referred to go there to legislate for themselves on their own affairs. Too much of that had already been the case, or there would not be so much of the kind of law Mr. Ellis had mentioned. They ought to be thankful that the Reform Bill of 1832 was passed to admit of another element going into the House. They had had something like five years' Government under a Liberal Premier, and he believed good service had been done. Mr. Paget had been to Parliament, and although he only remained there a short time, he did good work. One part of his work was to strip the rags—the fancy ornaments—from around the Reform Bill Mr. Disraeli brought in, and they owed it very much to Mr. Paget that they had household suffrage pure and simple. The same kind of trickery which was manifested when Mr. Disraeli was over the Government, the same clique were practising at the present time. Coming down Granby-street that night he saw posters professing to be issued by working-men in London, asking working-men to support Church and … should not wonder much if those working- … servative working-men they … and rings on their … were strange … among the … servative. … in- … not …

… progress. The Con… but with the combined efforts … would not be able to prevent the car from progressing. The time was rapidly coming when people would see that the Liberal Government was the only one they could look to for the protection and the equalisation of the laws affecting the different classes of the community; that it was, in fact, the only Government they could welcome with any degree of confidence. (Hear, hear and cheers.) There was one pleasing feature in connection with the county elections generally, and that was the passing of the Ballot to protect the voter. Mr. Merrick then went on to show that in some villages the clergyman was regarded with fear by the villagers, instancing a case in which he himself saw sixteen to twenty men who were standing round a public-house corner ran away on the approach of the clergyman, and came back when he had gone. He also pointed out that there were instances on record of men having been turned out of their houses for voting in accordance with the dictates of their conscience, and then said under the Ballot no one need fear, as the voting would be secret. If a man in town or country now voted contrary to his convictions and principles it would be his own fault. He wished the people in the country to feel that now they could throw the blame upon no one else but themselves if the election should be lost. The Liberal Government had thrown around them a shield of protection and under it they might rest and bid defiance to the landlord, parson, or squire. If Mr. Paget consented to stand for the Southern division of Leicestershire, let them work night and day if required, earnestly and thoroughly determined. This was an important national crisis, and it was for them to say who should be returned to govern—a man who would throw the nation altogether into debt, or a man who had steered them on safely, and who would lead them on to still greater results. Let them work in earnest, and then if Mr. Paget were not returned at the head of the poll, he would at least be sent to Parliament as one of the representatives of the Southern Division of the County. (Cheers.)

The resolution was then put and carried with an enthusiastic "aye," followed by repeated cheers.

Mr. W. STANTON, who was received with cheers, said they might expect very shortly to have the pleasure of seeing and hearing Mr. Paget, and he should not therefore occupy much of their time. He had listened with great pleasure to the speeches that had been delivered that evening, and especially to the speech of Mr. Ellis of Glenfield. (Cheers.) That gentleman spoke from experience, and therefore his testimony was reliable. They were all aware that a man in business in Leicester, in order to keep pace with the times, must avail himself of all the new appliances which were introduced so as to obtain for himself and for his workmen too—all the advantages that were to be obtained, and to make progress in his business. Now he didn't see why farmers in the county should not be placed on an equality with the manufacturers in Leicester. (Cheers.) He had heard that if the farmers of this country were placed in such a position as that they could invest their capital and adopt all the new appliances that could be brought to bear upon their farms that they would have a much larger produce of corn. Well, if they had a larger supply of corn, of course they would have it cheaper, and with cheaper corn there would be increased prosperity in the country. (Cheers.) That being the case he thought it was essential that they should send to the House of Commons gentlemen like Mr. Paget. They had heard that he was a very good landlord, and that he always did what was just and right between landlord and tenant. (Cheers.) Many of the landlords studied only their own interests and their own pockets, and therefore he thought they should endeavour to improve the position of the farmers and graziers in this respect, and in order to do that they must return gentlemen like Mr. Paget. (Cheers.) Now they must all do their best to return him, and if they were defeated they would have the consolation of knowing that they had done their best. He had no doubt they would secure a very good majority for the Liberal candidates in the Borough, and that would inspirit those in the county and give them courage. He was quite sure Mr. Paget would do his share of the work. (Hear, hear.) He worked wonderfully hard on the last occasion, and he then made for himself a host of friends. He felt that it would not have been right if they had not asked Mr. Paget to come forward now. They were in altered circumstances, and they must work with a will, and see what the ballot would do for the southern division of the county. (Cheers.)

Mr. Paget entered the room, accompanied by two or three gentlemen, and was received with loud and continued cheers. The Chairman came to the front of the platform and read to Mr. Paget the resolution which the meeting had passed with so much unanimity and enthusiasm.

Mr. PAGET, in coming forward to address the meeting, was received with enthusiastic cheering, again and again repeated. He said:—Gentlemen, after having heard the kind opinions and wishes so kindly read to me by your chairman, you cannot for one moment believe that I shall hesitate one single instant as to cordially and heartily responding to them. (Loud cheers.) I throw myself entirely upon your support, and more especially must I do so to-night, for having spent nearly the whole day in London, and having only a short time ago arrived in Leicester by train, any speech which I may make will be a matter wholly and entirely unprepared. I don't know that it is any the worse for that, for it is often the case that that which is unprepared is the most frank. My journey to London to day has been almost exclusive for the purpose of ascertaining from head quarters how things are going on—(hear, hear)—and to tell them how remarkably well we went on here last night. I think the meeting of last night was a grand success. (Cheers.) I entirely agree with one or two remarks I heard fall from Mr. Stanyon as I entered the room. We do enter into the contest in an entirely different position to any contest that has been fought within my recollection. (Cheers.) I think however formidable our opponents may seem to us, and however considerable the majority may be by which they defeated me last time—(a voice: It was not much.) Well it was something. It was more than I should like to be defeated by this time. Giving them all that to the good, I want to show you that we are in a totally different position, from one particular circumstance, and that circumstance is, we have the Ballot. (Cheers.) Now I think that considering that altered circumstance, and considering also the peculiar circumstances in which we are placed by our leader—I say that considering these, every constituency is bound to be tested. (Cheers.) I am afraid I shall commit a great deal of tautology, for many of you here heard me last night, and you must excuse me if the few remarks I have to make savour somewhat of repetition. (Cheers.) I think there are two reasons why every constituency in the kingdom should be thoroughly tested. The first is to try the working of the ballot, and the second is the clear and absolute line of demarcation by which our Premier has given to us a choice between a continuance of his policy, and of a ministry under his guidance, and a transference of that power into other hands. I say I am no advocate, and never shall be for transferring the powers from such men as Mr. Gladstone to be crooked and spoiled by any Tory leader whatever. This is the question now before the constituencies of this country, and it is our duty to answer yes or no to the question. Will you continue to support Mr. Gladstone, or will you transfer the power to Mr. Disraeli? I recollect saying the same thing when I appeared before you five years ago, and I have not altered my opinions or my principles one iota. (Loud cheers.) I ask you whether I am not justified in my preference when you cast your eye across the Parliamentary work of the last five years. Four Acts which have been passed during that period stand conspicuously before my mind. The first will never be forgotten by me, because I had, through your kindness, some part in the earlier and later divisions which took place on that question—I mean the Irish Church. If there were no other measure passed by Mr. Gladstone's ministry, that great measure alone would have been considered tantamount to a beneficent revolution. (Cheers.) What followed? The Irish Land Bill. It is an abstruse question, and I shall not go into that to-night, but I think that has proved a most beneficent measure also. And what followed? The Judicature Bill, which has yet to ripen and bear fruit in simplifying the law of this country. And lastly comes the most triumphant work of all—the Education Act. I am well aware that I think more favourably of that Act than some of you do—(hear, hear)—but I believe that when certain modifications, reforms, improvements, and repeals—(applause)—which that Act is certain to undergo if you keep the present men in office have been effected, that Act will prove to be one of the greatest statutes which has ever been passed in the Parliament of England. (Cheers.) It will place us, where we are not now, on a level with Prussia and other Continental States. With all our natural cleverness, our natural solidity, and our natural perseverance, in competing with those countries, we are as far behind them in the matter of education as it is possible for us to be, and hold our own. (Hear, hear.) And unless we compete with them in the matter of education we shall not be able to hold our own. (Hear, hear.) Therefore I prize the Education Act, and would tr…

Magnificent Mercury

History of a Regional Newspaper:

The first 125 years of the
Leicester Mercury

Magnificent Mercury

History of a Regional Newspaper:

The first 125 years of the

Leicester Mercury

by

Steve England,
Leicester Mercury Librarian

KAIROS PRESS
Newtown Linford,
Leicester
1999

First Published in Great Britain by
KAIROS PRESS
552 Bradgate Road, Newtown Linford, Leicester LE6 0HB
1999

ISBN 1-871344-21-2

Book design and layout by Robin Stevenson, Kairos Press
Body text in Aldine 721 BT 10.5 pt.
Imagesetting by CDS Imaging, Leicester
Cover design and film by Geoff Sanders, Creative Design Studio, Leicester Mercury
Printed in Great Britain by Norwood Press, Anstey, Leicester
Bound by BadmintonPress, Syston, Leicester

CONTENTS

Page No

CHAPTER 1 7
Setting the Scene
Before 1874

CHAPTER 2 13
The Birth
1874 – 1900

CHAPTER 3 21
Private Limited Company
1900 – 1910

CHAPTER 4 27
First World War
1910 – 1920

CHAPTER 5 38
Public Company
1920 – 1930

CHAPTER 6 46
Unemployment & Newspaper Wars
1930 – 1940

CHAPTER 7 57
War & Peace
1940 – 1950

CHAPTER 8 63
Mr Hewitt Sells Control
1950 – 1960

CHAPTER 9 68
Momentous Years
1960 – 1970

CHAPTER 10 81
Centenary Celebrations
1970 – 1980

CHAPTER 11 100
The Arrival of Automation
1980 – 1990

CHAPTER 12 118
Looking To The Future
1990 – 1999

Dedicated to:
Mr Terry Dwyer and the late Mr F Brian Thompson for their work
on the official 'Blue' History of the Leicester Mercury; Miss Lisa
McQue for the loan of her PC; Janet Rowlands, Leigh-Ann Holland
& Carole Inman; Mr Tony Foy, for helping me with the technology
behind the writing of this history; my wife, Sue, who now has me
back under her feet on Sunday mornings; all former staff who have
contributed to this history.

A LASTING MEMORY MAKES A PERFECT GIFT

Many of the photographs in this book are available to order and make an excellent gift or an ideal reminder of personal memories.

These reprints from the original photographs reflect the changing face of Leicester over the years*.

Reprints are available framed in a choice of quality mouldings for only £19.95 (postage extra).

Unframed prints are available at only £9.95 inc postage and packing.

Telephone orders 0116 222 4256 (24 hour answer phone).

Or write giving details of the page number and subject to:
Martin Webbon, Leicester Mercury, St George Street, Leicester LE1 9FQ.

*print quality may vary dependent on the original.

Back cover photograph: A printer checks the first edition.

Endpapers: The first issue of the Leicester Daily Mercury, from Saturday January 31st 1879. The front page was reset to match the original at the time of the Mercury centenary because the only copy in existence was too mutilated to reproduce. Pages 2, 3 and 4 however are from the original type.

Chapter One

Setting the Scene

Before 1874

Queen Victoria had reigned since 1837 and was to continue until her death in January 1901. In November 1871, however, she was 'deeply distressed' by a speech by the radical MP Sir Charles Dilke at a meeting in Newcastle. He had denounced 'the political corruption that hangs about the monarchy' and called for Victoria to be deposed and a republic established. Republicanism had been given a boost by the novelist William Makepeace Thackeray, who had delivered a series of sneering attacks on Victoria's Hanoverian ancestors in his public lectures on The Four Georges. When he died in 1863, Victoria refused to allow him to be buried in Poets' Corner in the south transept of Westminster Abbey.

Liberal William Gladstone had been Prime Minster since December 1868. The disestablishment of the Irish Church, the Irish Land Acts, the Education Act introducing compulsory national elementary education and the Ballot Act were among the great domestic measures of his government.

In Leicester, the population stood at 95,083 according to the Census in 1871. A population which rose from 17,000 to 219,000 during the century not only had to be clothed, fed and housed, it also had to be provided with water, sanitation, transport, schools, hospitals and open spaces, as well as workhouses, asylums and prisons.

To provide clean water, Thornton reservoir was created in 1853, Cropston in 1866 and Swithland in 1894. Each in turn proved inadequate. For sewage, a pumping and drying station was erected near Leicester Abbey. A number of obstructive mills were blown up and the River Soar straightened to prevent floods after the passing of the Leicester Improvement, Drainage and Markets Act in 1868 and a further Improvement Act in 1874.

The death rate began to fall and Leicester gradually changed from a most unhealthy to a fairly healthy town after the end of the century.

Below: Leicester in 1868: Horsefair Street looking from Gallowtree Gate before the Town Hall was built.

◆ The first mechanical press, a hand-press with a mechanism for laying on and taking off sheets and automatic inking, was made by Friedrich Koenig and Andrew F Bauer. It was not a success. The first cylinder presses, also built by Koenig, were used by The Times in 1814, producing 1,100 sheets an hour. Readers were proudly informed that they held in their hands 'the greatest improvement connected with printing since the discovery of the art itself.'

◆ Edward Cowper patented perfecting presses in 1818, which printed both sides of a sheet for book and periodical production. These were called 'Applegarth and Cowper Royals' and were driven by steam and could later print between 800 and 1,000 perfected sheets an hour.

◆ The first typesetting machine was devised by Dr William Church. Type was stored in boxes and released by keys and transferred to a channel which acted as a composing stick.

◆ The Times was printed on Applegarth and Cowper flatbed 'four feeder' presses for 10 years from 1828. They reached a speed of 4,200 impressions an hour and took four men to lay on white paper and four to take off printed sheets.

The Mechanics' Institute closed in January 1870 and its books were freely presented to the Central Library, which was given by philanthropist Andrew Carnegie and erected on a site provided by the City Council. The Town Museum had opened earlier in 1849, formed with a collection from the Literary and Philosophical Society, at the former Proprietary School Building on New Walk.

The Council had been meeting in the Chamber of the Old Guildhall, but discussions had been taking place on the subject of a new Town Hall. Two sites divided the opinions of the Council. The old Cattle Market in Horsefair Street and the property in Friar Lane formerly belonging to the late Mr Beaumont Burnaby and purchased by the Council in 1866. Friar Lane was decided upon, but rescinded in September 1872 in favour of the site of the Old Cattle Market, which had closed on April 6, 1872 and moved to Aylestone Road. Competitive designs were advertised for, the cost not to exceed £30,000. The first prize was awarded to Mr F J Hames of London, who was appointed architect for the work. A memorial stone was laid near the main entrance by the Mayor, Alderman William Kempson on August 3, 1874, and the building formerly opened on August 7, 1876.

In November 1872, two competing companies gave notice of an application to Parliament through the Board of Trade for a Provisional Order to authorize the construction of tramways in Leicester. The Belgrave Road line was constructed first by the Leeds Company and opened for horse tram traffic on December 24, 1874.

By 1800, there were many newspapers in the country, but they were being printed, page by page, on handpresses and typeset, letter by letter, by hand compositors. News had to released as soon as possible to readers and mechanisation of the press was required. In 1800, the 3rd Earl of Stanhope developed stereotyping using plaster moulds. They were however too small for newspaper formats. Curved metal stereo plates for newspaper presses were not made until over 54 years later.

Newspapers locally began as early as 1695 with the *Rutland and Stamford Mercury* (no connection with the *Leicester Mercury*), which was published in Stamford and is reputed to be the oldest newspaper under the same title in Britain.

Leicester's first newspaper – *the Leicester and Nottingham Journal* – was published on May 12, 1753, by J Gregory, in the Market Place. It had four pages, each eleven inches by sixteen and a half inches, with three three

and a quarter inch columns per page and sold for two and a half old pence.

News reported tended to be predominantly national and its politics Tory. The date of each cable reproduced was given, often a fortnight old. In its early days, advertisements were few and far between. Some interesting ones included an appeal by a promoter for gentlemen to enter birds for a cockfight between the counties of Leicestershire and Warwickshire; a notice about the London to Nottingham stage coach, which left every Monday and Friday at 5am and arrived in Nottingham on Tuesdays and Saturdays, and an announcement of the forthcoming sale of the Manor of Halstead, two freehold houses, three cottages, 464 acres, the tithes of Marefield and third presentation to the living of Tilton, let at a yearly rent of £274/15s.

The outbreak of the American War of Independence and later the wars with France whetted the appetite for news and led to the setting up of newsrooms in the town. Mr W Simpson, of the Wheatsheaf, Gallowtree Gate, boasted he could obtain the London newspapers 20 hours sooner than any other newsroom keeper, as he was a clerk to the stage coach.

Several weekly papers began in Leicester, usually in opposition to the Government. They had various fates, finding that the Journal had become quite established.

First came the *Leicester Herald* and the *Leicester Chronicle* in 1791. Twenty-five year-old Richard Phillips was the founder of the Herald. He had started a commercial academy, followed by a bookseller's business, a pamphlet room with 'the most extensive assortments of new publications in Europe,' a music and pianoforte department, a 'Navigation Office' for the buying and selling of canal companies' shares and a department for the sale of patent medicines.

He ran a Literary Society and it was to members he suggested starting a newspaper with Liberal leanings. On the eve of publication he found to his surprise that there was a rival. Another bookseller by the name of Thomas Combe issued placards announcing the birth of the Chronicle. Phillips contacted him and suggested an amalgamation, but Combe did not agree and so the Herald and the Chronicle came out together. Both fought hard, against each other and against the Government, but soon failed. The Chronicle went first, early in 1793, threatened with prosecution by the Government for 'much political animadversion calculated to make the people discontented with the Government.' Two months later, Phillips was prosecuted for 'publishing seditious literature' and was sent to prison for 18 months. He carried on publishing from prison, but soon after he was released, he had to close it down in June 1795.

For 15 years, the Journal continued as the sole newspaper in the area. In 1810, the *Leicester Chronicle* was re-launched with a staunch Whig outlook and had among its proprietors Walter Ruding, Whig squire of Westcotes Hall. It appealed, it claimed, to

> 'the modest and judicious of all parties – the middle class of respectable and patriotic men in which the moral and intellectual health of Britain lives.'

Leicester philatelist and friend of Keir Hardie, Mr P H Cooper, of Greenhill Road, who died in 1965, had in his possession a 'proclamation' made by Thomas Martin, printer, of Market Place, Leicester. The pamphlet records the original announcement of the publication of *The Leicester Chronicle*, No 1 issue, dated November 10, 1810. It was subtitled the *Commercial and Agricultural Advertiser*. The final note in the pamphlet states:

> 'They (the proprietors) make their appeal to the moderate and judicious of all parties – TO THE BIGOTS OF NONE. They address themselves to that middle class of respectable and patriotic men, in which the moral and intellectual health of Britain lives, not languidly, but vigorously. If they obtain the suffrage of this portion of their countrymen, they will console themselves for the neglect and enmity of the remainder.'

In a continuing, unsuccessful attempt to find a suitable editor, the paper was sold to a Lancastrian, Thomas Thompson, who became proprietor, printer, publisher and editor.

Above: The proclamation made by Thomas Martin, printer, of Market Place, Leicester, announcing the publication of The Leicester Chronicle in 1810.

The Chronicle had vicious opposition from the rival Journal, now owned by Gregory's son-in-law, John Price. However, both papers flourished and it was 17 years before another dared to challenge them.

In 1827 came the second *Leicester Herald*, founded as a Corporation organ, with a Tory outlook. In an era when the Press was shackled and not allowed to criticise local or national government, owners and editors continually ran into trouble. The Leicester Corporation prosecuted the Chronicle's owner for severely criticising the administration of justice in the borough – the case was dismissed on technical grounds.

George Brown, a prominent 19th century Leicester Radical, poured scorn on the city's first Tory newspaper, the *Leicester Journal*, and its owner, John Price. He said:

> 'These curs (the Journal mongrels) were quiet and inoffensive before they were infested with the Price Mange; then they became vicious and almost rabid, snarling at their betters almost every Friday.'

The quotation is included in a review of 'The Press in Leicester' as it was in the late 18th and early 19th centuries, by Derek Fraser, published by the Leicestershire Archaeological and Historical Society.

Mr Fraser relates that provincial newspapers in the 19th century 'could both guide and reflect local public opinion.' During the 1790s, the presence in Leicester of two radical newspapers forced the Leicester Journal to become outspoken in its political bias and this continued for the first decade of the 19th century. There was in Leicester then a Tory journal willing to express Tory opinions, though the editorial as a separate column had not yet arrived. The development of the editorial in the Leicester Journal was accelerated by the presence of John Price, first as a partner in 1803, and then as proprietor in 1806. That it was Price who was responsible for a consistent use of the editorial did not go unnoticed by the Radical George Brown. From 1807 the editorial in the 'Leicester' column, where a strong Tory point of view was expressed, became the central feature of the newspaper. John Price was an important figure in the provincial Tory Press from 1803 to 1831. In many towns it was Radical editors who pioneered editorials and the leading of public opinion.

In many towns, also, the Tory press was slow to copy its rivals. In Leicester, though, Price was by no means the first to use editorials. He made full use of this new expedient and under his guidance the Leicester Journal became an effective force in local affairs. During the proprietorship of

◆ Stereotyping was invented in 1829 using 'flongs' – layers of paper sandwiched with glue, which were impressed on the type by beating or rolling and used as matrices to cast metalplates. It was 1845 before curved stereos for rotary presses were made and 1855 before they were produced for newspaper printing.

◆ Wood engraving reached a high standard in newspaper illustration during the 1860s. The photographic halftone plate, invented in 1881, replaced them and by the end of the century there were 95 process engravers working in London and many more outside the capital.

◆ The first newspaper rotary press to print from a continuous reel of paper was invented by William Bullock in 1865. He met an untimely end when his clothes were caught up in one of his American presses. His machine was improved on by Hoe in Britain and it was to become one of the commonest and most durable letterpress machines for newspaper printing. The Hoe Double Supplement press printed 24,000 copies an hour and by 1887 eight of them were used in this country.

Below: John Biggs.

John Price, the Leicester Journal was never the tool of the Corporation, but another Tory paper, the Leicester Herald, definitely was. Begun in 1827 by Henry Joseph Wilkinson, later to be dismissed for irregularities from the post of retiring officer, it supported the interests of the 'Old True-Blue Flag.' It was a completely scurrilous publication, claiming that its editor had duties more important than animadversions upon matters of general policy – a reference to its frequent malignant attacks upon individuals. Its remarks soon involved Wilkinson in libel suits and in one of them he was ordered to pay Richard Cooke £50 and Cave Brown £30. His inability to pay resulted in a prison sentence, during which time the Leicester Herald was run by William Vickers, under whom, to his cost, was revealed the influence of the Corporation over it.

The weekly *Leicestershire Mercury* burst on to the scene in 1836. Staunchly nonconformist, it was edited, printed and published by Albert Cockshaw from offices in High Street. At first it cost 7d, but with the reduction of the stamp duty on newspapers this was reduced to 4d within a few weeks.

Mr Walter Cockshaw of Shropshire Road in Leicester informs me Albert Cockshaw was his great great uncle and he describes the Leicestershire Mercury as the forerunner of a free independent press, a symbol of the future. Walter left school in 1934 and his first job as copy boy in the proof-reading department of the Leicester Mercury.

Mrs Enid Allison of Wicklow Drive, Leicester, also tells me Albert Cockshaw was a relative, her third great great uncle. She says he was quite a character and a pioneer in his day. His father Isaac was an art master, book seller, engraver and printer. He ran an academy for young gentlemen and had one of the earliest circulating art libraries in the country. After his death in 1818, his two sons, Albert and Isaac Junior, carried on the business in High Street, but later Isaac Junior opened a shop in Gallowtree Gate opposite the Three Crowns Hotel, which was then located at the corner of Horsefair Street.

Albert was a dedicated radical and non-conformist. Acutely aware of the poverty and misery that surrounded him, he used the printed word to help to change the order of things. Along with other reformers, he advocated the disestablishment of the Church, the abolition of slavery, extended suffrage and the abolition of the Church rate.

His former news room at his house was let as a general committee room and it was here that the Leicester Literary and Philosophical Society was launched on May 15, 1835. Alfred Paget was the provisional Secretary and George Shaw, Esq, MD, was in the Chair. The Leicester Medical Society also used the premises.

He was always in conflict with the town's Corporation. After publishing one of his many pamphlets in 1833, entitled 'A letter to the People of Leicester on Corporate Reform, dedicated (without permission) to the Mayor and Magistrates,' he was charged with libel along with the editor of the Leicester Chronicle, who also published it. The whole affair provoked questions in the House of Commons. The charges were dismissed, however, when it came before the King's Bench Division, on an objection by the defendant's counsel. This was certainly a blow to the town's Corporation, who had brought the case.

On the Mercury staff was the local eminent Chartist, Thomas Cooper. He was found to be contributing to another new paper, the Midland Counties Illuminator. He was sacked and became the Illuminator's editor in 1840, at 30 shillings a week. He eventually owned it, but it failed and for two years he ran a succession of other unsuccessful Chartist newspapers – Chartists' Rushlight, The Extinguisher, Commonwealthian and Chartist Pioneer.

Albert Cockshaw was overwhelmed by the many enterprises he was engaged in and he was declared bankrupt in 1840, but his strong beliefs were unshaken. He moved to

London, where he was appointed to the executive committee of the Anti-State Church Association. He was also a member of the Liberation Society and was associated with the publication of the 'Nonconformist' journal.

Albert Cockshaw died on December 10, 1870, at his son-in-law's house at Oulton Hall, near Stone, in Staffordshire, where he had resided for some years. The final words in his obituary in the Leicester Chronicle of December 17 say: 'He no doubt with vivid remembrance of the past is happy in the change to the Great Presence in which he now lives' – a final epitaph to a man who struggled to change the shape of our society.

The *Leicestershire Mercury* continued, but with one proprietor following another. In 1843 it was in the hands of J Burton. Seven years later, Burton's former partner, G H Smallfield, took charge, but found it was too much to manage and sold his interest to the Biggs family, hosiery manufacturers. J F Hollings, a headmaster and brother-in-law of John and William Biggs, was entrusted with the job of running the paper.

In Loughborough, the town's first newspaper, The Loughborough Telegraph, was born in 1837. It must have achieved some success, because its wider circulation resulted in the title change to The Leicester, Nottingham and Derby Telegraph. But it did not last, because of the crippling government stamp duty of 4d a copy. In 1859, Mr John Gray started the Loughborough Monitor, which was printed in the Angel Yard, off Market Place. It was later renamed the Loughborough Monitor, Castle Donington, Ashby and Melton Herald, showing its increased circulation. Mr Rollings Lee bought it for £45 in 1862 and merged the title with the Loughborough News in 1870 to become the Loughborough Monitor and News. Two more new publications, the Loughborough Advertiser and Loughborough Herald, were later bought by the Monitor.

The Leicester Herald had, for the second and last time, gone out of existence in 1842. The Leicester Advertiser, named originally Payne's Leicester and Midland Counties Advertiser, was launched as an auctioneer's sheet, published 'for the purpose of facilitating business' and it cost two and a half pence in contrast to the four and half pence charged for most other papers by now. Its original neutrality and commercial aim was sacrificed to become the second Tory paper.

James Thompson, the historian, took control of the Leicester Chronicle. He was a man highly regarded in Leicester, having helped to found the Mechanics Institute and

Above: James Thompson, historian, who took over The Leicester Chronicle.

the Leicester Historical and Archaeological Society and was honorary curator of the town's museum. The paper made rapid progress. He was soon able to acquire the Leicestershire Mercury as well and in 1864 he merged the two under the banner of Leicestershire Chronicle and Mercury, with offices in the Market Place. It became the most 'sympathetic' newspaper in its attitude towards Chartism in the county. Between 1846 and 1850, the Leicestershire Mercury's circulation rose from 750 to 1,100.

In 1848, two young men anxious to learn the printing trade entered Mr James Thompson's office. They were Francis Hewitt and Thomas Windley – both were destined in due course to become Mayors of Leicester. Francis Hewitt was born in May, 1832, into a family of farmers, who lived in the Naseby area on the county border of Leicestershire and Northamptonshire. His father died when he was twelve and he had to earn a living. Thomas Windley recalled 'They were the days of Tom Cooper and the Chartist risings, the days when Leicester mustered perhaps 40,000 population, when the staple industry was the hosiery trade and the Leicester working man was noted over

Above: Thomas Cooper, Leicester Chartist Leader.

the country for his gaunt visage and his extreme poverty; times when the municipal franchise was limited to a few hundreds of burgesses, when strikes and lockouts were annual occurrences, when books were scarce and newspapers were dear. Those were the days of toil and struggle for freedom, for justice, for enfranchisement, for civil and religious liberty.'

Hewitt and Windley were indentured with two others at four shillings a week, rising annually by one shilling a week for the following six years. Not exactly model apprentices, (on one or two occasions, they were known to have taken half-days off and even return from a weekend at Hewitt's uncle's farm at Welford a day late, having walked there and back – a round trip of 40 miles), they did however progress well and Hewitt eventually became an assistant reporter, having learnt Pitman's shorthand. Francis Hewitt saw the prospect of advancement in sales and in 1859 went into partnership in a stationer's and bookseller's business at Caxton House, 80 Granby Street, opposite the former Picture House. Very soon, his partner retired, leaving him as sole proprietor.

He asked Francis Drake, a Leicester architect and Fellow of the Society of Arts, to design him a new shop front in 1868. Two years earlier he had been elected to the Board of Guardians of the Poor and was renowned as a reformer.

Chapter Two
The Birth
1874 – 1900

James Thompson had for a long time toyed with the idea of starting a daily Liberal paper in Leicester and the failure of other people's attempts did not deter him. He published the very first evening newspaper in Leicester on January 31, 1874, at 3 St Martin's, Leicester.

Above: St Martin's, Leicester, in 1974 with its traffic and modern lighting – No. 3 St Martin's, in the centre, was the first home of the Leicester Mercury.

James was born five years after his father bought the Chronicle and his main education was entrusted to the minister of Great Meeting, the chapel in which the very soul of Leicester piety and radicalism was nurtured in the 18th and 19th centuries. After joining his father as a Chronicle reporter, he became joint proprietor in 1841 and sole owner in 1864.

His evening publication was a halfpenny paper, consisting of four pages, each 20 in by 14 in, with five columns to the page. The front page was devoted entirely to advertisements, with more on page two. Most were Liberal election addresses or notices in the first issue, as the General Election was due to be held. Readers were told that it was 'published daily (except Fridays) at 3pm and 6pm.' It was physically impossible to publish

two papers (including the weekly Leicestershire Chronicle and Mercury) on Fridays and so the Leicester Daily Mercury, as it was named, did not appear on that day. After only three weeks, the publishing times were changed to 4pm and 6pm.

In the first issue, the leader, not unexpectedly, extolled the Liberal viewpoint and the back page was devoted to a report of a 'Great Liberal Demonstration' at the Corn Exchange to adopt two Liberal candidates for the Borough, P A Taylor and A McArthur. Page three contained news, much of it about Liberal prospects in other constituencies. In a three-line paragraph, readers were informed that 'the laying down of the tramway rails have been commenced – the first rail was laid on Tuesday near the horse-trough on the Belgrave Road.' Note the grammatical error – it was certainly not the last mistake. For the first three days of the following week, the date above the leader column appeared as: Monday, February 2; Monday, February 3 and Monday, February 4!

Amusingly, on the front page of the first edition, there was an advertisement which informed the reader:

First edition of The Leicester Daily Mercury. (The full four pages of this edition are reproduced on the end-papers of this book.)

Above: No. 3 St Martin's in 1974 from the rear.

1874

◆ Advertisements were accepted at the minimum rate of twenty words for 6d for one insertion rising to sixty words for six insertions for 5/6d. Each additional word would cost one halfpenny and six insertions qualified for one free insertion in the Chronicle as well.

◆ The principal agents from whom copies could be bought were published, with Mr Hewitt of Granby Street heading the list. It also mentioned Mr Oldershaw of Granby Street, Mr Bent of Town Hall Lane, Mr Catlow of Humberstone Gate, Mrs Emery of Belgrave Gate and Mr Bradley of Welford Road.

1874

◆ The rateable value of property in Leicester (on March 25 1874) was £289,508 and the rates stood at 7/4d in the pound, but this caused no concern compared with that over the income tax of 4d in the pound. Organisations rose up all over the country to put pressure on the Government to abolish income tax, which was then in its 33rd year. It was at its lowest (it had been 1/4d in 1856-57) but it was claimed that it was a grossly unfair and unnecessary tax. When, on April 16, 1874, the Chancellor of the Exchequer (Sir Stafford Northcote) announced a useful surplus, he also calmed the public agitation somewhat by reducing income tax to 3d. In 1875, it fell another penny, but from that point started the upward trend which, in spite of spasmodic small fluctuations, resulted in the 10/- in the pound rate during the Second World War.

'Whereas a paper has been published connected with the Advertiser, a Tory print called the Leicester Evening Times, the imprint being J Hunter, 3 Horsefair Street, Mr James Hunter, of 26 New Walk, begs to inform the public that he has no connection with the miserable production in question and upon calling upon Mr Cox for an explanation he said it was his Super-intendent's wife's maiden name.'

Leicester went to the polls on its fourth day of publication and the leader of the previous evening made it clear what it intended the voters to do:

'Tomorrow between the hours of 8 and 4 the electors of Leicester will record their suffrages under the ballot for the candidates of whom they approve. We cannot doubt what will be the result. Messrs Taylor and McArthur will obtain a majority of thousands over the misguided young gentleman who has consented to be politically pilloried to please the Tories of Leicester.'

In the event, Taylor received 7,408 votes, McArthur 7,283 and the 'misguided young gentleman' named Warner, 5,615. Despite Leicester's preference for Gladstone, Disraeli had won.

With the election over, more room was found for news and advertisements. The paper gave much space to the progress of the Ashanti War and a certain amount also to the bringing home of the remains of David Livingstone and the internment in Westminster Abbey.

As a historian, James Thompson wished to continue to tell the story of Leicester, not from hindsight, but day by day, as it happened. Production was largely by hand – handwriting, hand typesetting and handcarts for the distribution of his editions. The sale in the early days was small at about 5,000 copies a day. James employed 25 people, not counting the newsboys, who were apparently so unruly that each afternoon a policeman had to be on hand to keep them in order.

Thomas Windley recalls: 'It was to advocate reforms that the Leicester Mercury was started and among its contributors were the Rev J P Mursell, Edward Miall, William Biggs and other well-known reformers.'

James was an energetic campaigner for the preservation of old Leicester and for the creation of modern facilities to meet the city's growing needs. He called for a 'People's Park' in an area of land reclamation in Abbey Meadows on the River Soar. Eventually, the park was designed by a Derbyshire firm, but it was so like the one James imagined, that it would be natural to suppose they knew of his ideas.

Through the columns of his newspapers, he was a fiery crusader in matters of public welfare, campaigning vigorously for better sanitation and drainage in the city, which, he believed, was far more important that building a new Town Hall, extending the Market Place or renovating the Post Office. The Town Council, which held its meeting just round the corner at the Guildhall, constantly came under fire.

James Thompson died on May 20 1877 at the age of 60 after years of fighting off the effects of an incurable disease and the town mourned the passing of a great editor, who, it was said, had brought 'dignity and authority' to the status of newspapers.

The tributes spoke of him as a reforming leader writer (he had written practically every leader in the Chronicle for 30 years), a most courageous opponent of abuses, ever ready with his pen to advocate local and national reforms.

Early in 1877 he saw a threat to Leicester's 14th century Guildhall and came out strongly on the side of its conservation. He did not live to see the outcome of his plea, nor was he to see the construction of Abbey Park.

When he died, a pocket edition of his great history of Leicester, which he had published in two parts, in 1849 and 1871, was being distributed as a timely memorial to a great man of Leicester.

Francis Hewitt was 45 years of age when James Thompson's death gave him the opportunity to buy the Leicester Daily Mercury and the Leicestershire Chronicle and Mercury from Thompson's executors. The late Mr P H Cooper of Greenhill Road, Leicester, had in his possession the original transfer agreement of the Leicester Chronicle to Mr Hewitt.

After just over three months, staff felt the need for a more powerful printing press. It had started with a Wharfedale, which it now advertised for sale:

'To newspaper proprietors. To be sold, cheap, second-hand two-feeder single cylinder news machine now used in the printing of the Leicester Chronicle and Mercury and sold in consequence of setting up more powerful machinery. Will print a sheet 52" x 32".'

To print with this machine meant cutting each page first, printing each side separately and then passing it through a folding machine. The type used was bourgoise, brevier, minion and nonpareil. Headings were never across more than one column and they were inclined to contain adjectives which expresses an opinion: horrible, tragic, amusing, etc.

A Victory web machine was bought and it was an improvement, although the process was still extremely laborious judged by today's modern standards.

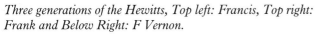

FRANCIS HEWITT
Proprietor 1877-1897

F. VERNON HEWITT
Chairman 1911-1954

FRANK HEWITT
Proprietor 1897-1906. Chairman 1906-1911

Three generations of the Hewitts, Top left: Francis, Top right: Frank and Below Right: F Vernon.

Below: F Hewitt, Bookseller, Stationer and General News Agent of 14 and 15 Granby Street, Leicester – his advertisement in 1865.

Orders carefully executed in approved styles and selected materials.

Old Carriages taken in exchange or repaired.

F. HEWITT,

BOOKSELLER, STATIONER, and GENERAL NEWS AGENT,

14 and 15, GRANBY-STREET, LEICESTER.

1866. ─ALMANACKS, DIARIES, & POCKET BOOKS for the year 1866.

CHEAP MUSIC.─5,000 Copies of the "Musical Bouquet," at 3d. per Copy (full size), including the newest Songs and Pianoforte Pieces, always in stock.

PLAYING CARDS, a large assortment of the newest Designs for the present Season, Just Received.

Mr Tony Waddington of Witney, Oxfordshire, has send me an eight-page pamphlet, entitled Sixty Years With The Press (1881-1941) by former sports writer Sam Berridge. He writes: 'It was on May 2, 1881, when young Sam Berridge walked into the Mercury office in St Martin's for an interview with the manager, Mr James (Jimmy) Thompson. He was not alone either, for another boy was there also and each, we found out later, thought we were competitors for the vacancy. That was not so, for there were two openings and we both got a job. Thus Sam Berridge and J E ('Jimmy') Blockley, who later became head of the stereo-typing department, where closely associated for many years. The first thing that attracted my attention whilst waiting for that interview was a placard standing against the wall in the vestibule that read 'Death of Lord Beaconsfield,' which had occurred a week or so previously. In due course I was apprenticed as a compositor. By the way, I am writing these recollections on the late Mr Francis Hewitt's desk on which I signed my indentures, situated, I was told, in the room in which Mr T T Paget, the subsequent banker and MP for South Leicestershire for many years, was born.

Besides the *Leicester Daily Mercury*, as it was then titled, the *Loughborough Herald* and the *Melton Mowbray Mercury and Oakham and Uppingham News* (two bi-weeklies) and the *Leicester Chronicle and Mercury*, a weekly publication largely sought for its serial stories and general and district news of the week, were the papers turned out by a comparatively small staff. But all were happy in their lot and made the most of the opportunity as piece-time compositors, whilst the apprentices were set a task according to age, with a few coppers per 1,000 ens in excess of that task. We apprentices were not confined to the case all the time.

There were other jobs to do. Every Saturday morning I was detailed to take the 'L C and M' second edition forme from St Martin's to Lamb and Palmer's in Granby Place. It was only a single slip-in sheet that constituted the second edition, but that forme hung rather heavy before the journey either way was complete.

The Francis Hewitt and Son enterprise made rapid headway. It really commenced when everyone was astounded when the Saturday issue containing 12 pages for half a penny made its appearance. From that time, the Mercury became an even more household necessity as a result of its news value and advertising medium.

A further step along the path of progress was when Mr Francis Hewitt acquired the Leicester Daily Post, previously controlled by the Rev Joseph Wood, chairman of the Leicester School Board and Minister at Wycliffe Congregational Church. Mr Angus Galbraith, editor of the Mercury, was transferred to the Post in a similar capacity, with Mr Harry Hackett, the chief reporter, commencing a long and honoured career as editor of the *Leicester Mercury* (in 1882).

In my early days at St Martin's, the only transport available was a handcart, supplemented by a cab in an emergency. It was on a Friday morning after the Chronicle run had not been any too smooth. 'Fetch a fly,' ordered the manager. A four-wheeler was obtained from a nearby cab rank and off we go post haste for the Midland Station in Campbell Street, but not for far. At the top of Grey Friars, there was a sudden stop and it was found that a piece of the cab floor had given way under the weight of the parcels. That cabby didn't half let go. What he said about the Chronicle and everyone connected with it would not pass any editor in these enlightened days. But we weathered the storm and remained to see many alterations for the better.'

Triumphal Arch Belgrave Gate (Opening of Abbey ... 1882.

The Granby Street bookseller had served his apprenticeship with James Thompson in what historians now record as the 'Hungry Forties,' when the people of Leicester, in great masses, were workless and starving, a grim forerunner to the prosperity which the 20th century was to bring to the city of Leicester.

For ten years after becoming the owner of the Mercury, he retained his bookshop and his flair for knowing what the public wanted was shown when, during the Egyptian wars, he placed in his windows copies of the Illustrated London News and other pictorial periodicals with their graphic reproduction of war scenes – the police had to be called to control the crowds surging round the shop to look at the pictures.

He had been elected to the Board of Guardians in 1866 and in 1871 had beaten a Tory by 255 to 18 votes for a seat on the Town Council, representing North St Margaret's Ward. He had also given active assistance to Liberal parliamentary candidates and shortly after the general election of 1880, which saw Gladstone and the Liberal Party at the head of the polls, the Liberals of the North Leicestershire constituency persuaded him to establish two more newspapers, the Loughborough Herald and the Melton Mowbray Mercury. Two years later he bought the Leicester Daily Post, a morning newspaper which had been founded by a Nottingham man. It was published from 39 Humberstone Gate, now the Mannie Social Club, with the Rev J Woods as editor.

Ready-set type used to be taken from the Leicester Mercury offices in St Martin's to Humberstone Gate by hand-truck. On one occasion this truck collapsed under the weight in Cank Street and the type was spilled all over the road. He now owned five newspapers.

Francis left the Town Council for health reasons after his first term ended, but in 1878 he had sufficiently recovered to allow his name to go forward in the place of his friend Thomas Windley, who had been made an alderman. He was returned unopposed and in 1882 he was elected Mayor of Leicester. During his year of office, the Mayoress presented him with a son and to celebrate the event they were presented by the borough with a silver cradle. His son was given the name Leicester to mark the occasion. This was Francis Hewitt's second son in seven children. By his first wife he had a son, Francis, and a daughter. After her death, he married Miss Elizabeth Cook, by whom he had four daughters and a son. Both sons were destined to join their father's business, the elder at the age of 27 becoming a partner with his father in 1888 by which time the Mercury had doubled its circulation to 10,000 a day.

1888 was an important year in the Leicester Mercury's history. The premises in St Martin's had become wholly inadequate. The publications were being even more widely read and set a standard of journalism which was fully recognised. The business acquired property in Albion Street and Wellington Street. It had been up for auction

Opposite page: A Triumphal Arch erected in Belgrave Gate specially for the Royal Visit of the Prince and Princess of Wales when they came to open the Abbey Park in May 1882.

Left: Albion Street offices were completed for occupation in 1890 – the architect had incorporated this striking heraldic griffin sculpture.

Right: Harry Hackett, the Leicester Mercury's first non-proprietor editor.

1895

◆ The average wage of a compositor was between 28 shillings and 30 shillings a week and there was no limit to the amount of hours he might be asked to work. If he could write, he would double up as a reporter as well.

◆ To be first with the story was the name of the game – even if it meant setting the type for a court case held elsewhere at a local firm of printers and bringing it back. A simultaneous fire bell as that which would alert the Fire Brigade in Bowling Green Street would sound and the fire engine would have a place reserved for a reporter from the Leicester Mercury!

in 1883 and when it came on to the market again Francis bought it for £4,900. It contained three cottages in Albion Street, numbers 25, 27 and 29, an engineer's shop, stables and three malthouses. The cottages made way for the boiler-house entry and publishing office, the engineer's premises for the front office and the stable for the side entrance. Completion came in 1890 and the move from St Martin's was made. It was to be the home of the evening paper and its associated weeklies for nearly 80 years until the move the St George Street in 1967.

Francis found he could no longer combine the editorship with his many other duties, therefore in 1890 he appointed Mr Harry Hackett, an employee of 12 years, as the first non-proprietor editor. Francis was on the Board of directors of the Press Association and in 1892 he was elected chairman (an honour in the newspaper world) and he took part in the moving of the headquarters from Wine Office Court, off Fleet Street, to better premises in New Bridge Street, Blackfriars. Later, he was also President of the Newspaper Society, the provincial newspapers' employers' organisation and did much to unite managements under the Society's banner.

To celebrate the move to Albion Street, he entertained staff and a few leading Leicester business men to dinner in what eventually became the composing room.

Mr Sam Berridge recalls the move: 'It was a great day when we entered the more

spacious and convenient premises in Albion Street in 1889, which really marked the beginning of rapid growth of an up-to-date and enterprising newspaper venture. Before the actual commencement of business in the new building, however, Mr Francis Hewitt entertained the staff to dinner in what was to be the composing room in celebration of the occasion. Mr Hewitt's guests included several personal friends and well-known local businessmen. Thus the composing room made history at the very outset. We had already replaced the Wharfdale with a Victory web machine whilst at St Martin's, but it was not long before that was scrapped in favour of the more up-to-date and rapid Hoe Rotary presses. This was a revelation indeed, for where in the old Wharfdale days a paper had three operations – printing each side separately and then feeding each sheet through a folding machine. But the Hoe did away with all that by feeding from a reel of paper some four and a half miles long to produce the finished article and counted into dozens into the bargain.'

It was not long before the first four linotype setting machines were bought, the first to introduce linotype in Leicester and one of the first in the Midlands. By 1894 the Leicester Mercury circulation figures hit 15,000 copies a day and extra staff were continually being engaged and new machinery purchased. In 1895 a second one-unit web press was bought.

Left: The Francis Hewitt shelter at Hunstanton.

Below: The News Room on the corner of Belvoir Street and Granby Street, Leicester, built in 1898.

Bottom: Detail of the carvings in a archway at the News Room. It has been suggested the two figures represent Thought and Study.

Francis was spending more and more time in the healing environment of Hunstanton as his health was failing, leaving his eldest son, Francis, more usually called Frank, more and more in charge. In 1897, at the age of 65, Francis died after a long and distinguished career of public service. A shelter was erected to the memory of Francis in Hunstanton on the cliff tops overlooking the sea in 1898. The local council renovated the shelter in the early 1980s.

The newspaper undertook changes in the editorial make-up, in line with many other papers. Readers were more educated and wanted general knowledge as well as the latest news in their paper. Useful hints on housekeeping and cookery found their way into the weeklies, with supplements containing a serial story by a well-known author. Illustrations in the form of drawings, mostly portraits, were frequently used.

Frank's early training had been on the commercial side of the business and he often joked that the editorial side constituted the 'overhead expenses.' He started daily editorial conferences, attended by himself, the editor, chief sub-editor and the manager, Mr James Thomson, a genial Scot who had been in the position since 1877.

For half an hour, they would discuss the main news items of the day and decide what and how they should be featured. Special editions with outstanding news of the day became more frequent. 1892 saw the first one – the death of the Duke of Clarence, eldest son of the future King Edward VII – and others followed – an account of the execution of a Loughborough murderer in 1894 and a train disaster at Wellingborough in 1898.

THE LEICESTER DAILY MERCURY, TUESDAY, JULY 24, 1863.

THE DAILY MERCURY,
Leicester, July 24, 1883.

The London Office of the Daily Mercury and Chronicle and Mercury is at East Temple Chambers, Fleet-street, E.C., Mr. R. HARRIS, Manager. Advertisements received until 6.45 p.m. will be in time for the following day's publication.

Loughborough Branch Office:—42, Baxter-gate.

Mr. Gladstone announced in the House of Commons last night that the agreement with M. de Lesseps in reference to the projected new Suez Canal would be withdrawn. Thus, as we remarked yesterday, the Ministry have admitted that the terms to which they assented have failed to meet the views of those in the country who are interested in the question, and we fear that this admission will not do them much good. It must not be supposed that this decision on the part of the Cabinet will remove the subject from the region of discussion either in Parliament or out of it. The Conservatives profess a certain amount of pleasure that the Government have abandoned the scheme, but they will not fail to make use of what has occurred for the purpose of harassing the Cabinet. It is indeed, indeed, that they should adopt every means in their power to discredit Ministers, and the surrender of the latter to the outcry which has been raised will give some colour to the assertions of the Opposition. If, however, the terms of the agreement are fairly stated, and the facts of the case thoroughly understood, it will be the Government, at any rate so far as the issues between the Ministry and the Opposition are concerned.

The course which the Government have decided to take will be regretted in many quarters; but it must be admitted that both Earl Granville and the Prime Minister assigned very good reasons for it. Mr. Gladstone pointed out that he and his colleagues were pressed to enter into negotiations with the Suez Canal Company on account of the desire which existed in commercial circles in England that the maritime highway should be improved. In the course of those negotiations he believed considerable concessions were obtained from the shareholders—at all events they were such as the Government thought fair, though the Premier granted that it was for the House and the country to say whether they were a sufficient equivalent for the engagements which Great Britain undertook to fulfil. The right hon. gentleman recognised that this was the part few days a change has been observable in the tone of the communications addressed to Ministers on the subject, there is not sufficient unanimity in the public mind to justify the Government in adhering to the agreement, and consequently they have decided not to press it upon the attention of Parliament.

From Mr. Gladstone's statement—and the Premier was fully supported by the briefer explanation of the Foreign Secretary in the other House—it would seem that in the first instance the Government had some doubts as to whether they ought to enter into negotiations with a commercial company on such a matter. We are not surprised that this should have been the case, and it is doubtful whether they acted quite wisely in doing so. The circumstance, however, were somewhat peculiar. Not only were commercial circles dissatisfied with the accommodation provided by the canal, but we had already a great pecuniary interest in the company, and then the state of affairs in Egypt was altogether singular, and gave us opportunities for exercising a good deal of influence. This being so, Ministers may have felt justified in dealing with M. de Lesseps instead of leaving commercial men to regulate a commercial undertaking. But it is very satisfactory to have the assurance of the Government that notwithstanding all that has occurred they will not use the peculiar position in which they now find themselves in Egypt to wring from the company terms inconsistent with justice and honesty. As Mr. Gladstone observed, the Cabinet will be put by to asserting the dominion of England over the waterway of the isthmus, notwithstanding that what Lord Salisbury may desire, neither will they take advantage of the exceptional position they occupy in Egypt to procure the abatement of any right possessed by the company.

But what is likely to be the outcome of the decision of the Government? The canal cannot be maintained in its present state. Lord Salisbury congratulated the Ministry on withdrawing from the agreement, but what will this incur? M. de Lesseps will now proceed either with the extension of the present stream or with the construction of a second canal upon land already possessed by the company, but in this case the parallel way will not be so advantageously situated as it would have been under the scheme submitted to Parliament by the Chancellor of the Exchequer. In a letter to Mr. Gladstone the Chairman of the Company states that the reduction of dues will be carried out according to the terms of the agreement when the second canal is made, but this reduction cannot take effect so early as was promised, because it will cost more to raise the capital required than the English Government proposed to charge. Thus English shipowners have not very much to be congratulated upon. Then the proposal that Great Britain should be more fully represented upon the directorate will

The second Liberal candidate for South Essex is no "weak-kneed Whig," to judge by his "profession of faith" as made at a meeting in the Town Hall of Stratford last night. Mr. Cook said he was an ardent follower of Mr. Gladstone, was in favour of the reform of the House of Lords, and would like to see a scheme developed for the creation of life peers and the House relieved of the presence of the bishops; he desired to see fair play in religion and in land, and was theoretically in favour of the nationalisation of the land, which was a big question and wanted a big man to handle it. If Mr. Cook is a sample of the gentlemen likely to be accepted as Liberal candidates for English counties in the immediate future Radicals in the boroughs will have to look to their laurels.

The cholera is still causing sad havoc in Egypt. It is said that five hundred deaths have taken place in Cairo, and the scenes described by the correspondents as having occurred in the city are heartrending. At length it would appear that the sanitary arrangements are to be thoroughly overhauled. A commission comprising General Wood, General Stephenson, and Baker Pasha has been appointed to look into these matters, and it has been decided to establish three additional hospitals and to organise an ambulance corps, while twelve English doctors, well versed in the disease, will leave this country for Egypt to-day by order of the Government, taking with them a large supply of medical stores. It is to be hoped that these measures will prove effective, and check the extension of the complaint.

Local and District News.

PRESTON'S BOOTS are acknowledged to fit well, look well, and wear well, at prices defying competition.—Tower Buildings Depôt, Haymarket.—[Advt.
GEO. BROWN'S for Men's Cardigan Jackets, Boys' Jerseys and Jersey Suits, 42½, Humberstone-gt.—[Advt.
ROYAL OPERA HOUSE.—This house re-opened last evening with Buckstone's famous drama, "The Green Bushes," which was satisfactorily presented by Mr. Nelson Wheatcroft's dramatic company, and sympathetically received by a moderate audience. The most noticeable feature in the performance was the thoroughly natural acting of Miss Lizzie Scobie as Nelly O'Neil, a part she presented in a charmingly unaffected manner. Miss Maude Brennan was the Geniviere, and altogether was satisfactory in her undertaking, as also was Miss Clinton as Geraldine. Mr. Nelson Wheatcroft was Connor O'Kennedy, and was most favourably received, but we have seen him to better advantage in lighter parts. The George O'Kennedy of Mr. Vincent Sternroyd was somewhat lacking in power, but otherwise it was a careful representation. Mr. Edmund Tearle was particularly pronounced as Wild Murtough, whilst the Messrs. Deacon and Belford proved themselves thorough comedians. ABOUT (Bird Eyevett v. COLACERIAY)—This match was played at Ashby on Wednesday, and resulted in a victory for the visitors. Score:—

LEICESTER, No. 1.		SHEEPSHED, No. 2.	
Rowell, b Standley	12	Smedley, c and b Williams	7
radford, b Dunmore	2	Foster, b Bradley	6
Grigsby, c Wootton	8	Batson, b Williams	3
Brumby	5	Dunmore, st. Potter	1
Brownlow, c Bullen, b Dunmore	11	Stott, run out	5
Poulter, c and b Dunmore	6	Preik, b Williams	4
Pullen, c b Potter	3	Bullen, b Potter	0
Allen, c and b Preik	3	Dunmore, st. b Potter	4
Jackson, c and b Smedley	7	Mun, not out	3
Thornley, not out	1	Chaplin, b Williams	0
Hull, run out	1	Extras	4
Bownman, run out	0		
Extras	4		
Total	**63**	**Total**	**41**

NEW TALE by Miss BRADDON, "PHANTOM FORTUNE," has commenced in the Chronicle and Mercury.

THIS DAY'S POLICE

TOWN HALL.
TUESDAY.—Before W. Bowlett (in the chair) and J. P. Clarke, Esqrs.

BREACHES OF BYE-LAWS.—Wm. Watts was charged with leaving a horse and carriage for an unreasonable length of time, thus causing an obstruction of the thoroughfare.—The offence was proved by P.C. Neal, who stated that the defendant left the vehicle in the street three-quarters of an hour.—He was fined 5s.

—Geo. Newitt Jones was charged and remanded with neglecting to comply with a notice served upon him on the 19th of June to remove a certain nuisance.—The Town Clerk (Mr. John Storey) appeared, and said that since the adjournment of the case the defendant had consented to carry out the order, and he therefore asked that the summons be dismissed.—The Bench thereupon dismissed the summons, expressing their gratification that the defendant had consented to do the work necessary to abate the nuisance.

WANTING TO SEE THE RACES.—John O'Brien, a young man, was brought up in custody charged with travelling on the Midland Railway without a ticket.—Frederick Daniels, porter in the employ of the railway company, stated that he was appointed to collect tickets by the 5.10 special train arriving at Leicester from London this morning, and asked the prisoner for a ticket. He stated that he had given it up to witness, and afterwards said that a person with whom he was travelling had given witness two tickets. On being searched about 5s. was found upon him.—The prisoner, in reply to the charge, adhered to the statement that a fellow passenger had given the porter a ticket for him.—The Bench said they did not believe him, and ordered that he be imprisoned for seven days in default of paying a fine of 20s.

OBSCENITY.—Henry Marrs, a young man, handed guilty to using obscene language in Gallowtree-gate on the 7th of July.—He was fined 2s., or 14 days' imprisonment.

A DISORDERLY SHOEMAKER.—Henry Bruce, a shoemaker, was charged with committing two pairs of boot tops on the 2nd of July, the property of Wm. Minard.—The prisoner pleaded guilty.—The prosecutor stated that on the 2nd of July he gave the prisoner 18 pairs of tops and bottoms to rivet, and expected him to return them the next day. Several days elapsed, and as witness did not receive them he sent to the prisoner's house, but found that he had gone to work elsewhere. A man named Lewin returned 16 pairs, and two pairs were still missing.—The prisoner had nothing to say in answer to the charge, and he was committed to prison for a month with hard labour.

THE MAYOR'S OPEN-AIR CONCERTS.

The following is the programme of music to be performed by Mr. Nicholson's Band, in the Market-place, this (Tuesday) evening, from 8 to 9 p.m., weather permitting:—

Pas Redouble	Royal Standard	Vandi
Overture	Nino	Verdi
Serenade		Schubert
Operatic Selection	Maritana	Wallace
Valse	Volantine	Sullivan
March of the Israelites	Eli	Costa
Gavotte	Coriolan Brothers	Lord Duppill
Pas de Patineurs	(Piccolo solo)	Oliver
Descriptive piece—The Turkish Patrol	Michaelis
Selection	La Mascotta	Audran
March	Boccaccio	Audran
Polka	Hippo's	Barrett
Overture	Tancredi	Rossini
Valse	La Barcarelle, b Naples	Waldteufel
Finale	Gioia di Lammermoor	Donizetti
Galop	Brighton	Reyloff
Pot Pourri	National Airs	Nicholson
God save the Prince of Wales.
God save the Queen.

THE SUEZ CANAL QUESTION.

LETTER OF M. DE LESSEPS TO MR. GLADSTONE.

PARIS, July 23.—M. Ferdinand de Lesseps addressed the following letter to Mr. Gladstone on the 20th instant:—

"My dear and honourable friend,—You are aware with what cordiality the fixed mind of admiration and the representatives of the Government of the Queen on that board have directed themselves unceasingly up to the present time, within the limits of the law, to the legitimate interests of the shareholders and the clients of the universal maritime canal. This constant accord has just been concluded in a written agreement which gave to this twofold interest such just rights as were permitted on the one hand by the obligations of a company employing an exclusive monopoly for 99 years of constructing a maritime canal in the Egyptian Isthmus, and, on the other hand, of the shipowners whose fleets makes use of the work accomplished after so much outlay and such great efforts. This agreement, examined and concerted with the Ministers of the Queen, aimed at giving effect to the principal objects of both parties by securing within the shortest possible term the construction of a maritime canal parallel to the present one, and by holding out a prospect of reductions of rates in conformity with the progress solemnly made at a former time to the shareholders and shipowners. In frank public opinion, forgetting the past, has unanimously applauded this accord. In England, it appears to me, a section of public opinion, which has perhaps judged hastily, has not understood the whole bearing of the equitable arrangement which has been arrived at, and the result has been unpleasant discussions between two friendly nations—discussions which I fear may prejudice deeply, and for a long time, the necessary sentiments of strong friendship which have united the two peoples. I should personally be much grieved if a work of peace, executed in Egypt with French capital in the interest of universal commerce, should become a motive of discord, and if Europe were to witness the development in the English Parliament and under your Liberal Ministry of an error of judgment fatal to right. In the interest of general peace, to which you give attachment, for the English alliance, indispensable to the civilization of the world, I beg you not to consider yourself bound towards myself by the terms of the agreement we have signed. Our board of administration possesses by the statutes of the company sufficient powers to decide upon the construction of a second maritime canal and to settle the dues to be levied, and our shareholders are in a position to furnish the means for cutting a second canal. Consequently regard it as expressly understood that if our agreement be suspended or even withdrawn, the construction of a second maritime canal will be immediately carried out, and all the reductions of dues foreshadowed in that agreement will be enforced, and we shall continue to undertake that peace as hitherto, and in accord with the representatives of the Queen's Government on the board, to work and improve the maritime canal in accordance with the exigencies of a work made to render freely open and safe for the fleets of all nations, without exclusion or favour, according to the terms of our concession.—Accept, my dear and honourable friend, the expression of my affectionate sentiments and my high esteem.
(Signed)
"FERDINAND DE LESSEPS."

A town's meeting convened by the Mayor in accordance with a requisition of the leading Conservatives of the town was held in the Town Hall, Birmingham, on Monday night, to consider the question of the second Suez Canal. The hall was crowded, and throughout the proceedings party feeling was so high that not a single speaker was allowed an uninterrupted hearing. Fearing a great disturbance, the chief of police, by order of the Mayor, stationed a large body of police in various parts of the building, besides having a reserve of about one hundred men in one of the ante-rooms.—Mr. Satchell Hopkins, chairman of the Birmingham Conservative Association, moved a resolution expressing approval of the action of the Government in deferring the consideration of the scheme. He thought it was about the wisest thing that the Government had done.—Mr. Edward Gem seconded the resolution.—Mr. George Dixon, chairman of the Birmingham Liberal Association, moved as an amendment, "That this meeting, considering the substantial concessions contained in the provisional agreement, expresses its full confidence in the ability of Mr. Gladstone and his colleagues to secure for this country all the advantages which can be obtained by further negotiations conducted with a due regard for the rights and interests of other nations." Throughout the course of Mr. Dixon's speech the greatest uproar prevailed, and the remarks were inaudible.—Mr. R. Tangye seconded the amendment, which was carried amidst applause, yells, and hisses, by a large majority. It was resolved to forward copies of the amendment to Mr. Gladstone, Mr. Chamberlain, and Mr. Childers.

Thomas Sperr, money lender, was committed for trial by the Doncaster magistrates on Monday on a charge of forging the endorsement to a bill of exchange.

The members of the congregation assembled in Youlgreave Church were on Sunday much startled by the appearance in a man that misled who called for "silence," and said he was the bearer of a message from the King of Kings. He turned out to be a lunatic.

A woman named Agnes Beach was on Monday found with her throat cut in a Nottingham alms-house, occupied by a man named John Friezle. The latter said he knew nothing of the case further than that he found the woman—who lies in a critical condition—but he is in custody pending inquiries.

A lady named Austin has died in Paris possessed of property worth upwards of half a million sterling. She died intestate, and as there is no next-of-kin the question of her domicile has arisen with a view to decide whether her fortune shall go to the British Crown or to the Government of the French Republic. Most of the property is in this country. The case was mentioned in the Probate Court on Monday, and was postponed in order that the French Government may have an opportunity of intervening in the case.

On Monday afternoon an event of a very unique and exceptional character—being, we believe, the first of the kind known in the history of the borough, took place in the Council Chamber, Town Hall, when Alderman Chambers, the ex-Mayor, on behalf of the subscribers presented the Mayor and Mayoress with a silver cradle in commemoration of the birth of their son, Arthur Leicester, during Worship's year of office. Though the opportunity had never previously occurred in the town for such a ceremony, it was known to be customary throughout the country when the occasion presented itself, and being anxious to observe the congratulatory practice followed in other municipal towns, a number of gentlemen formed themselves into a committee for the purpose in May last. Alderman Chambers was elected chairman, and the following were the committee, with Mr. J. Storey (Town Clerk), hon. secretary:—Ald. Barfoot, Ald. Bennett, Mr. Wm. Hilton, Mr. W. J. Brda, Mr. A. H. Burgess, Mr. E. Clephan, Mr. J. H. Cooper, Mr. W. H. Ellis, Mr. H. E. Emberlin, Mr. W. Gleadow, Mr. James Green, Mr. C. Gordon, Mr. I. Hart, Mr. J. E. Hodges, Mr. Holyland, Ald. Kempson, Mr. Geo. Oliver, Ald. Paget, Mr. J. G. F. Richardson, Ald. Stafford, Ald. Stevenson, Mr. S. F. Stone, Ald. Stretton, Mr. Underwood, Ald. Viccars, Mr. Robt. Waite, Ald. Windley, and Mr. T. Wright. They decided to open a subscription list, the subscribers not to be limited to members of the Town Council, and subscriptions not to exceed a guinea each. A ready response was made to the suggestion of the committee by their friends, and designs for the ornament were invited from the following:—Messrs. Cort and Paul (Market-place), Mrs. Rowland (Gallowtree-gate), Mr. Curtis (Market-place), Mr. Kirby, late Gray (Cheap-side), Mr. Bott (Granby-street), Mr. W. F. Johnson (Gallowtree-gate), and Mr. R. Osmond (Market-place). After due consideration the committee selected the design submitted by Mr. Kirby, of Cheapside, who was accordingly entrusted with their instructions, and provided the piece of plate—a cradle-épergne—which is of an exceedingly handsome and beautiful design, prepared specially for the purpose. On an oval base of bright silver, elaborately and delicately ornamented with foliage filled with fruit and vine-work, emblematic of fruitfulness, stand two angels exquisitely modelled in snow-white frosted silver, standing dos-à-dos. Their arms are uplifted, and thus they bear the cradle—the chief feature in the ornament—between them. The cradle itself is of bright silver, and contains an infant of frosted silver. In the front of the base is a shield to high relief, on which is engraved the following inscription:—"Presented, on the 23rd July, 1883, to Francis Hewitt, Esq., Mayor of Leicester, and Mrs. Hewitt, in commemoration of the birth of their son, Arthur Leicester, on the 4th May, 1883." At the back is a corresponding shield containing the borough arms. On smaller medallions on the base is the monogram F.E.H.—the initials of the Mayor and Mayoress. At each end of the base, at the feet of the angels, sits a cherub of frosted silver, with instruments of music. From the platform on which the angels stand rise partly branches of silver, supporting glass dishes, richly engraved with festoons of fruit and flowers. These branches may be removed and smaller épergnes put in their places, so as to give the ornament the character of a centre-piece only instead of an épergne if desirable. The child forms also a lid to the cradle and may be removed, the cradle thus serving the purpose of a flower or fruit holder. The plate rests on a stand of maroon velvet, which considerably adds to the effect. The total weight is 126 oz., the base proper being 19 inches in length, and 15½in. wide. The height is about 17in., and the branches referred to extend 29 in. measured from edge to edge. The design is most original and artistic, and the workmanship exceedingly chaste and skilful. The figures are a splendid work of art, being perfect in execution in every detail. The expression of the features is very pleasing, the engraving ornate, and the whole effect most admirable. The approaches to the Council Chamber were bedecked with bunting and choice flowers and plants on the occasion of the presentation, and a quantity of superb roses and other blooms were placed in artistic profusion about the room itself. A number of the subscribers, with a lady escort, were invited by the committee to be present, the full list of invitations being as follows:—Mr. W. W. Stretton and lady, Mr. and Mrs. W. N. Reeve, Mr. and Mrs. J. Pilgrim, Dr. Shaw and lady, Mr. W. Bowmar and lady, Mr. and Mrs. C. R. Crossley, Mr. and Mrs. Emberlin, Mr. and Mrs. T. M. Evans, Mr. and Mrs. R. Argrave, Mr. and Mrs. J. Sarson, Mr. and Mrs. Higginson, Mr. and Mrs. T. F. Johnson, Mr. and Mrs. Howlett, Mr. and Mrs. Richardson, Mr. and Mrs. Howcutt, Mr. and Mrs. T. D. Paul, Mr. and Mrs. J. P. Clarke, Captain and Mrs. Goodchild, Mr. Crow and lady, Ald. and Mrs. Chambers, Ald. and Mrs. Stretton, Ald. and Mrs. Kempson, Ald. and Mrs. Stretton, Ald. and Mrs. Stevenson, Ald. and Mrs. Paget, Ald. and Mrs. Bennett, Ald. and Mrs. Windley, Ald. and Mrs. Viccars, Ald. and Mrs. Almond, Ald. and Mrs. Barfoot, Ald. and Mrs. Wood, Councillor and Mrs. Butcher, Councillor and Mrs. Mott, Councillor and Mrs. Carey, Councillor and Mrs. Black, Councillor and Mrs. Swain, Councillor Burgess and lady, Councillor and Mrs. Green, Councillor and Mrs. Clifton, Councillor Leonard and Mrs. Leonard, Councillor and Mrs. Franklin, Councillor Cleaver and lady, Councillor Haines and lady, Councillor and Mrs. G. Ellis, Councillor and Mrs. Holyland, Councillor and Mrs. Hart, Councillor and Mrs. T. Goddard, Councillor and Mrs. Wilford, Councillor and Mrs. Rowley, Councillor and Mrs. Dicks, Councillor and Mrs. Grimes, Councillor Sheen and lady, Councillor and Mrs. Meadows, Councillor and Mrs. Colton, Councillor and Mrs. Oliver, Councillor and Mrs. Wood, Councillor and Mrs. Butcher, Councillor and Mrs. Mott, Councillor and Mrs. Carey, Councillor and Mrs. Black, Councillor and Mrs. Swain, Councillor Burgess and lady, Councillor and Mrs. Green, Councillor and Mrs. Clifton, Councillor Leonard and Mrs. Leonard, Councillor and Mrs. Franklin, Councillor Cleaver and lady, Councillor Haines and lady, Councillor and Mrs. G. Ellis, Councillor and lady, Councillor Deacon, Mr. and Mrs. G. F. Harrison, Mr. W. Billson (Borough Treasurer) and Mrs. Billson, Mr. Walters and lady, Mr. and Mrs. R. Toller, Mr. and Mrs. R. S. Toller, Mr. S. F. Stone and lady, Mr. and Mrs. J. H. Cooper, Mr. and Mrs. W. H. Ellis, Mr. and Mrs. J. Levy, Mr. and Mrs. W. Waite, Mr. and Mrs. Clephan, Mr. and Mrs. I. Hart, Mr. and Mrs. W. Gleadow, Mr. and Mrs. Downing, Ald. and Mrs. S. Davis, Mr. J. J. Corah and lady, Mr. A. Corah and lady, Mr. A. B. Cooper and lady, Mr. C. S. Burnaby and lady, Rev. J. Went and Mrs. Went, Rev. A. F. Dawson and lady, Mr. and Mrs. A. R. Bird, Mr. and Mrs. J. A. Wykes, Mr. and Mrs. Tabberer, Mr. and Mrs. Wilshere, Mr. and Mrs. J. G. Chambers, and others.

The CHAIRMAN said he was sure the company would be anxious to express their thanks to the ladies and gentlemen for the musical treat they had provided, and to express their hearty thanks. He wished proceedings to be most splendid manner. He wished to include also Miss Deacon, who had kindly given the use of the piano for the occasion. (Loud cheers.)

The National Anthem was then sung, and after inspecting the piece of silver the company gradually dispersed.

The present would be exhibited in Mr. Kirby's (late Gray's) window in Cheapside for a few days.

The Royal Commission on the crofters' question closed its sittings in Orkney on Monday. The most exciting event of the meeting was the refusal by one landlord, General Burroughs, of Rousay, to give an undertaking that he would henceforth adopt the tenants in consequence of the evidence they might give. He said he would accept no such pledge and give. He said to do would be to condone law-breaking by the tenants, and that he was bound to protect the other members of his community against them. A warm discussion ensued, but the witnesses who had given evidence were all adamant.

With a view to the resumption of regular diplomatic relations with the Mexican Republic, there arrived at Liverpool, on Monday, by the White Star steamer Britannic, from New York, Señor Marisco, who has for some time represented Mexico at Washington. Señor Marisco, who comes to England as Envoy Extraordinary to Great Britain, was received by the Mayor of Liverpool at the Town Hall, and last evening departed for London.

The committee of management of the Liverpool Liberal Association met on Monday evening, and resolved that its Ninth Hundred should record their satisfaction with the conduct of the Government in dealing with the current practice at elections, and to express the hope that the Government will at the earliest moment restore that pledge to introduce into the Ballot Act Continuance Bill a clause extending the hours of polling.

MALARIAL FEVER.—Malarial fevers, constipation, torpidity of the liver and kidneys, unreliability, nervousness, and neuralgia, arising from them, are all dispelled by Hop Bitters. It strengthens and builds up the system as nothing else will do. Observe.—At the druggists' call for Hop Bitters, and try them before you sleep. Take no other. Dr. Soule's Hop Bitters cures with a few doses. Remarkable cures effected where all else fails.—See advt.

Chapter 3
Private Limited Company
1900 – 1910

The turn of the century did not see any special treatment in the Leicester Daily Mercury. Indeed, New Year's Eve was a Sunday and there does not appear to be an issue for January 1. However, the edition for Saturday, December 30, had nearly four columns with the title 1899 – A Retrospect and the national survey was taken from the Leicester Chronicle.

'Leicester in 1899' had the following foreword:

> Leicester has shared very fully in the national prosperity in the past year and also in the anxieties of the war which is an unfortunate blur on that prosperity. Trade has been good and employment regular – where not interrupted by strikes – the people generally are, we are glad to know, better off today than in previous seasons and prospects are promising. Our local bodies have had much work to do and the public burdens have had to be augmented, but it cannot be pretended that the people are unable to bear them. Religious and educational institutions have put forth renewed energies, there has been more political activity, we have been, happily, free from calamity and serious crime and the death-roll is not a heavy one, though it includes several well-known and honoured names. There is trouble in many homes on account of absent ones in peril on the battlefield, but Leicester has nobly borne its part in assuaging the sorrows of wives and children left at home. Whatever the future may have in store, the past has given us much to be thankful for.

Queen Victoria's health had been showing signs of strain over the year and appeared to be seriously ill when at Osbourne House on the Isle of Wight in December. A woman, whose apparent refusal to acknowledge the effect of any sickness had only embellished her image as the very cornerstone of the empire she rules, is at last weakening. The death of her son Alfred in July came brutally sudden and the continuing tales of reverses and defeats in South Africa had seriously distressed her.

At 6.30pm on January 22, 1901, she breathed her last, surrounded by her children and grandchildren at Osbourne House. Outside, a pack of pressmen yelled 'Queen dead!' and raced to be first to the telephones.

So the era to which Victoria gave her name had come to an end. She had graced the throne for nearly 64 years of great change.

The next day, black-bordered newspapers carried the details of the Queen's passing, not only in Britain but also around the world as the news reached the far-flung parts of the world's largest empire. Sombre citizens queued to buy special editions of newspapers which chronicled the reign of the only monarch whom almost everyone could remember.

The Leicester Daily Mercury too issued a special edition. The edition of January 23 still carried advertisements on the front page, but inside it reported how the news was received in Leicester – in fact, the first intimation that she had died was received at 7.18pm the day before 'through the medium of a Central News telegram' and a special edition was immediately published. Within the next half-hour, 'the bulk of the inhabitants were made aware of the irreparable loss which the nation had sustained.' Its opinion column carried the headline The New Order and said:

> 'We do not realise as yet all that the death of the Queen involves. To most men and women now living the name of Victoria is inseparably associated with the national life. The majority have never known a King. Even those whose recollections carry them back to the days of George III and George IV can only have dim youthful remembrances of that far-off time. The Queen virtually saw the beginning of modern England. Her reign has been contemporaneous with the remarkable growth of British trade and commerce and the extension of British influence.'

The first seeds of competition to the Leicester Mercury were sown in 1901. Lord Cecil Manners, MP, Dr C H Marriott, Mr J H Marshall and others launched an appeal for £30,000 'to establish a Daily Evening Half-penny Paper for the Town and County

Opposite page: Page 2 of the Leicester Daily Mercury for July 24, 1883

Above: Sir John Rolleston.

Left: In lament of the short-lived rival Leicester Evening News.

Opposite page: Report of the Coronation of Edward VII, on page 2 of the Leicester Daily Mercury of August 9, 1902.

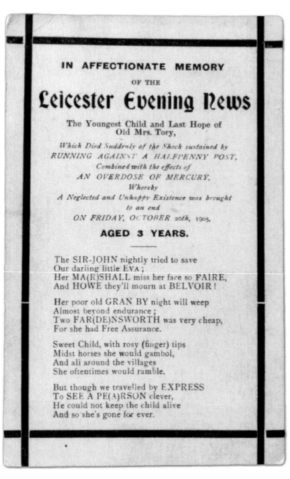

IN AFFECTIONATE MEMORY

OF THE

Leicester Evening News

The Youngest Child and Last Hope of
Old Mrs. Tory,

Which Died Suddenly of the Shock sustained by
RUNNING AGAINST A HALFPENNY POST,
Combined with the effects of
AN OVERDOSE OF MERCURY,
Whereby
A Neglected and Unhappy Existence was brought
to an end
ON FRIDAY, OCTOBER 20th, 1905,

AGED 3 YEARS.

The SIR-JOHN nightly tried to save
Our darling little EVA;
Her MA(R)SHALL miss her face so FAIRE,
And HOWE they'll mourn at BELVOIR!

Her poor old GRAN BY night will weep
Almost beyond endurance;
Two FAR(DE)NSWORTH was very cheap,
For she had Free Assurance.

Sweet Child, with rosy (finger) tips
Midst horses she would gambol,
And all around the villages
She oftentimes would ramble.

But though we travelled by EXPRESS
To SEE A PE(A)RSON clever,
He could not keep the child alive
And so she's gone for ever.

of Leicester.' By the end of 1901, £25,000 had been raised and on March 1, 1902, a meeting of all those interested was held at the Conservative Club under the chairmanship of Sir John Rolleston, MP. Among those present was a future director of the Leicester Mercury, Mr John Parsons. It was felt the time had come when any further postponement of deciding something definite would be detrimental to the Tory party and it was decided to approach Mr C Arthur Pearson of the Daily Express to find out whether he would be prepared to help in starting a newspaper.

Mr Pearson proposed that the sum of £30,000 was to be subscribed to a company formed locally and invested by such company in debentures of the Daily Express Limited, carrying interest at £5 per cent per annum. 'Such debentures to rank pari passu with the £200,000 debentures of the Daily Express Limited already issued and to be a first charge on the assets of the Daily Express Limited. In respect of these £30,000 debentures, 100 shares (being 5 per cent of the total share capital) of the Daily Express Limited will be transferred to the local company, so that whenever it is desired to pay off the £30,000 debentures, the local company will retain an interest in the Daily Express Limited and be entitled to one-twentieth part of the net yearly profits. Upon this investment being made, the Daily Express Limited will forthwith secure premises, provide the necessary machinery and plant and establish in Leicester a high-class Daily Evening Half-penny Paper, for circulation in the Town and County of Leicester, containing all the latest news affecting commercial, business and other interests; giving every attention to local affairs and matters conducing to the well-being of the population in the Town and County and promoting in a broad and comprehensive Imperial and Unionist principles.'

A committee was formed to raise the remaining £5,000 and to form a company and in July of the following year the paper was established, under the title of Leicester Evening News. Viscount Churchill was chairman of the Board and the offices in Belvoir Street on the site later occupied by Joseph Johnson and Co. A fire occurred a year later and a move was made to Granby Street. The public were told buying the Leicester Evening News meant a contribution to Tory funds, but neither benefited. It ceased publication in 1905 and issued an 'obituary' post card for sale.

By reason of its holdings of debentures in the Daily Express, the company was able to continue and pay dividends. For the period

KING EDWARD VII.

CROWNED

AT

WESTMINSTER ABBEY.

THE CORONATION CEREMONY.

FULL DESCRIPTION OF AN HISTORIC FUNCTION.

Amidst a scene of great pomp and splendour, King Edward VII. was, at 12.17 to-day, crowned at Westminster Abbey by the Archbishop of Canterbury with all the rites and ceremony customary on such an historic occasion, and his gracious wife, Queen Alexandra, was subsequently crowned as Queen-Consort by the Archbishop of York.

When the sun rose this morning the sky was cloudless, and there was every prospect of a brilliant day. By 9 o'clock the sky had become somewhat overcast; nevertheless all appearances favoured the hope that the weather would remain fine, and that the crowning of King Edward VII. would be carried out under every condition auspicious to the great pageant. Further, the King himself suffered no ill-effects from the labour entailed in the multiplicity of State duties yesterday, and was reported well able to undergo the strain of to-day's ceremonial.

THE EARLY SCENES.

POLICE AND SOLDIERY.

NO CRUSH.

THE DECORATIONS.

THE KING IN GOOD HEALTH.

SCENE IN PARLIAMENT-STREET.

ARRIVAL OF THE NAVAL BRIGADE.

OUTSIDE THE ABBEY.

AT BUCKINGHAM PALACE.

THE KING AND QUEEN START.

AN ALARMING ACCIDENT.

MAGNIFICENT SPECTACLE ALONG THE ROUTE.

THEIR MAJESTIES IN THE ABBEY.

OFFICIAL ORDER OF PROCESSIONS.

THE PRINCE OF WALES'S PROCESSION.

THE KING'S PROCESSION.

THE ABBEY.

LORD MAYOR AND COLONIAL PREMIERS.

ARRIVAL OF THE PRINCE OF WALES.

THE CORONATION.

THE STATE COACH.

THE KING AND QUEEN.

IN THE ABBEY.

A NEVER-TO-BE-FORGOTTEN SCENE.

A BEAUTIFUL SIGHT.

ONE GLORIOUS HARMONIOUS WHOLE.

THE TWO THRONES.

THE PEERS AND PEERESSES.

WEALTH AND BEAUTY.

HIS MAJESTY'S FAITHFUL COMMONS.

ARCHBISHOPS AND THE BISHOPS APPEARED.

THE KING ACCLAIMED.

THE ADMINISTRATION OF THE OATH

THE CEREMONY OF ANOINTING.

THE INVESTITURE.

PUTTING ON THE CROWN.

HIS MAJESTY ENTHRONED.

DRAMATIC INCIDENT.

THE CORONATION OF THE QUEEN

THE KING FREE FROM FATIGUE.

CELEBRATIONS IN INDIA AND THE COLONIES.

Reuter's Telegram.

The Leicester Tramway Siege in 1903.

1904

◆ Frank Hewitt at the Leicester Mercury replaced the old Wharfedale equipment with rotary presses, popularly called 'flyers.' Finished newspapers appeared at the end of the line at the rate of 7,000 to 8,000 copies an hour. This was very necessary if the rapid growth of readership was to be maintained. By 1904, the Leicester Mercury sold 25,000 copies daily – five times the number only 30 years previous.

of the General Election in 1906, it ran another evening paper, the Evening Times, but the Leicester Mercury was well established and the public did not support the newcomer, even though it had Arthur Pearson's experience and ability behind it.

Under the terms of Francis Hewitt's will, Frank inherited one-quarter share of the business and the trustees decided not to sell until after the death of Mrs Hewitt or when the youngest son, Leicester, had reached 23 years of age, whichever event was the later. As it happened the later event was Leicester's 23rd birthday in 1906 and the decision was then made to form a private limited company called F Hewitt and Son. Frank assumed control, with his brother and sisters as fellow-shareholders.

Frank served as a Justice of the Peace for a number of years and was greatly interested in sport, particularly golf, cricket and tennis. He became President of the Leicestershire Golf Club and the Town Cricket Club.

The Edwardian era is generally regarded as a period of gaiety, but it also produced the Right to Work campaign, the workless marchers and the Passive Resistance movement. It heralded the arrival of trans-Atlantic radio, the first flights of heavier than air machines and the start of motoring for all.

The Boer War had dragged on for three years, with peaks of exhilaration at moments of relief such as Mafeking and Ladysmith,

but primitive communications which made news too often outdated by events before it was published aroused public distrust of good news when it came. They had believed too often that peace was at hand to be disillusioned by later disclaimers from the faraway battle fronts. So when peace finally did come in 1902, there were doubters. The official news of the ending of the war reached London on Sunday evening, June 1, out of normal publishing times. The authorities told the church authorities and the news was passed along the line. So at the evening services ministers and clergymen announced the greatest news from the pulpit.

In Leicester, the Leicester Mercury on June 2 recorded that as the congregation of Victoria Road Chapel came out after hearing the news from the minister, they found special editions of the Mercury giving the official bulletins from Lord Kitchener waiting for them. Never, it seems, has there been such a scramble for a newspaper. Under the heading 'Newsboys have a good time,' it said:

> 'Newsboys with the extra edition of the Daily Mercury last night had a rare good time. Newspapers were eagerly bought, sixpences and shillings being tendered with the remark 'Keep the change'. One gentleman gave half a crown, saying the announcement in the paper was

well worth it. This newsboy will not forget Peace Sunday in a hurry.'

The following day Leicester celebrated from dawn to dusk with church bells ringing for hours. Schools were given the day off and many places of work closed.

Within two months there was another occasion for Leicester to rejoice. Edward VII's coronation took place eventually after a postponement when he was taken ill on June 24 and had to undergo an operation. As Prince of Wales, he had visited Belvoir Castle and Bradgate House, where his friend, the Earl of Stamford, lived.

The 1901 census returns revealed Leicester's growth had reached 211,579 – almost double the figure recorded in 1881. Even allowing for borough extensions in 1891 bringing in Aylestone, Belgrave, Humberstone and North Evington, this surge was tremendous. Losses of lucrative war contracts for the hosiery and boot industry after Peace Sunday put an immense strain on the town's economy. The Mayor opened a relief fund, a Distress Committee was set up to find public works for idle hands and the unemployed themselves launched their own Right to Work campaign which provoked the now famous 1905 march of Leicester unemployed to London, led by Amos Sherriff and the Rev Lewis Donaldson, vicar of St Mark's, to seek help from the King himself.

Out of this march came the Unemployed Workmen's Acts and then the establishment of Labour Exchanges throughout the country, Leicester's being established in 1910.

Despite this distress, there was no serious crime in the town and judges of assize had no work to do in Leicester. Traditional white gloves were received in the spring, summer and autumn of 1906, because there were no cases to try. Lay magistrates however had their hands full dealing with the activities of the passive resistance movement. Many hundreds of eminent Leicester citizens, aldermen, councillors, chapel ministers and prominent businessmen appeared before the courts for non-payment of their rate bill. They were refusing to pay that part of the rate which related to education, because as a result of the 1902 Education Act, which ended School Boards and made education a State responsibility, voluntary schools, including church schools, became rate-aided. Chapel-goers objected strongly to having to pay for sectarian schools and took their opposition to the final lengths of non-violence: summonses for debt and distraint on their household goods.

The Edwardian era ended on May 6, 1910, with the death of King Edward VII. It stopped the nation in its tracks and millions mourned his passing. In June the next year, King George V had a spectacular coronation and a month later, His Majesty invested his eldest son (the future King Edward VIII/Duke of Windsor) as Prince of Wales at Caernarvon. Altogether it was a year of great ceremony.

Below: Return of the Leicester Unemployed March to London in June, 1905.

Right: Coronation of King George V on June 22, 1911 – celebrations in the Market Place, Leicester.

Below: Celebrations in Loughborough Market Place.

CORONATION SERVICE LEICESTER JUNE 22ND 1911.   T.E.S.L.

Chapter 4
First World War
1910 – 1920

A third attempt was made on January 1, 1910, to launch a paper in competition to the Mercury. The Leicester Mail struggled for 21 years until its debts finally proved too heavy. The Conservative paper was backed by so many of the town and county's influential people. Sir Herbert Marshall was the first chairman and among its directors were Lord Churchill, Mr Samuel Faire, Mr Charles Bennion and Sir J F Rolleston.

Readers in January 1911 were captivated by reports in the Mercury of the highly dramatic story of the Siege of Sidney Street, which developed into the Hounsditch Murders. One Peter the Painter and his gang of Russian anarchists clashed with police in Hounsditch and, after shooting a number down, escaped and took refuge in a house, which they barricaded. Troops were called in and a battle commenced. The siege was personally directed by Winston Churchill, then Home Secretary. It all ended when the house caught fire and the Russians perished, except Peter the Painter, who is believed to have escaped in the confusion and was never found.

On the occasion of his 50th birthday in October, 1911, Frank Hewitt entertained the staff to dinner at the Grand Hotel. Speeches made illustrated the fact that there was a happy relationship between management and staff.

Nobody was aware, however, of his impending illness. Shortly afterwards, he was taken seriously ill. He undertook an appendix operation and seemed to be recovering well, but had a relapse and died. He was survived by Mrs Hewitt, a son and two daughters. His son, Francis Vernon Hewitt, succeeded him as the head of F Hewitt and Son.

Vernon had been in control for little more than a year when his manager, Mr James (Jimmy) Thompson, died. A severe blow, for James Thompson had been manager during the whole 36 years of the Hewitt regime. Chief cashier, Mr W J Basford, who had been with the firm for 30 years after leaving Wyggeston Boys' School, was appointed in his place. He started as a junior clerk in 1883, when the staff numbered just 27.

After coverage of the Titanic disaster in 1912, the following year brought more news drama. A haunting story of human endurance, the story of Scott and Oates in the Antarctic, one of the greatest epics of success – and failure – of all time. Amundsen, the Norwegian explorer, had reached the South Pole before them, but the full story was not told until more than a year later, when the expedition ship Terra Nova reached New Zealand on February 10, 1913. Captain Robert Falcon Scott and Captain Oakes both died during the expedition. Scott's last entry in his diary called on our rich country to provide for those who depended on them. and the Mercury leader writer headed his tribute 'An appeal from the tomb.' A Leicester man, a Mr Day, son of an architect, was the engineer of the motor sleigh, but the Mercury reports 'it is unlikely that he was with the advance party' and there the local angle was laid to rest!

Stories about the suffragettes were scattered across the pages of the Mercury, telling of the raids on Downing Street, Parliament, the battles with the police and the astonishing tragedy of the woman suffragette who threw herself in front of the King's horse at the 1913 Derby at Epsom and brought it down, losing her life in the process. Locally, they tried to burn down Blaby railway station, attacked shops, poured sticky black ink into pillar boxes and damaged the Leicestershire Golf Club links.

In the summer of 1914, the lasting years of peace were to be shattered when the Archduke Ferdinand, the Serbian heir, was assassinated at Sarajevo on June 28. This triggered off a chain reaction and five weeks later all Europe was at war.

On the Saturday after the declaration of war, wages had to be paid without the customary gold sovereign. The country had decided to substitute paper money for gold and until the bank note came along, staff had to be paid with money orders, postal orders, silver and bronze. Eventually, paper money became as accepted as gold had been.

Newspapers became involved fully and quickly in the general upheaval of everyday life. Enlistment was voluntary (it was two years before the need for some form of

1912

◆ The year saw some of the most vivid journalism the Mercury had experienced in its 38 years. Readers' appetite for sensation was whetted with the reporting of the world's greatest sea disaster. They had read about the 46,000-ton White Star liner Titanic's departure from Liverpool in a blaze of glory and were shocked when in mid-April the news came through that it had struck an iceberg and had plunged to its doom while its passengers were revelling at a luxurious dance party. The stories covered wireless calls for help, the desperate attempts of other ships in the area to steam to the rescue, the loss of all but 700 of the 2,200 people on board, the tales of heroism and sacrifice and the searching inquiries afterwards as to why it had happened.

Overleaf: Page 2 of the Leicester Mercury for Wednesday August 5, 1914, following the declaration of War. As with all newspapers at that time the front page was used exclusively for advertisements, so that even news as momentous as this could only be reported inside the paper.

28

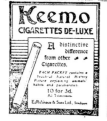
WORLD CONFLICT.

GREAT BRITAIN DECLARES WAR
BECAUSE GERMANY INVADES BELGIUM.

RIVAL NAVIES IN THE NORTH SEA.

THE GERMAN ADVANCE.

BRITISH ARMY MOBILIZING.

GOVERNMENT CONTROL OF RAILWAYS.

Owing to the summary rejection by the German
Government of the request made by his
Majesty's Government, that the neutrality of
Belgium will be respected, his Majesty's Ambassador at Berlin has received his passport, and
his Majesty's Government has declared to the
German Government that a state of war exists
between Great Britain and Germany, as from
11 p.m. on August 4th.

—BRITISH OFFICIAL ANNOUNCEMENT.

At midnight, in accordance with the terms of her
ultimatum, Great Britain declared war on
Germany. The above is the official Government statement of the fact, and it sets forth
the reason why Great Britain has felt compelled to join in the world-conflict.

Seven nations are already involved in the titanic
struggle, viz.:

Great Britain.	Germany.
France.	Austria.
Russia.	Servia.
Belgium.	

It may be that others will be speedily drawn in.
Ranged on one side as Austria (who set the
torch to the conflagration by making war on
Servia) and Germany; on the other, Great
Britain, France, and Russia, and we suppose
Belgium, which has been forced into the con-
flict to defend her liberties and her integrity
against German invasion.

France and Russia are linked by defensive treaty.
England has been associated with both in close
friendship but without committal to even a defensive alliance; the logic of events has brought
us in. Germany and Austria have an offensive
and defensive treaty, and, with Italy, made up
the Triple Alliance. Italy's committal to the
Alliance was of a defensive character. Regarding
the present as a wave of aggression merely,
brought on by Austria, she has declared her
neutrality, though in certain eventualities may
intervene.

Apart from Italy, the United States and Japan are
the only Great Powers clear of the conflict, and
if the enemy attempted to carry war into Asia,
then our Far Eastern Ally would come in. She
has already stated that she will make good her
promises should the need arise.

The British Ultimatum was despatched to Germany
yesterday morning. It required that Germany
should give an unequivocal assurance that she
would respect the neutral territory of Belgium,
guaranteed by her under the Treaty of 1839—a
guarantee endorsed in writing in 1870. It also
intimated that, failing this assurance, Great
Britain would declare war on Germany at midnight.

The steps by which the Prime Minister and the
Government of Great Britain approached the
momentous decision were as dignified as they were
unmistakable. Following upon Sir Edward Grey's
statement in the House of Commons on Monday,
the German Ambassador at Berlin, protesting
against the violation of Belgian neutrality by
Germany and asking for an immediate reply.

The reply came quickly. On the same morning the
German Government telegraphed to the German
Ambassador in London, instructing him to
repeat most positively "the formal assurance
that, even in the case of an armed conflict with
Belgium, Germany will not under any pretence
whatever annex Belgian territory."

The German Ambassador was also instructed to
inform Sir Edward Grey that Germany had
disregarded Belgian neutrality in order to
"prevent what means to lose a question of life
and death, the French advance through
Belgium." Thereupon followed the British
ultimatum.

In the House of Commons yesterday the Prime
Minister, with admirable dignity and concise-
ness, set before the nation the action which the
Government had thus found it necessary to take
in vindication of British honour. Then proceeding to the Bar of the House, he handed to
the Speaker a Proclamation by the King,
providing for complete mobilisation of the
Army

Vice-Admiral Sir John Jellicoe has assumed command
of the Home Fleets, with the acting rank of
Admiral. The King has sent him a message, in
which he says—

"At this grave moment in our national history
I send to you, and through you, to the officers
and men of the fleets of which you assume command, the assurance of my confidence that, under
your direction they will revive and renew the old
glories of the Royal Navy, and prove once again
the sure shield of Britain, and of her Empire, in
the hour of trial."

The British Government have taken over the two
Turkish battleships built in this country, now
completed and the other nearing completion,
and two Chilian destroyer leaders.

By way of naval news there are reports that the
Germans have sunk a British mine-layer; that
a "foreign" (not Danish) torpedo boat has been
sunk off Denmark with a loss of 29 lives, and
that the French fleet in the Mediterranean has
sunk the German cruiser Panther, which played
an important role as the emblem of the "Mailed
Fist" at Agadir during the Morocco crisis.

Two British Ministers, Lord Morley and Mr. John
Burns, finding themselves unable to approve of
the action taken by the Government, have resigned from the Cabinet.

German troops have entered Belgian territory, and
it is reported that a battle has taken place near
the frontier, resulting in the Germans being thrown
back. Belgium was already mobilising when
Germany flung her ultimatum at the little
kingdom, and at the moment she probably has
100,000 soldiers in the field.

On the German frontier more minor incidents between
French and German troops have taken place. Near
Belfort German detachments are making requisi-
tion upon the inhabitants of French territory.

The King has issued a Proclamation to the Dominions,
expressing their deep hope for their loyalty and their pro-
fered help, and expressing his "confidence belief
that in this time of trial my Empire will stand
united, calm, resolute, trusting in God."

The Colonial Office has received a message from the
Governor-General of Australia, saying that the
Australian Navy will be placed under the control
of the Admiralty when this is desired. The Australian Government is also prepared to place at
the disposal of Great Britain an expeditionary
force of 20,000 men, made up in any way which
may be suggested. The expenses of maintenance
of this force will be wholly borne by Australia.

In Canada Volunteers are pouring in in hundreds.
The Prime Minister of Manitoba has offered to
raise a force of 10,000 men.

The War Office has issued a notice instructing all
Regular Reservists to proceed immediately to their
appointed posts without waiting for the receipt of
any official call.

The committees of the Cabinet appointed to deal with
food supplies had last night issued a statement, in
which they say that there are no conceivable circumstances in which a wheat famine could arise.
The situation with regard to meat is not less satisfactory. There is no justification for any present
increase in the price of meat or bread.

STATE INSURANCE OF SHIPPING.

THE GOVERNMENT'S SCHEME.

On the motion for the adjournment of the House,
Mr. Lloyd George made a statement with reference
to the question of insurance against war risks. He
said the problem was how, having regard to the
narrow limitation of the insurance market for war
risks, and the difficulty of taking on reasonable
terms, or possibly any terms, in case of war in which
this country might be engaged, we might secure
that our vast overseas trade should go on, and
avoid an undue enhancement of the prices of food
and raw material for our industries. The subject
had recently been reported upon by a strong committee of experts, and the Government proposed to
give immediate effect to a scheme based upon that
report. (Cheers.)

The scheme of the Government was in no sense a
purely scheme. About four-fifths of our overseas
shipping was now insured against war risks through
mutual associations. This form of insurance, although admirably adapted to protect the interests
of shipowners, added greatly to the peril of the interruption of our overseas trade, because on the
outbreak of war all vessels would immediately run
for shore. What was wanted was a scheme that
would encourage shipping to keep the sea. A State
insurance office in connection with the scheme had
already been opened in London. Sir Douglas Owen
had placed his services at the disposal of the Government, and associated with him would be men of
weight and representative character in the commercial and insurance world.

Should the necessity arise, the Government hoped
and believed that by this scheme they would be
able to do something to relieve the anxiety of the
mercantile and shipping world, and ensure the continuity, in spite of every emergency in the free
flow of food and material for the population of
this country. (Cheers.)

Mr. Austen Chamberlain expressed approval of the
Government's scheme, which he thought would secure
this country against any alarming scarcity of
supplies.

DISTRIBUTION OF FOOD SUPPLIES.

Mr. Arthur Henderson pointed to the possibility,
notwithstanding the steps outlined by the Chancellor of the Exchequer, of the poor feeling without
food during war, and appealed to the Prime
Minister to see that some scheme of organisation
to deal with starving people was introduced.

The Prime Minister agreed that the steps already
outlined by the Government would not be adequate
to emergencies which unhappily were now contemplated, unless they went a step further and
contemplated the problem of distribution. That he
had been engaging the anxious attention of the Government, and in the course of one or two days
there would submit proposals in regard to it which
would complete the scheme. (Cheers.)
The House then rose.

KING'S MESSAGE TO THE COLONIES.

SPONTANEOUS ASSURANCES OF SUPPORT.

The Press Association states the following cable-
gram was sent yesterday by the Colonial Secretary
to the Governor-General of Canada, the Governor-
General of the Commonwealth of Australia, the
Governor-General of New Zealand and the High
Commissioner of South Africa:—

August 4, 4.50 p.m.

Please communicate to your Ministers the following message from his Majesty and publish:

"I desire to express to my people of the
Oversea Dominions, with what appreciation and
pride I have received the messages from their
respective Governments during the last few days.
These spontaneous assurances of their fullest
support recall to me the past to the Mother
Country. I shall be strengthened in the discharge of the great responsibilities which rest
upon me by the confident belief that, in this
time of trial, my Empire will stand united,
calm, resolute, trusting in God."

"GEORGE R.I."

SUPREME COMMAND.

APPOINTMENT OF ADMIRAL JELLICOE.

KING'S MESSAGE.

The Admiralty issued the following last night:—
With the approval of his Majesty the King,
Admiral Sir John R. Jellicoe, K.C.B., K.C.V.O.
has assumed supreme command of the Home
Fleet, with the acting rank of Admiral, and
Rear-Admiral Charles E. Madden, C.V.O., has
been appointed to be his Chief of the Staff.
Both appointments date from to-day.

The following message has been addressed by his
Majesty the King to Admiral Sir John Jellicoe:—

At this grave moment in our national history I send to you, and through you to the
officers and men of the Fleets of which you
have assumed command, the assurance of my
confidence that under your direction they will
revive and renew the old glories of the Royal
Navy, and prove once again the sure shield of
Britain and of her Empire in the hour of trial.

GEORGE R.I.

The above message has been communicated to
the senior naval officers on all stations outside of
home waters.

The Men We Trust.

Vice-Admiral Sir John Rushworth, who has
assumed supreme command of the Home
Fleets, is 55 years old, and has had an active
and stirring career. He entered the Navy in
1872, and saw fighting in the Egyptian War of
1882. As commander he was on board the ill-
fated H.M.S. Victoria which was rammed by
H.M.S. Camperdown off the coast of Syria
and sank with Vice-Admiral Sir George Tryon
and 22 officers and 356 men. He commanded
the Naval Brigade and acted as Chief of Staff
to Vice-Admiral Seymour in the attempt to
relieve the Pekin Legations besieged by the
Boxers. He is a sturdy, silent man, clean
shaven, with a resolute face. He is married
and has three daughters.

ADDITIONS TO THE FLEET.

TURKISH AND CHILIAN VESSELS TAKEN OVER.

The Secretary of the Admiralty announces:—
His Majesty's Government have taken over
the two battleships, one completed and the
other shortly due for completion, which had
been ordered in this country by the Turkish
Government, and the two destroyers—leaders
ordered by the Government of Chile.

The two battleships will receive the names
Agincourt and Erin, and the destroyer-leaders
will be called Faulknor and Broke, after two
famous naval officers.

THE ARMY.

SIR JOHN FRENCH'S NEW POST

THE EXPEDITIONARY FORCE

The "London Gazette" of last night announces
that Field-Marshal Sir John D. P. French, G.V.O.,
G.C.V.O., K.C.M.G., is to be Inspector-General of
the Forces. Dated August 1.

As Private Secretary—Major A. F. Watts, Yorkshire Hussars Yeomanry, Territorial Force.

As Aides-de-Camp—Lieutenant - Colonel S. L.
Barry, D.S.O., Commanding 4th Battalion the
Northamptonshire Regiment; Major and Brevet
Lieutenant-Colonel Lord Brooke, Warwickshire
Royal Horse Artillery, Territorial Force.

It is probable that after the mobilisation of the
Regular Army at home Field-Marshal Sir John
French, G.C.B., G.C.V.O., K.C.M.G., will be ap-
pointed to the command of the six divisions of
Infantry and one of Cavalry constituting the Ex-
peditionary Force. His Chief of Staff will be Major-
General Sir Archibald Murray, K.C.B., C.V.O.

Each pair of divisions will constitute a Corps.
The 1st Corps will probably be commanded by
Lieutenant - General Sir Douglas Haig, K.C.B.,
K.C.I.E., A.D.C. to the King, and will consist of
the 1st and 2nd Divisions. The 2nd Corps will be
under Lieutenant-General Sir James Grierson,
K.C.B., C.V.O., C.M.G., A.D.C., and will be composed of the 3rd and 4th Divisions. The 3rd Corps
will be made up of the 5th and 6th Divisions, and
will be under Major-General W. P. Pulteney, C.B.,
D.S.O. The Cavalry Division will presumably be
commanded by Major-General Allenby, C.B., now
Inspector of Cavalry. The command of the divisions will probably remain unchanged, but as Sir
Archibald Murray will be taken for the 2nd Division when he joins Sir John French's staff, it is
likely that Major-General C. C. Monro will take
his place.

A number of distinguished officers, including
General Sir Bruce Hamilton, K.C.B., K.C.V.O.,
will command certain Corps of Territorials.

THE RIVAL FLEETS.

BRITISH SUPERIORITY IN STRENGTH

GERMAN STRATEGY.

The strength of the main British and main
German Fleets in the most powerful type of ships
is as follows:—

	Pre-Dreadnoughts	Battle-Cruisers
	Dreadnoughts	Dreadnoughts	
British ...	20	8	4
German ...	13	5	4

Both Great Britain and Germany have also brought
up large numbers of older and smaller ships.

The weight of metal from the heavy guns in the
British main Fleet is equal to 91 per cent. so
that in the German main Fleet. This is due to
the fact that the British Dreadnoughts carry 12in.
and 13.5in. guns, whereas the German Dreadnoughts only carry 11in. and 12in. guns.

In submarines the British Navy has a very very
great strength: the British total available is
about 70 boats, and the German force is not believed to exceed 30.

The British Fleets are manned by at least
100,000 officers and men, the German Fleets by
about 65,000 men.

The "Daily Mail," which indulges in these
comparisons, adds:—"In a weighing support can
be given to the British Navy by the French, who
have an enormous number of torpedo-boats, and
some 30 submarines ready in the North Sea or
Channel.

The German strategy is best generally understood. To save the strong ? the British Fleet were con-
centrated and ready, not to attack, but to mass their
action, to attack the British fleet with mine
layers, submarines, and torpedo-boats, and
British commerce with cruisers.

Only if the British Fleet were unready and scattered
was it proposed that the German battleships should
come forth and deal a shattering blow. Whether
these were the real plans, whether Germany will now
act upon them the next few hours will show.

NO FEAR OF FAMINE.

REASSURING STATEMENT BY THE GOVERNMENT.

The Committee of the Cabinet appointed to
deal with food supplies last night issued a statement in which they say that in addition to wheat
supplies sufficient to last four months already in
this country there are large consignments now on
the way here, much of it being close at hand.
There are, therefore, no conceivable circumstances
in which a wheat famine could arise, and high
prices can only be due to fears of scarcity. There
is no actual scarcity.

The position with regard to meat is not less
satisfactory. There is no justification for any
present increase in the price of meat or bread.

BRAZILIAN PRESIDENT DECREES BUSINESS HOLIDAY.

Rio de Janeiro, Tuesday.

At a meeting of Ministers and Financial Commis-
sions of the Chamber and Senate under the pre-
sidency of President Hermes Da Fonseca, it was
decided to decree a business holiday until August
13, and to ask Parliament to vote a moratorium.

The Minister of Finance also proposed that
the inconvertibility of the Conversion Fund notes
in order to prevent the export of gold. These
measures will meet the urgent necessity of assist-
ing trade in the critical situation created by the
events in Europe.—Reuter.

BRITISH ULTIMATUM TO GERMANY.

PREMIER'S STATEMENT.

When the Speaker took the chair at a quarter
to three, in the House of Commons, yesterday
afternoon, there was again a crowded attendance
of members.

Mr. Asquith, in reply to Mr. Bonar Law, said in
conformity with the statement of policy which was
made by the Foreign Secretary the previous day,
a telegram was sent early that morning by him
to our Ambassador at Berlin. It was to this effect—

That the King of Belgium had made an appeal
to his Majesty the King for diplomatic intervention on behalf of Belgium. His Majesty's
Government are also informed that the German
Government has delivered to the Belgian Government a Note proposing friendly neutrality
pending a free passage through Belgian territory, and promising to maintain the independence and integrity of the Kingdom and its
possessions on the conclusion of peace, and
threatening, in the case of refusal, to treat
Belgium as an enemy, and that an answer
was requested within twelve hours.

We also understand that Belgium has categorically refused this flagrant violation of the
laws of nations. (Cheers.) His Majesty's Government are bound to protect against this
violation of a treaty to which Germany was a
party in common with ourselves, and must
request an assurance that the demand made
upon Belgium will not be proceeded with, and
that her neutrality will be respected by Germany. (Cheers.)

We asked for an immediate reply. (Loud
cheers.)

GERMANY'S THREAT TO BELGIUM.

His Majesty's Government, proceeded the Prime
Minister, received this (Tuesday) morning from
their Minister in Brussels the following telegram:—

The German Minister has this morning addressed a note to the Belgian Minister for
Foreign Affairs stating that as the Belgian
Government has declined the well-intentioned
proposals submitted to them by the Imperial
Government, the latter, deeply to their regret, will be compelled to carry out, if necessary, by force of arms, the measures now considered indispensable, in view of the French
menace.

Immediately afterwards, continued Mr.
Asquith, we received from the Belgian Legation
in London the following telegram from the Belgian Minister for Foreign Affairs:—

The General Staff announce that territory
has been violated at Verviers, near Aix la
Chapelle. Subsequent information tends to
show that a German force has penetrated still
further into Belgian territory.

We also received late this morning from the
German Foreign Secretary, and communicated by
the Ambassador to us—

Please dispel any mistrust that may subsist
on the part of the British Government with
regard to our intentions by repeating most
positively the formal assurance that even in
the case of an armed conflict in Belgium Germany will not under any pretence whatever
annex Belgian territory. (Cries of "Oh," and
laughter.)

The sincerity of this declaration is borne
out by the fact that we solemnly pledged
our word to Holland strictly to respect her
neutrality. It is obvious that we could not
profitably annex Belgian territory without
making at the same time a territorial acquisition at the expense of Holland.

Please impress upon Sir E. Grey that the
German army could not be exposed to a
French attack across Belgium which was
planned, according to absolutely unimpeach-
able information. Germany has in consequence
disregarded Belgian neutrality to prevent
what means to her a question of life and
death—the French advance through Belgium.

BRITISH ULTIMATUM.

I have to add this on behalf of his Majesty's
Government, continued Mr. Asquith: We cannot
regard this as in any sense a satisfactory communication. (Cheers.) We have in reply to it
repeated the request which we made last week to
the German Government, that they should give
us the same assurance with regard to Belgium by
France last week. (Cheers.)

We have asked in reply to this telegram of this
morning, which I have read to
the House, should be given before midnight.

(Loud and prolonged cheers.)

The Prime Minister then brought to a message
from the King, intimating that the Army Reserves were to be called out on permanent service,
and that the Territorial Force was to be embodied
in pursuance of the resolution moved by the
Prime Minister and agreed to without discussion.

All outstanding Votes in Supply for the Civil
Army and Naval Services were agreed to without
comment, and in Committee of Ways and Means
payment out of the Consolidated Fund of a sum of
nearly a hundred and five million pounds was
authorised.

The Anglo-Persian Oil Company (Acquisition of
Capital) Bill passed through committee, as also
did the Expiring Laws Continuance Bill.

Mr. Herbert Samuel, in reference to the latter
measure, gave an assurance to Mr. Edmund
Harvey that the Road Board and the Development Commissioners were considering measures
for relief of unemployment.

The Education (Provision of Meals) Bill was
considered on report, and read a third time.

STATE CONTROL.

WAR OFFICE ANNOUNCEMENT.

The War Office announces that an Order in Council has been made declaring it is expedient that
the Government should have control over the railroads in Great Britain.

This control will be exercised through an Executive Committee, composed of the general managers
of the railways, which has been formed for some
time, and has prepared plans. Although railway
facilities for the public may be somewhat restricted
for a time to meet the special requirements of the
naval and military authorities, more normal conditions will in due course be restored.

The order, which does not apply to Ireland, has
been made under the Regulation of the Forces Act, 1871.

In order to make clear the scope of the announcement made of the Government's assumption of
the control of the railways, the Central News is
authorised to issue the following statement:—

In view of the announcement made that the
Government have taken over the control of the
railways, it is desirable that the public should
understand exactly what this means. The control of
the railways has been taken over by the Government for the purpose of ensuring that the railways,
locomotives, rolling stock, and staff, shall be used as
a complete unit in the best interests of the state,
for the movement of troops, stores, and food
supplies.

The necessity for this action must at once become
apparent, when it is realised that certain ports
through which the bulk of our food supplies enter
this country may be closed for the purpose of such
food supplies, and, in that event, the rolling stock,
locomotives, etc., may have to be diverted to other
lines for the purpose of serving other ports.

The staff on each railway will remain under the
same control as heretofore, and will receive their
instructions through the same channels as in the
past. The Act of 1871, which deals with the control of the railways in time of national emergency,
is as follows:—

REGULATION OF THE FORCES, 1871.

(16.) When her Majesty, by an order in Council,
declares that an emergency has arisen in which it is
expedient for the public service that her Majesty's
Government should have control over the railroads
in the United Kingdom, or any of them, the Secretary of State may, by warrant under his hand, em-
power any person or persons named in the
warrant to take possession in the
name or on behalf of her Majesty of any
railroad in the United Kingdom, and of the plant
belonging thereto, or of any part thereof, and may
take possession of any plant, without taking possession of the railroad itself, and to use the
same for her Majesty's service, at such times and
in such a manner as the Secretary of State may
direct, and its directors, officers, and
servants of any such railroad shall obey the
directions of the Secretary of State as to the use
of such railroad or plant, as aforesaid for her
Majesty's service.

There shall be paid to the said Secretary of
State in pursuance of this section shall remain in
force for one week only, but may be renewed from
week to week so long as, in the opinion of the
said Secretary of State, the emergency continues.

There shall be paid to any person, or body of
persons, whose railroad or plant may be taken
possession of in pursuance of this section, out of
moneys to be provided by Parliament, such full
compensation for any loss or injury they may
have sustained by the exercise of the powers of
the Secretary of State under this section, as may
be agreed upon between the said Secretary of
State and the said person or body of persons, or
in case of difference, may be settled by arbitration
in manner provided by the Lands Clauses Con-
solidation Act, 1845.

Where any railroad or plant is taken possession
of in the name or on behalf of her Majesty, in
pursuance of this section, all contracts and engagements between the person or body of persons, their
railroad is so taken possession of, and the directors,
officers, and servants of such person or body of persons, or between such person or body of persons, and
any other persons in relation to the working or
maintenance of the railroad, or in relation to the
supply or working of the plant of such railroad,
which would, if such possession had not been taken,
have been enforceable by, or against the said person or body of persons, shall, during the continuance
of such possession, be enforceable by or against her
Majesty.

For the purposes of this section the railroad
shall include any tramway, whether worked by
animals or mechanical power, or otherwise, and
partly or wholly in the other, and any stations,
sidings, works, and premises connected with or
required for the working of such railroad or tramway; and plant shall include all engines, tenders,
carriages, waggons, trucks, sheds, machinery and
other things whatsoever belonging to, or
used for working, maintaining, or repairing the
railroad, or any station, sidings, works, and
premises connected with or required for the working
of such railroad, or in the working of the railway.

It will be seen that the control of
all the railways in Great Britain has been vested
in a committee composed of the general managers of
the railways as follows:—

Mr. D. A. Matheson, general manager Cale-
donian Railway;
Sir Sam Fay, general manager Great Central
Railway;
Mr. C. N. Dent, general manager Great
Northern Railway;
Mr. F. Potter, general manager Great Western
Railway;
Mr. Robt. Turnbull, general manager Great
London N.W. Railway;
Mr. J. A. F. Aspinall, general manager Lanca-
shire and Yorkshire Railway;
Mr. D. A. Walker, general manager Land
S.W. Railway;
Sir Guy Granet, general manager Midland
Railway;
Sir Alexander K. Butterworth, general manager
North-Eastern Railway;
Mr. F. H. Dent, general manager S.E. and C.
Railway.

The official chairman of this committee is the
President of the Board of Trade, and the acting
chairman is Mr. H. A. Walker, general manager of
the London and South-Western Railway. The
railway secretary to the committee is Mr. Gilbert.
Szlumper.

We are officially advised that in order to give
due effect to the instructions received from the
War Office and Admiralty for the movement of
troops, etc., it may be necessary to discontinue
at short notice a portion of the advertised service,
or to close certain of the lines against ordinary
traffic. Under these circumstances, no responsibility
can be accepted for any delay or loss that may
occur.

GERMAN LINER OFF ILFRACOMBE.

SHORT OF BUNKER COAL.

The Hamburg-America liner Belgia, from Bos-
ton to Hamburg, called off Ilfracombe early yesterday morning, and remains at anchor off the
port. The captain landed, and endeavoured to
get into communication with the German Consul
at Newport, but up to the present had been unable
to do so. He says he has run short of bunker
coal, but it is believed that he is apprehensive of
proceeding down the English Channel for fear of
capture by the French. It is stated that he had
a large amount of private passengers on board.

THREE CHILDREN HAD ECZEMA.

50, Carlisle Rd., Hereford, Essex. Eng.—"My three
children, aged nine, seven and five had a breaking
out of running sores on their scalps. They used to
burn and scream and a very contagious kind which
we should have great trouble to get them cured of.
It was continually discharging a sticky yellow liquid
which dried and then crusted. Starting on the crown of their
heads it travelled down behind their ears to their
necks and where the children scratched they had a
few little sores on their hands. But too worse and we
were behind their ears where the children scratched they had a
few sores.

"We were given a box of ointment but I cannot
say that it did any good at all. Seeing the Cuticura
Soap and Ointment advertised we sent for a sample.
Upon sending some to found them a greatly
better, also applied the Cuticura, so we bought
some of each and with their help our children were
perfectly cured." (Signed) Mrs. A. J. Duckett, May 13,
1914. Although Cuticura Soap and Ointment are sold
by chemists throughout the world, a sample of
each with 32-p. Skin Book will be sent post-free upon
application. Address post-card: "F. Newbery & Sons,"
27, Charterhouse Sq., London, E.C.

conscription was needed). Most of the younger members of the Mercury staff were soon in uniform and were joining large numbers of men enlisting at the Magazine, hoping to join the regular Leicester battalions, which were already on their way to France to take on the German foe.

The responsibility of producing a newspaper under increasing difficulties fell upon the rest at the paper. Vernon Hewitt, soon to be without his uncle and co-director, Leicester Hewitt, who joined the Army, felt that the Mercury could still help the war effort by doing more – each Christmas an appeal was made for funds to send parcels to local men in the various theatres of war and the despatch of these gifts continued until the staff became too depleted.

Another Mercury enterprise was the meeting of women to consider allowances to wives and children of serving men. The cost of living rose with the progress of the war and these allowances became totally inadequate. A stream of letters of protest were sent to the editor. A committee was set up with the Mayor, Alderman J North, as chairman and the editor, Mr Hackett, as hon secretary. Pressure was brought to bear on the Government to supplement their scale of allowances. Communication was entered into with other towns and cities and support was readily forthcoming. Local MPs were stirred into action and eventually the Government made substantial increases to dependants.

Some pacifist members on the Town Council attempted to keep Leicester neutral and stay out of the war. In fact, Leicester had

1914

◆ Before 1914 was ended, it had become apparent that the cost of production was going to rise fast, so the price of the Mercury was raised to 1 penny. It was a big shock to readers and the sale, then in the region of 35,000 copies a night, was affected at first. The Mercury was smaller and it was the first time it had to submit news to the censor. Newsprint became scarcer and dearer as the years went by, but it was never rationed. In 1914 it cost £9 15s a ton; by 1918 the price was £56. Mr Basford, as general manager, made countless journeys to London and other centres, calling not only on the manufacturers but on other newspapers as well, begging and bargaining for any precious newsprint which might be spared. The result was that all the Hewitt papers were able to publish continuously, reporting the war between August 4, 1914 and November 11, 1918, although often working with no more than a week's supply in hand.

Above left: Newsprint delivery in Albion Street in 1915.

Below left: The Albion Street machine room.

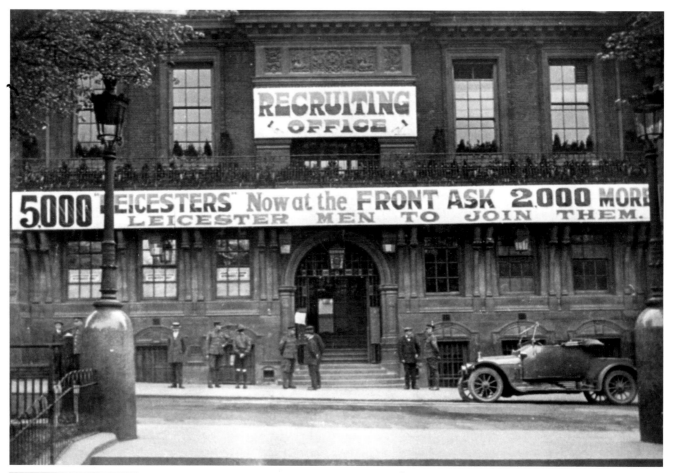

Above: The Town Hall – Leicester's recruiting office during the First World War.

◆ Efforts were made in the columns of the paper to solve the riddle of Ramsay MacDonald, senior MP of the town since 1906, whose talk of 'our German Friends,' letters to German newspapers and frequent anti-war outbursts were in marked contrast to some recruiting speeches he made, one in particular on May Day, 1916, in Leicester's Market Place. Readers' comments left no doubt he was heartily disliked for his pacifism and he was thrown out at the 'khaki' election. He, of course, survived and became the first Labour Prime Minister and eventually an honorary freeman of Leicester.

the worst recruiting figures of the whole country. At the recruiting special meeting on March 30, 1915, it was stated Leicester had recruiting figures of 2.6 per cent; Newcastle 18.5; Nottingham 18.5; Swansea 10.5 and Hull 7.1. Councillor W E Hincks noted there was business as usual, pleasure as usual, racing as usual and frivolity as usual. With the hordes of Germany almost knocking at our doors, this was an insidious and hideous mockery, he said. A senior officer of the Leicestershire 2/4 TA battalion, who was also a member of the Town Council, came back from his unit to try to personally recruit 1,000 men and was astonished to see 'hundreds of young fellows who ought to be serving.' He organised a procession of captured machine guns and car loads of wounded men with banners which said: 'Your pals are at the front, won't you go to?' Soon after a huge banner appeared outside the Town Hall which said: 'Recruiting office; 5,000 Leicesters now at the front ask 2,000 more Leicester men to join them.' Alderman North (later to be knighted for his war work) was Mayor of Leicester for all but a few weeks of the entire war. His age did not prevent him accepting a Government invitation to go to the Western Front to see for himself what was happening. He returned unscathed from

Ypres early in 1916, after being caught by shell fire.

Mercury headlines hailed the Battle of Jutland in June 1916 as a 'Glorious Page in History.' It was the last great sea battle of big ships of the war and the hero was Admiral Sir David Beatty, who had made his home at Brooksby. Three days after the news of Jutland came a heavy blow, the sinking of HMS Hampshire after striking a mine while on its way to Russia. On board was Lord Kitchener, whose parents lived at the Manor House, Cossington. Leicester grieved for the man, whose immense efforts at the start of the war had raised a citizen army.

The war years were noted for two momentous developments in Albion Street – the introduction of motor transport and the beginning of full-scale photo-journalism. In 1915, the Chronicle and Mercury became the *Illustrated Leicester Chronicle* with four or five pages of pictures, very badly processed initially, but pictures nevertheless and something quite new to Leicester. The first editor of the new Chronicle was Mr C J Tonsley, a member of the Mercury editorial staff for 13 years.

The first motor vehicles were bought in 1915 and were a Saxon car and two Belsize vans. There was no garage to keep them in, so at night they were taken to a public garage in Braunstone Gate and in the daytime, when not in use, they were parked in a yard on

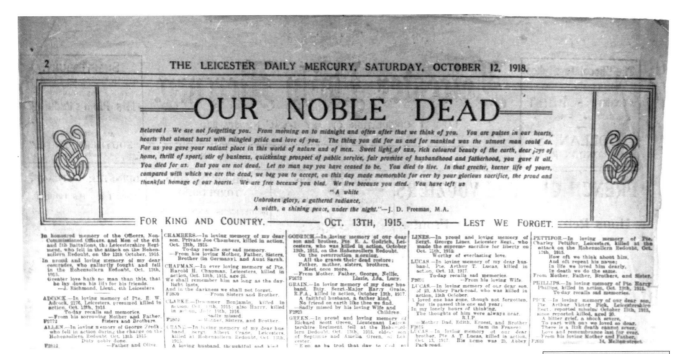

Wellington Street. Hand-trucks had been for so long the means of transporting papers in the town and pony-and-traps had been used to deliver papers to many parts of the county. No longer would readers in Anstey and

Above: This memorial across the top of a wartime edition of the Leicester Daily Mercury on the anniversary of October 13, 1915, tells more effectively than words what the Hohenzollern Redoubt meant to the people of Leicester and county.

Below: A Leicester Mercury Belsize van purchased in 1915 and thought to be the first to enter the fleet.

Enderby have to put up with just two deliveries a week – three days papers on Wednesdays and Saturdays! The Mercury was also now available in countless villages. Two more vans were bought in 1917 and by then 23,000 miles were covered and 1,000 gallons of petrol used in the year.

Mrs M Jebbett of Brailsford Road, Wigston, remembers her uncle, Mr George Wright, came to Leicester from Preston, Lancashire, and started the Process Department at the Mercury during the 1910s. He was joined later by Mr Harold Taylor, also from Preston. Mr Wright left during the 30s to start his own photo-engraving business in

1917

◆ Mr Donald Cumming of Wallis Close, Hunters Green, Thurcaston, remembers entering a competition for youngsters in the Mercury in 1917. He was 9 years of age at the time and confesses to receiving assistance from his father. The competition required him to write down his full name (Donald Arthur Cumming) and then make a sentence from the letters (And murmur a cold night). He received half a crown as just reward.

◆ Mr Charles Green of Greencoat Court, Greencoat Road, Leicester, remembers his uncle, Bill Green, who suffered shell shock during the First World War, began selling copies of the Mercury outside the Saracen's Head public house and later at Kemp's Clock at this time. He continued selling until he died in the 1950s.

*Above: A world 'first' –
the town's first morning
newspaper, the Leicester
Daily Post, was
delivered by air from the
old county ground at
Aylestone to a field 12
miles away beside the
Ashby Road in
Loughborough on
November 30, 1912 –
Gustav Hamel was the
pilot in a 50 hp plane.*

Albion Street, but Mr Taylor stayed until his retirement.

Mr Tom Mitchell of Main Street in Markfield has a lasting memory of the Mercury in 1917. Due to manpower shortages, people were needed to harvest the turnips and marigolds to feed the cattle in winter. Schools closed for 14 days to allow as many boys as possible help. He well remembers the farmer asking him to go and fetch a Mercury from a lady who passed by the field a few times. She was Mrs Turner, who used to sell the Mercury in the village of Newton Burgoland and used to collect them from Shackerstone Station. He remembers readers used to get Monday's four-page Mercury on Tuesday morning. The Evening Mail came the same way and both cost 1d.

Mr Harry Limbert of Catherine's Close, Quorn, has informed me of the 'oldest newsagent who sold Leicester Mercuries.' Mr William Armston bought a shop next door to

the White Horse Inn in Leicester Road, Quorn, as a security for his wife, Sarah, and five children. He prepared it as a newsagents in 1915, but then found he could not obtain permission to sell Mercuries, owing to the fact that there were two other newsagents in Quorn. He did however sell Nottingham papers and his first day's takings amounted to 4 and a halfpence. Soon afterwards, one of the other newsagents, Mr Facer, decided to sell up and Mr Armston seized the moment and bought his Mercury rounds. Mr Limbert describes it as a colourful shop, where people used to love to stop and have a chat with Mrs Armston, particularly Pc Bobby Norman, who used to stop outside the shop in a little corner to smoke a cigarette. He would ask Mrs Armston to pull the curtain across so that the light did not shine on him in his little corner. His story-teller is Hilda, the youngest of the Armston family, who remembers all the Mercury editions, the Monitor, the Post, the Mercury Mid-day and the Sports Mercury. Big fights at the Granby Halls warranted special editions in the 1920s. Her sister Edith Ann worked for the Evening Mail as Aunty Molly. There was a commotion in the shop during the war, when a German Zeppelin flew over Quorn on its way to bomb Loughborough. The word spread that it was passing over Mountsorrel, when a lady named Miss Webster dashed into the shop and jumped on to the counter and put the light out. All the family went to the darkened window, as Sam, the youngest son, was out delivering Mercuries while the Zeppelin was still overhead. Mr Armston received a surprise visitor one day – it was Mr Vernon Hewitt, who had come to live at Quorn, (first at Oaklands, Chaveney Road, then at White Lodge, Buddon Lane, Quorn). He had called in to see how the newspaper shop was progressing and they became firm friends. Hilda used her memory when putting morning and evening rounds together. 'That's the training I had as a young girl going up one street and down another for 1/6d a week in all kinds of weather.' She did all the Quorn rounds at one time or another.

The Post, purchased in 1882, made history on November 30, 1912, with an 'Aerial Edition,' the first in the world. A certain Gustav Hamel took off in a 50 hp aeroplane from the old county ground at Aylestone and at 35 mph covered the 12 miles to a field beside the Ashby Road in Loughborough, handing over copies of the Post to the Mayor's representative. Post staff had to help hold the tail of the aeroplane as it prepared for take off and the 'intrepid aviator,' as he was named, then followed the main Leicester-Loughborough road at about 200 feet, every now and again dropping papers to the crowds waving to him from below. He sat on a seat between the wings, exposed to the frost and mist and was numb with cold when he landed.

On June 14, 1913, the Post was also the first newspaper in the world, it was believed, to run to 28 pages and become the largest edition ever published. It was a special industrial issue, with a leading article in English, French, German and Italian and cost one halfpenny. It found its way to many parts of the world.

The ordinary man's attitude to the war – 'I'll wait till they fetch me' – appalled the city council and members attempted to alter their views by the decision in mid-war to erect a temporary war memorial in Town Hall Square to the fallen. When seeking approval, the Mayor said: 'It will bring home to many people, especially young people, who still seem to be regarding the war with

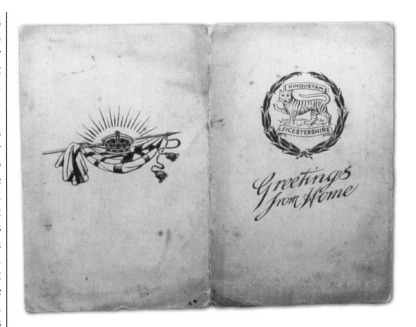

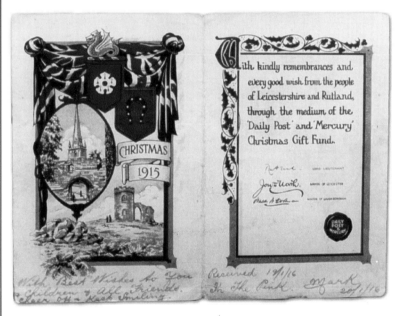

indifference, the seriousness of the times in which we live.' It was unveiled in June 1917 and had two wings with the words carved 'They Did Not Fail Us: We Must Not Fail Them.' The names numbered 2,129, just one fifth of those who were ultimately to appear in the Roll of Honour compiled at the end of the war, totalling 9,348. Many others had been prisoners, wounded or discharged disabled.

Armistice was signed between the Allies and the Central Powers on November 11, 1918, and a general holiday was declared. Four days later, the Duke of Rutland presented medals for Gallantry to over 100 soldiers on Victoria Park and on November 17, United Thanksgiving Services were held in De Montfort Hall at the cessation of hostilities.

Leicester faced the return to peace with some of the euphoria of the ending of the war still hanging over and it reached a climax on

Above: Christmas 1915 and a card received 'in the Pink' by a local soldier at the front.

Overleaf: Leicester Mercury front page for Armistice Day, November 11, 1918. Between 1914 and 1918 the news and headlines had displaced the adverts on the front page.

Leicester Daily Mercury.
LARGEST CIRCULATION OF ANY LOCAL NEWSPAPER.
Registered as a Newspaper.]
Estab. 1874. MONDAY, NOVEMBER 11, 1918. ONE PENNY.

THE GREAT NEWS.

GERMANY SUBMITS.

Armistice Signed This Morning.

FIGHTING ENDS AT MONS.

At about 10.25 this morning the great news was received at our office that the German plenipotentiaries had accepted Foch's armistice terms.

Their signatures were appended at 5 a.m., and by the terms of the agreement fighting on all fronts was to cease as from 11 a.m. to-day, French time.

From that hour the Allied armies were not to advance beyond the lines they then occupied.

For the British the fighting is a glorious ending, for a few hours before the armistice put an end to hostilities Canadian troops captured Mons.

PREMIER'S ANNOUNCEMENT.

The Prime Minister makes the following announcement:—

> Armistice was signed at five o'clock this morning, and hostilities are to cease on all fronts at 11 a.m. to-day.

Thus ends, as we may hope and believe, the greatest and also the most unholy war in history. The armistice does not mean a formal peace. It brings about a cessation of hostilities while peace terms are discussed at what will be the most momentous Conference on record, but for the actual peace we shall have to wait. That peace will come in due course we may have every confidence, for Germany, beaten and facing ruin, must be ready to accept with what grace she can the conditions that the Powers, acting as vindicators of an outraged civilisation find it their duty to impose.

FIRST PEACE SUGGESTIONS.

The first suggestion of peace came in December of 1916. At that time Germany was at the zenith of her strength, and the state of the "war map" favoured her pretensions. The peace she then sought was a German peace. President Wilson asked the belligerents for their terms. The Entente Powers answered with as much detail as the circumstances then warranted, the reply being practically based upon Mr. Asquith's famous avowal that there must be restitution, reparation, and guarantees by Germany against repetition of the crime of August, 1914. The German Government made no adequate response whatever, a fact that the President could not fail to point out. The object of Berlin obviously was to draw the Allies into a controversy, in the hope of dividing them and thus securing a permanent advantage. The game failed.

GERMAN SCHEMES FOILED.

Subsequent alusions to peace by German spokesmen indicated some divergence of opinion. but in the main it was clear that their purpose was to secure in the west an equivalent of the aggrandisement they secured in the east by the treaties of Brest-Litovsk and Bucharest. As the fortunes of war waxed or waned their demands went up or down. but it is no injustice to them to say that the German Government schemed to make Belgium an appanage of the Confederation, with the design of dominating France and Great Britain. That these were the hopes entertained when the great offensive of March was entered upon seems evident enough. The promise to the German people was still of "a German peace." The course of that offensive was peremptorily stopped in July, since which date the Germans have passed from one defeat to another. Bulgaria went out in September Turkey and Austria followed in a short time, and under stress of continued defeat, and a rapid crumbling internally, the German Government at last had to accept Mr. Wilson's Fourteen Points and apply for an armistice with a view to peace upon that basis. The Allies agreed upon the terms, and left Marshal Foch to communicate them upon request.

THE POURPARLERS.

On Friday morning the accredited representatives of the German Government met Marshal Foch, with whom were General Weygrand and Admiral Wemyss, Herr Erzberger being the spokesman of the enemy emissaries. He requested an immediate suspension of hostilities. Marshal Foch said the armistice terms must be accepted first. These werre then communicated, and the plenipotentiaries referred them to Headquarters at Spa. This led to delay, of course, and in the meantime the abdication of the Kaiser and the formation of a new Government led, as it is stated, to the arrival of new representatives at Spa. But only one course was inevitable, that indicated by the Prime Minister. The armistice was signed at five o'clock this morning, hostilities ceased at eleven, and the bloodshed is at an end. And the cause of righteousness and civilisation has won.

FRENCH NOTIFICATION.

Admiralty, per Wireless, through the French Wireless Stations:—

> Hostilities will cease on all fronts as from November 11th, at 11 o'clock, French time.
>
> Allied troops will not, until further orders, go beyond the line reached on that date and at that hour.

JOY IN PARIS.

Paris, Sunday.

The news of the abdication of the Kaiser was announced in all the theatres and cinemas in Paris last night, and provoked scenes of indescribable enthusiasm.

The "Matin" says: "The Empire of the Hohenzollerns is defeated, and capitulation may perhaps be regarded as already signed."

The "Petit Journal" writes: "Let us get our flags ready. The armistice is imminent. It is not impossible it will be signed to-day."—Central News.

THE ARMISTICE DELAY

GERMAN EXPLANATION.

The following was yesterday transmitted through the wireless stations of the German Government:—

Regarding the delay in communicating the conditions for an armistice, the following official statement is made:—The courier charged to convey the armistice conditions radiotelegraphed during the night of Nov. 8/9 from the Eiffel Tower that he was not able to cross the lines as the Germans had not yet ceased fire. He had evidently been led to this conclusion by the circumstance that on the German side a munition depot had caught fire, and blown up with continuous detonations. The courier was notified to this effect by wireless, and received the order to cross the lines at once. The arrival of the armistice conditions in Berlin is to be expected hourly.

RECEIVING THE DELEGATES.

Paris, Saturday night.

Details of how the German plenipotentiaries reached the French lines are now available. On Thursday evening, in a driving rain, the German motor-cars pulled up at Haudroy. French soldiers, headed by a superior officer, approached the automobiles, verified the papers of the occupants, and then proceeded to bandage their eyes. The cars were then driven by the French to the appointed residence. On Friday morning the plenipotentiaries were taken to Marshal Foch, the journey taking four hours.

The interview between Marshal Foch and the German delegates was purely a formal one no discussion taking place. They seemed discouraged when Marshal Foch declined to suspend hostilities at once. They asked that they might be allowed to get into telegraphic communication with Spa, and this request was granted on condition that cipher was not used. A courier was also placed at their disposal.—C.N.

The signing of the armistice was announced to the public of London at eleven o'clock this morning by the sending up of maroon signals.

KAISER'S SUCCESSOR.

Grandson or Republic.

In Berlin it is reported that Prince August Wilhelm will act as Regent for the eldest son of the Crown Prince, and that Von Payer will be President of the Prussian Cabinet. In many circles, however, it is considered that the Hohenzollern yesterday is completely compromised, and that the only issue can be a Republic.

THE MEETING WITH FOCH.

Historic Interview.

Paris, November 9th.

The following are details of the journey of the German plenipotentiaries to the French lines and their reception by Marshal Foch:

The plenipotentiaries, having received word that they should present themselves between 8 and 10 p.m. on Thursday on the La Capelle road at a point specified and marked by aerial searchlights arrived at this point in three motor cars at 8.15. The French officers detailed by Marshal Foch received them at the French lines, and took their seats in the motor cars, lowering the blinds. The delegates were then conducted to the Chateau de Francport, near Compiegne. where quarters had been prepared for them.

On account of the lateness of the hour their reception by Marshal Foch was adjourned till the following day, and took place at 9 o'clock on Friday at Rethondnes Station, where Marshal Foch awaited them in hsi train, accompanied by General Weygand and Admiral Sir Rosslyn Wemyss, the British Naval Delegate. The German parlementaires listened in silence to the reading

(Continued in Next Column).

FINE FINISH BY BRITISH.

MONS CAPTURED.

(British Official.)

France, 10.10.

Shortly before dawn this morning Canadian troops of the 1st Army, under General Horne, captured Mons.

RUMANIANS INVADE HUNGARY

Amsterdam, Sunday.

A Vienna telegram states that Field-Marshal Mackensen's Army, without waiting further developments, has started to march through Hungary. Rumanians have penetrated into the South Hungarian town of Lugos, and have occupied it, as well as Grosskenisen.

Eighty Russian prisoners of war were killed and 28 seriously wounded in an affray in Hungary.—Central News.

of the armistice terms without any signs of feeling, but requested Marshal Foch to allow them to deliberate among themselves, and returned to the Chateau de Francport, where they conferred together.

The result of their dleiberations was the request to Marshal Foch to be permitted to communicate with their Government. This was granted on condition that their communication was drafted in French. They then decided to despatch a courier to Spa. The courier selected was a subordinate member of the delegation.

The "Matin" adds the following details: Marshal Foch gave orders for the delegates to be brought to him about nine o'clock. The proceedings began with the examination of the credentials with which the parlementaires were furnished, after which Herr Erzberger, speaking in French, announced that the German Government had appointed himself and his colleagues as plenipotentiaries for the purpose of taking note of the conditions proposed by the Allies and eventually of signing the armistice. Marshal Foch then read aloud the terms, articulating every word distinctly. The full extent of the defeat of the enemy seemed to be brought home to the delegates for the first time as they listened. They made few observations, and merely pointed out certain material difficulties in the way of some clauses of quite secondary importance.

Herr Erzberger then requested, as a measure of humanity, that there should be an immediate suspension of hostilities. Marshal Foch replied that the only suspension of hostilities that could be agreed to was that which would follow the signing of the armistice. He then authorised the plenipotentiaries to despatch a courier to Spa, and to send a wireless notification to Spa of his early arrival. The delegates then retired.

Marshal Foch proceeded to draw up a message to M. Clemenceau, and consigned it to the charge of an orderly officer, who at once started for Paris in a motor car, reaching the Ministry of War at 11.55 a.m. The exact time of the despatch of the message as stamped on the envelope was 10.25 a.m.

The following semi-official statement is issued here:—

The German plenipotentiaries, who crossed the lines on Thursday evening after ten o'clock at Haudray, near La Capelle, spent the night at the Chateau de Rethondes, ten kilometres from Compiegne, on the Soissons road. At nine o'clock yesterday morning they arrived and were received at Marshal Foch's headquarters. Marshal Foch was accompanied at the interview by General Weygand and Admiral Sir Rosslyn Wemyss. The German delegates asked for a provisional suspension of hostilities, which Marshal Foch categorically refused. This refusal will be unanimously approved. The enemy parlementaires also asked in formal terms for the conclusion of an armistice. The text of the conditions decided upon by the Versailles Conference was read to them and then handed to them. They decided to send a courier to German Headquarters at Spa, where the Kaiser now is. The interview ended at eleven o'clock.

Military events enable us to await the result of the pourparlers now in progress with perfect tranquility. The German armies have been flung back towards the narrow defiles of the Belgian Ardennes. They are driven against a wooded and mountainous labyrinth, and are there in danger of a real debacle. Moreover, the internal situation in Germany is every day assuming a more serious character. These considerations cannot fail to weigh with the decisions of those who will have to pronounce on the armistice terms offered by France and her Allies.—Reuter

CLEARING FRANCE.

ONLY A FRINGE LEFT.

Marshal Foch is making excellent use of the period of 72 hours allowed Germany for considering whether or not to sign the armistice. We are into one of the suburbs of Mons, and the capture of the whole is hourly expected. General Debeney is said to be before Chimay—the point of junction with the British—the 3rd French Army are near Rockroy, and General Gouraud has crossed the Meuse, and is proceeding, with United States troops and his own, against Montmedy. The United States troops have cleared the Forest de Woeuvre, and have taken Jametz, which is 19 miles due north of Verdun. The enemy now hold but a fringe of Northern France—an important and valuable district, but of no great size.

The army under the King of the Belgians is playing its part. It has crossed the Scheldt in a new place, and is threatening the Germans with a disastrous outflanking movement.

The British 1st, 3rd, and 4th Armies are threatening further south, and are finding their chief difficulty that of maintaining touch with the retreating enemy. Touch was actually lost east of Tournai. The Germans shelled Tournai after evacuating it, damaged the cathedral, and killed some civilians.

PAST MONS.

Paris, Sunday midnight.

The Central News special military correspondent writes: The pursuit continues on the whole front between the Sambre and the Meuse. Mons has been passed, and more to the south the Ardennes reached. Between Charleville and Sedan the enemy offered some resistance, even directing counter-attacks on the bridge-head established at Vregnes-sur-Meuse, but the energy of the attack soon yielded before our soldiers, who pushed towards the first strongholds near Vrignes-au-Bois.

The 2nd American Army in the Wœvre took the offensive in the direction of Metz and Briey, and immediately obtained important results, which contributed to the destruction of the German army, for the advantages obtained will certainly be developed even during the few hours separating us from the German decision concerning the armistice.

MONTENEGRO OCCUPIED BY THE SERBS.

Surrender of Isolated Austrian Forces.

A Serbian despatch issued on Saturday stated:—

Everywhere in Bosnia and the Banat people received our troops with enthusiasm, and give them a most cordial and solemn receptionn. Joy reigns everywhere in the newly-liberated territories. A number of groups of the old Austro-Hungarian army which are isolated are surrendering to our troops and to our National Guard.

According to news received our troops occupied Montenegro on October 30, and Scutari on November 1. The strong positions of Bredica and Tarabos, which were defended from the south and western part of the town of Scutari, were taken on the same day.

On November 2 our troops occupied Podgoritza. More than 4,000 prisoners and 120 officers, together with a large amount of war material and munitions, have been captured by our troops.

Enthusiastic manifestations for the liberation and unity of our people of three names—Serbs, Croats, and Slovenes—are being received from all the newly-liberated territories.

A particularly solemn and cordial reception was given to our troops by the National Council and inhabitants at Serajevo on their entr, into that city.

The billiards match of 16,000 points between Stevenson and Falkiner (receives 2,000) was brought to a close at the Grand Hall, Leicester-square, on Saturday. Falkiner won by 7,279 points. The scores were:—Falkiner, 16,000, Stevenson, 8,721.

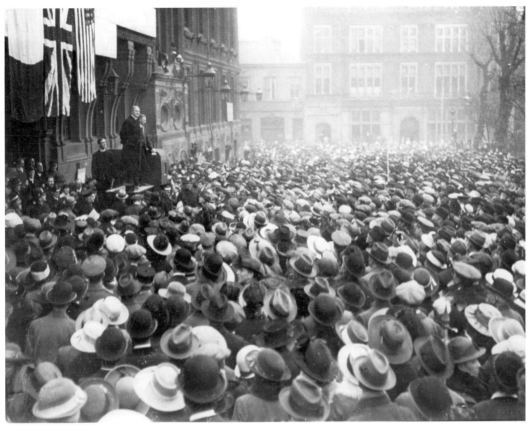

Left: Armistice Day, 1918 – Bishop Wood and the newly elected Mayor of Leicester, Walter Lovell, face the vast throng in Town Hall Square, Leicester.

Below: Front page of the Leicester Mercury for June 10, 1919, the day Leicester was declared a city.

June 10, 1919, when their Majesties King George V and Queen Mary visited the city and took part in a Royal procession through the principal thoroughfares. A march past was held on Victoria Park and honours were bestowed by the King to officers and men of various regiments for services rendered during the war. He publicly knighted the war-time Mayor, Jonathan North, at the De Montfort Hall and elevated Leicester to the rank of city, a status the town's leaders had been seeking since Victorian times. The population now stood at some 234,000 people. One immediate effect was a change of name for the local football club – Leicester Fosse FC was reincarnated as Leicester City FC. Leading figures in the city, including the Mayor, took a shareholding in the club.

On June 30, the 1st 4th and 1st 5th Battalion of the Leicestershire Regiment arrived home from France, amid a public welcome. On July 3, the King's Proclamation announcing the signing of Peace with Germany was read at the Castle and, on July 19, Peace Day was celebrated in Leicester.

Members of the Mercury staff began returning from the Forces and on August Bank Holiday Sunday the combined staffs of the Hewitt papers, totalling 120, went on an outing to Dovedale, in Derbyshire. Mr Vernon Hewitt presided at the meal at the Dog and Partridge Inn and Mr W J Basford, the chief cashier, proposed the toast of the firm, mentioning that 34 members of the staff had been with the firm for over 25 years. Mr

◆ Newsprint remained scarce and the cost rose to such an extent that before the end of 1919 the price of the paper was raised from 1d to 1 and a halfpence. A promise was given that if production costs fell, the penny paper would return. That day came quicker than had been anticipated and, in 1920, the price fell to 1d again and was to stay at that for nearly 20 years.

◆ Looking forward to more prosperous days, with more newsprint and a larger readership, a new press with a speed of 30,000 copies an hour was ordered and the battery of linotype machines was increased to 20.

Harry Hackett, as Editor of the Mercury, supported Mr Basford's toast, as did Mr W G Gibbs of the Post and Mr J K Berry, chief compositor, for the technical departments. After lunch, there were sports for those who wished, while others went for a walk. Before returning home, Vernon Hewitt presented a cheque for £10 to Mr W Davis, of the publishing department, who had risen from private to sergeant during his war service and won the Belgian Medal.

Top and above: The official welcome home to Admiral Sir David Beatty, on his return to Brooksby after the First World War.

The Sports Mercury was launched on Saturday, January 4, 1919. It was an unfortunate day to choose the launch – a heavy snowstorm caused the cancellation of football matches all over the country. This new venture, however, proved popular from the start and set a standard which many

sports papers in other parts of the country have failed to reach after many years of publication.

Harking back to Mr Armston's shop in Quorn, a crowd used to gather outside as soon as the 'final whistle' had gone and as soon as the Mercury van came into sight a big cheer went up and this brought the local village bobby running out of his house, still buttoning up his tunic, to organise the noisy crowd into an orderly queue. The Sports Mercury caused quite a stir amongst the sporting public, as it covered nearly all sports. Mr Vernon Hewitt visited one Saturday to see for himself how the new Sports paper was selling. When he saw how eager the crowd were to obtain the new 'Sports', he promptly took off his coat and started selling his own paper.

Top: Staff outing to Dovedale in 1919.

Left: The Leicester Mercury recorded the death of Sir Jonathan North, JP, DL, Honorary Freeman of Leicester.

Below: The Transport Fleet in 1919.

Chapter 5
Public Company
1920 – 1930

The Armistice was the signal for aid for those who had lost husbands and fathers in action and the suggestion was made in the Mercury columns that it would be some recognition of the sacrifices made if gifts of boots, hosiery and other necessities could be sent to war widows and their children. The next day a boot manufacturing firm offered half a gross of boots to start the undertaking. A constant stream of gifts resulted from the appeal. The Boot Manufacturers' Association promised to find all the boots required for the next twelve months and the hosiery trade was equally generous.

A vigorous committee did the work of distribution, with Mr Hackett again being honorary secretary. Over 7,000 pairs of boots were disposed of and an even larger number of hosiery parcels in two successive winters were forwarded to 1,300 widows and children. It was known as the War Widows' Charity and it was with the consent of the Charity Commissioners that the funds remaining after the distribution of all these gifts were handed over to the Charity Organisation Society for the benefit of the widowed and fatherless.

In March, 1920, F Hewitt and Son purchased the three old-established weekly papers which had been publishing in Chatham Street from brothers W P and W Cox. The three titles – the *Leicester Journal, Leicester Advertiser* and *Loughborough Monitor and News* – cost just over £20,000. Management found Leicester's oldest newspaper, the *Leicester Journal*, practicably impossible to continue and after 167 years it died. The *Leicester Advertiser* was carried on under the title it had borne since its formation in 1841 and Mr W H L Halls continued in office as Editor. The *Loughborough Monitor and News*, founded as the Loughborough Monitor in 1857, was combined with the *Loughborough Herald* under the title of *Loughborough Monitor and Herald*, with Mr Herbert Cook, a relative of the first Francis Hewitt, as the new Editor.

Mr Halls took on extra responsibility at the beginning of 1921. Mr Vernon Hewitt started a new venture, which no provincial newspaper had ever tried before. This was the establishment of the Poultry News and management and staff entered into the task with great enthusiasm. It was a weekly publication, often consisting of as many as 24 pages. It reported poultry shows throughout the land and held its own at the Junior Training Hall in Leicester. Circulation staff went to these shows and set up special stands advertising the paper. Unfortunately, its life was destined to be rather short and it faded from the scene in August, 1925.

Leicester's first morning newspaper, the Leicester Daily Post, which three generations of the Hewitt family had published for nearly half a century, met its demise with its final edition on March 31, 1921. The reasons were given in a concise leading article in the March 1 issue:

'We have to announce this morning that the times have proved too hard for our little paper. It has struggled on gamely under adverse circumstances for well-nigh half a century (it would have seen its jubilee next year), but it has always had many things against it. Its chief obstacle was that it tried to established itself in a town too close to London. It has thus always had to face the severe competition of papers run by much more wealthy combinations. It has always been handicapped by the fact that Leicester is not the centre of a very large population. It managed to survive so long as conditions remained fairly easy, but of late, as everyone knows, the cost of paper has gone up to an enormous extent, the remuneration of the staff has had to be greatly increased and the cost of news-service has advanced very considerably. This has made it impossible for the proprietors to continue publication, save at a loss which cannot reasonably be borne.'

Letters and messages of regret were received in great numbers at the Post's office. Fortunately, the whole of the Post staff was absorbed by the other papers.

Mr Vernon Hewitt presided at a dinner for the staff held at the Junior Training Hall (which became the Granby Halls) in 1923, which was attended by Mr Leicester Hewitt, who had retired a few years previously. Also among the guests was Alderman Windley who, naturally enough, recalled his early associations with the firm's founder. The

1921

◆Mr Arthur (Sam) Summerland of St Denys Road, Evington, was employed as an 'office boy' in the evenings and on Saturday mornings at the Leicester Advertiser before he left King Richards Road School in 1921. On the odd occasion, he had to run errands and met up with an uncle, Syd Carr, who was a linotypist in the composing room and lived at Rathbone Place, Wellington Street.

◆ Part of the new Chatham Street premises was given an entirely new use – a travel bureau under the name of the Midland Holiday Bureau. It was run on the lines of other travel agencies, but had the advantage of the Mercury and its publicity value behind it and continued until the Second World War.

event was held in honour of Mr Harry Hackett, the only non-proprietor editor the paper had had, who had served the firm for 45 years and was editor for 33 years. He retired shortly afterwards and was succeeded by Mr R Gittoes Davies.

Above: Mr Harry Hackett, who served as editor of the Mercury for 33 years.

Below: The Transport Fleet in the 1920s.

Mr Harry Hackett's daughters, Misses Gladys and Helena Hackett, lived on Greenhill Road in Leicester in 1965 and recall he had just retired when Sir Winston Churchill stood as Liberal candidate for Leicester West. Mr Hackett was on the committee of the constituency Liberal Party. Shortly after Mr Churchill lost the election, Mr Hackett died. Four days later, a letter came from Mr Churchill to his widow, offering his condolences on her husband's death, saying how much Mr Churchill admired him.

Mr Basford, who proposed the toast to the firm at the dinner, referred to its rapid growth. It had, he said, outgrown its present building in Albion Street and one had been bought in Granby Street, between Chatham Street and York Street. He had a vision of a building on the Granby Street site worthy of the city.

There were now ladies on the staff of the firm, but they were not invited to the celebration. Instead they were entertained two days later with a visit to the Opera House.

These were the early days of broadcasting and its possibilities were seized upon by those running the Mercury. Signor Marconi, the first practical user of wireless, on the occasion of the paper's jubilee in 1924, wrote to the editor:

'Please accept my heartiest greetings and good wishes on the occasion of

1923

◆ These were heady days of progress in Albion Street. Circulation had reached 50,000 copies a day and the entire circulation of 1874 could be printed and folded by the present machines in less than a minute. Every village in the county was now reached each evening by van, bus or train. The firm's fleet of vehicles numbered as many as 40, which were kept in a garage recently built in Brazil Street on land bought in 1921 for £887. Such was the demand for advertisement space that sometimes as much as 18 columns had to be left out of a 16-page paper.

Right: A Fiat van in the 1920s, decked out for a procession.

Middle: The Fleet at Brazil Street in the 1920s with an Albion lorry, Fiats, Morris vans and cars.

Bottom: A Ford Model 'A' van in the late 1920s.

the Jubilee of the Leicester Mercury, towards which I have always entertained a special feeling of grateful admiration for the interest it has always taken in wireless since the earliest days of its successful inception and for the enterprise with which it has followed and adopted most modern developments.'

Earlier, in 1923, a radio enterprise was reported and caused a mild sensation. A reporter had taken down on shorthand, while sitting in the Mercury newsroom, a special broadcast by Lord Robert Cecil by radio telephone from Marconi House and this was described as 'an achievement which demonstrates the immense possibilities of wireless in relationship to modern newspaper production.'

The Mercury formed the Wireless Club for the benefit of those keen to investigate the wonders of this invention. The Editor himself was one of its leading lights and members met frequently at the offices of the *Leicester Advertiser*. The BBC paid the Mercury the compliment of broadcasting a complete programme chosen by its readers.

The 50th anniversary of the Mercury, on January 31, 1924, brought messages of congratulation from eminent persons up and down the land, from the Prime Minister (Mr J Ramsay MacDonald) and other politicians, from churchmen, playwrights, authors, journalists, composers, businessmen and poets.

Special articles appeared on the events of the previous 50 years and on prospects for the future. Particularly prophetic was one by Robert Donald: 'By the end of the next quarter-century, newspapers will be fighting for their existence. There will be wireless news, accompanied by moving pictures in every home.' 25 years 4 months later, television, with its newsreels, first came into the homes of Leicester.

Professor A M Low, an eminent scientific writer of the day, also wrote about the scientific wonders of the next fifty years. His thoughts included:

'I think that roads will generally be better kept; horse traffic will certainly be excluded from the streets and the use of arcades and travelling platforms into shops may prevent pavements from becoming death-traps ... The main thoroughfares in our large cities will hardly be likely to be exposed to the ravages of fog, which must cost the shopkeepers enormous sums of money ... The police and other people will be in constant touch with their headquarters and will be able to call up the 'Yard' from their pocket.'

The Editor himself, Mr Gittoes Davies, stressed the advances of the previous ten years.

'During and since the war, the management has spent thousands of pounds in its determination to ensure an efficient and up-to-the-minute news service. The installation of a private telegraph wire in direct communication with the London offices, the purchase of new machinery, the institution of a photographic reproduction plant and an elaborate telephone system, the appointment of correspondents in all parts of the country, the

1923

◆ Mr Ernest Hall of Grange Drive in Melton Mowbray remembers his father, Reuben, 'started the Leicester Mercury and the Leicester *Evening Mail* in Melton Mowbray.' Ernest's eldest brother Bert worked in Leicester and travelled on the same train as the papers. He used to parcel them up *en route* and give them to the waiting paper boys, who quickly took off on their bicycles shouting their wares. Ernest also remembers a great demand for the Sports Mercury – he had his own parcel of 12 dozen and was paid 3 pence per dozen. Bert used to take copies to Waltham on the Wolds, about five miles away and charged six pence for delivery. Ernest remembers delivering copies to the local pork butchers, who would count them and then give him a sausage roll!

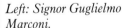

Left: Signor Guglielmo Marconi.

Near right: Editor R Gittoes Davies.

Far right: Editor H W Bourne.

Opposite page: Leicester Mercury front page on Monday May 3, 1926.

engagement of special writers, the opening of branch offices – all these moves illustrate the spirit of enterprise which permeates every department.'

A revolutionary wind was to blow through the offices of the Hewitt papers. Mr Hewitt decided, against the advice of many of his closest friends, to abandon the Liberal banner and make all papers politically independent. 'As soon as the news columns of the paper begin to reflect political bias, that journal ceases to be a newspaper,' said the leading article on January 31, 1924.

Staff and readers were unaware of the drama which took place behind the scenes at the time of this momentous decision. Mr Winston Churchill visited the city specifically to hold a meeting with Mr Hewitt. Churchill was then the prospective Liberal candidate for one of the Leicester divisions and quite a power within the party. He had not arranged the meeting, but eventually, sensing the reason for the meeting, Mr Hewitt agreed and went round to the Grand Hotel, where Mr Churchill was staying. The point was arrived at quickly. It was imperative for the Liberal cause, said Mr Churchill, that the Mercury, which he understood was considering becoming independent, continued on its present line. Mr Hewitt disagreed and stated his reasons. Churchill paced up and down his room and grew increasingly insistent, but to no avail. Finally, he told Mr Hewitt that if he would go back to his directors and persuade them to change their minds, he would promise him any honour he would care to name when the Liberals came to power!

Mr Hewitt was not one to be swayed and made this perfectly clear to Mr Churchill. He left, immediately called a Board Meeting. He told the story of his meeting to his fellow directors and the unanimous decision was to announce the Mercury's independence immediately. It was done that very night. Significantly, Mr Churchill himself forsook Liberalism within a few months in favour of Independence.

Editorially, it was found to be a difficult course to take and there were many deviations. It was not until Mr Henry W Bourne, a member of the sports staff, was appointed Editor of the Mercury in 1926, could it be said that the right course was finally and truly set.

Peacetime in Leicester had brought huge problems. There was a shortage of jobs and homes for the returning war heroes and industrial disputes escalated. Shortage of coal because of disputes led to cuts in electricity and gas supplies in the middle of 1921. Trams had to finish at 2pm and the number of names on the Distress Register, who were chronically unemployed, rose to 2,000 and efforts were made to create public work jobs to keep them occupied. The general level of unemployment rocketed to 15,000 out of work and 12,000 on short time. Unemployment demonstrations took place near the Clock Tower.

The result was the General Strike of 1926, which was destined to bring the country to a halt, but was called off after eight days, largely due to the way in which volunteers kept the vital services and food supplies going. When, on May 12, the Mercury went on the streets with a two-word flash 'Strike Off,' all traffic in the centre was held up while people frantically clamoured for a copy of the paper. In later editions, it was reported:

'Bus drivers and motorists stopped their vehicles, dashed towards the news sellers and bought copies by the dozen. These were distributed to the

ALL THE NEWS IN PICTURES

SEE THIS WEEK'S "Illustrated Leicester Chronicle"

Leicester Mercury.

Extra Special.

Estab. 1874. (REGISTERED AS A NEWSPAPER). MONDAY, MAY 3, 1926. ONE PENNY.

NET SALE at least FOUR TIMES that of any other local daily paper.

Sports Mercury

FOR BEST

CRICKET REPORTS.

GENERAL STRIKE ORDERED TO START AT MIDNIGHT

Breakdown of Negotiations in Early Morning.

SIR W. MITCHELL-THOMSON (Chief Civil Commissioner).

T.U.C. Refuses to Withdraw Call for National Stoppage.

VOLUNTEERS BESIEGING RECRUITING OFFICES.

Adequate Arrangements for Carrying on Vital Services and Maintaining Food Supplies.

Orders have been issued by the trade unions concerned for the general strike to begin at midnight. Almost a miracle will be required to avert it.

The negotiations broke down early to-day. The Government offered to extend the subsidy for a fortnight providing that the miners accepted a settlement on the lines of the Commission's report, and demanded as a condition that the general strike orders should be withdrawn before negotiations were resumed. The T.U.C. Council refused to call off the strike.

No further request has been received from the trades unions for a resumption of negotiations.

The Government state that the news from the country is eminently satisfactory. Offers of service are pouring in all over the country. Food stocks are normal.

Adequate arrangements have been made for the continuance of vital services, and the maintenance of food supplies.

London, To-day.

NOT the smallest gleam of hope broke through the gloom of the mining crisis this morning, and in the absence of some wholly unforseen development midnight will mark the opening of the general strike.

By this hour, unless almost a miracle intervenes to prevent it, the industrial life of the whole country will be almost completely paralysed.

Shortly after 1 a.m. to-day it was announced at 10, Downing-street, that the Government had informed Mr. Pugh that before negotiations could be continued there must be an unconditional withdrawal of the instructions for a general strike.

Such an abrupt and dramatic termination to the negotiations as was announced in the Prime Minister's message to the chairman of the Trade Union Congress (reported on Page 5), came as a profound disappointment to those who heard the encouraging message broadcast last night by the B.B.C. that it was believed that a basis for fresh negotiations had been found.

Significant Avowal.

In their reply to the Government's decisive attitude, the T.U.C. mince no words. "An unprecedented ultimatum" is how they describe Mr. Baldwin's letter, and they frankly state their belief that "the sincere work which the General Council has been engaged in to obtain an honourable settlement has been wrecked" by it.

The only encouragng aspect of the reply of the T.U.C. to the Government's message, is that the Trade Union leaders expressly state that they "cannot accept any responsibility" for acts of indiscipline which, it is alleged, have been taking place among certain of the men, and their reply to the Government emphasises that "measures are being taken to prevent any acts of indiscipline."

No New Peace Move.

This is a significant avowal, and one which Mr. Baldwin's ultimatum emphasised would be required before any further negotiations could be opened.

The ultimatum, however, also makes it plain that discussions cannot be resumed in the absence of "an immediate and unconditional withdrawal of the instructions for a general strike."

NOT TOO LATE!

Following a joint meeting between the Parliamentary Labour Party, the Miners' Executive, and the Joint Council of the T.U.C. at the House of Commons, a prominent trade union leader said: "It is not too late yet to avert disaster. A tremendous lot depends upon what happens in the next hour or so."

The following unions are definitely due to start the strike to-night:—

National Union of Railwaymen	350,000
Locomotive Engineers and Firemen	63,500
Railway Clerks' Association	60,000
Transport and General Workers' Union	300,000
Miscellaneous Transport Unions	30,000
Sailors' and Firemen's Union	60,000
Printing unions	120,000
Building Trades Unions	300,000
Electrical Trades Unions	25,000
Iron and Steel Trades' Confederation	100,000

STRIKE ITEMS.

The Railway Rates Tribunal to-day adjourned sine die in view of the emergency.

* * * *

London special constables have been ordered to report immediately.

* * * *

The Board of Trade is establishing a milk pool in London under the London Milk Pool Committee.

* * * *

Supplies at Covent Garden were about normal to-day, but there was no surplus.

* * * *

The general position with regard to electrical power stations and gas companies in London is described as "standing by and awaiting events."

* * * *

All persons are earnestly requested by the Government to exercise the greatest economy in the consumption of motor spirit.

* * * *

Enquiries to-day elicited the fact that both the electricity and gas undertakings of the Loughborough Corporation have satisfactory stocks of coal in hand and no difficulty is anticipated on that score in maintaining the town's supplies of heat, light and power.

CROWDS IN DOWNING STREET.

Special Meeting of the Miners' Executive.

When the trade union leaders left Downing-street early this morning, Mr. Thomas said, "It is a very sad affair." Mr. Cook said, "We must prepare now for the struggle. The Prime Minister has declared war."

Members of the National Executive of the Miners' Federation began to assemble early this morning at the London headquarters, in response to telegrams sent yesterday asking them to attend a specially summoned emergency meeting.

Interviewed prior to the meeting, Mr. Cook said the miners are locked out, denied the right of a living wage. The last proposals received were from the Prime Minister, with reductions in wages and longer hours. The whole Trades Union movement will prove to the Government the solidarity of labour. This is labour's greatest effort to protect the great mining community.

"We asked for peace and bread; the Government and coal owners are determined to give us a stone."

Crowds of people evinced keen interest in the coming and going of Ministers to Downing-street.

Many confessed they had been unemployed for some time.

At 10.30 the Miners' Executive left for Westminster Hall, with the object of consulting members of the Trades Union Congress.

Labour Party Meeting.

Soon after their arrival at Westminster, the Miners' Executive continued their special meeting in one of the committee rooms.

In an adjoining committee room the Special Industrial Committee of the Trades Union Congress and the members of the Parliamentary Labour Party met simultaneously.

Following a meeting between the Executive of the Parliamentary Labour Party and Trades Union Congress, a meeting of the full Parliamentary Labour Party was held. At this meeting were present also representatives of the Trades Union Congress General Council and of the Miners' Federation.

OFFERS OF SERVICE POURING IN.

Food Stocks Normal in Country as Whole.

WARNING BY RAILWAYS.

"NEWS from the country is eminently satisfactory. There is no excitement, everything is normal," said a Government spokesman this afternoon.

Offers of service are pouring in all over the country.

Food stocks are normal, taking the country as a whole, and in many cases are above the average.

The Government spokesman again expressed the view that the railwaymen were very reluctant to go on strike. Nothing could be further from the truth than to suggest that the Government were attacking the miners in order indirectly to attack the railwaymen.

Hyde Park as Milk Depot.

Hyde Park was entirely closed to the public to-day, in preparation for its use as the milk distributing centre for London.

"We have no reason to suppose that the Post Office staff will strike," was the reply to an inquiry at the G.P.O.

Sir William Bull, one of the Civil Commissioners, spent some time at the Government Whips' office, and Sir Hanky (Secretary of the Cabinet) was in consultation with Prime Minister.

The police were kept busy in Downing-street to-day, directing men and women to recruiting offices.

From time to time the crowd of volunteers at Whitehall had to be formed into a queue.

It was noticeable that the great majority of men offering their services were of the artisan class.

Troops at Liverpool.

Troops were disembarked at Liverpool landing stage from the Anchor liner Neuralia to-day, in connection with the Strike Emergency plans, to the number of about 1,000. The troops proceeded to the riverside station, where a train was waiting to take them to Aintree Racecourse, to be ready to proceed at a moment's notice to any centre of disturbance in Lancashire.

Glasgow is preparing for a general stoppage, but so far the shipyards are not affected.

Tramwaymen have been notified to prepare to stop at midnight, but the response is doubtful.

Coal supplies are adequate for immediate necessities. Retail coal prices were advanced sixpence per cwt. to-day.

Railway Companies' Statement.

The railway companies of Great Britain give official notice that in the event of the present general strike taking place, and necessitating a curtailment or interruption of trains, boat, and other services, they will be unable to accept or convey passengers' merchandise and livestock traffic in the usual course, and such traffic will only be accepted as it can be dealt with, and upon the understanding that the companies will not be liable for any loss, expense, damage, deviation, misconveyance, misdelivery, delay, or detention received from or in consequence of such curtailment or interruption of service.

NEWSPAPER STOPPED.

Interference With Rights of the Press.

The "Daily Mail" was not published to-day. The National Society of Operative Printers and Assistants demanded that an alteration should be made in the leading article headed "For King and Country," and the editor refused to comply. The Natsopa thereupon ceased work.

Although there was no issue of the "Daily Mail" from Carmelite House, to-day, it was printed in its Manchester office as usual.

The Government, realising the importance of getting news to the public in newspaper form, have this matter under consideration.

There will be broadcasting at 10 a.m., 1 p.m., 4 p.m., 7 p.m., and 10 p.m.

GREAT RECEPTION FOR PREMIER.

Loudly Cheered in the House.

THE KING'S MESSAGE.

Westminster, This Afternoon.

AS a result of the extreme gravity of the industrial crisis, there was a very large attendance of members in the House of Commons.

Owing to the general desire for enlightenment as to the actual position of affairs, only perfunctory attention was paid to the printed questions dealing with minor matters, of which 69 appeared on the paper.

Great Reception.

Mr. Baldwin made his appearance during questions, and was given a grat ovation by Conservative members. Rising in all parts of the House, they loudly cheered and waved order papers and handkerchiefs.

"The apostle of peace and goodwill," shouted a Labour member.

Ministerialists cheered loudly, and Sir W. Davidson called out: "No Soviets in this country." (Cheers.)

Mr. Baldwin then went to the Bar and announced the receipt of a message from the King, "signed by his own hand." Approaching the table, he handed a document to the Speaker.

The Speaker then read it—the declaring of the existence of a state of eemrgency—to the House. Mr. Baldwin thereupon rose and moved that an humble Address be presented to his Majesty, thanking him for his gracious message. The Speaker was about to put the motion when Mr. Ramsay MacDonald rose and asked if the matter should be debated at that stage.

The Prime Minister replied that this was purely a formal stage, and it was not usual to have a debate on such a motion.

They could, he said, have debate on the regulations on Tuesday or Wednesday.

Labour Challenge.

Mr. MacDonald said that so long as this was purely formal, and all the consequences arising out of it would be subject of debate later on, he would not press the matter.

Mr. Neil McLean asked who it was who had threatened to stop the coal trade which gave rise to a state of emergency. The Prime Minister replied that any Government which thought there was fear or stoppage on any extensive scale could declare a state of emergency. The speaker then put the motion.

The Labour party loudly challenged a division on the motion which was, however, carried by 308 to 108.

On the motion for the adjournment the Prime Minister, stating that the House was meeting to-day on one of the gravest occasions on which it had ever met, expressed confidence that the debate that might ensue to-day would be worthy of the occasion.

The whole of the machinery required radical overhauling. The Government had been repeatedly brought into relations with the coal trade in the past, and it had prescribed, but the patient's health had been but little improved. Recurrent crises always had certain common symptoms. Either the Mining Association gave notice of reductions, or the federation demanded advances.

HINCKLEY HOSIERY TRADE IMMUNE.

Interviewed at Hinckley to-day, Mr. John Bailey stated that so far as the Hinckley and District Hosiery Union is concerned, they are not affiliated to the Trades Union Congress, therefore at present no action would be taken.

The union has a membership of over 4,000 at Hinckley, Earl Shilton, Stoke Golding, Burbage and Nuneaton.

Work, it would appear, will be continued until supplies are stopped.

There are also 1,500 Union operatives on the finishing side of the local hosiery industry which will also not be affected at the moment.

NATIONAL NEWS GUILD.

A meeting of the National News Guild to discuss the general strike situation will be held at the Flying Horse, Wellington-street, Leicester, at 8 o'clock to-night.

'MERCURY' Amateur Photographic Competition. £100 In Prizes. £30 FOR ONE PHOTOGRAPH. No Entry Fee. :: Enter Now.

Leicester Mercury.

Extra Special.

Estab. 1874. (Registered as a Newspaper.) SATURDAY, MAY 21, 1927. ONE PENNY.

NET SALE at least FOUR TIMES that of any other local daily paper.

PLAYER'S WHITE LABEL 10 CIGARETTES 5½d.

LINDBERGH CROSSES ATLANTIC

Sighted 100 Miles off Irish Coast.

SPEED OF 200 MILES AN HOUR.

'Flying Fool's' Great Lone Adventure; Mascot Cat Left Behind.

CAPTAIN Lindbergh, who left New York alone on his attempt to fly to Paris, has succeeded in crossing the Atlantic. He is the first man to make the trip alone.

The first tidings of him since he passed over Newfoundland was the following cable from New York:

A wireless company states that its office in Ireland has received a report that Captain Lindbergh's aeroplane was sighted by a vessel 200 miles off the Irish coast at 6.30 a.m. New York time (11.30 British time).

This was later corroborated by a telegram from Dublin stating that the Valentia Cable Station, South-West Ireland, reported that Lindbergh had been sighted 100 miles off that island.

PARIS is excited at the prospect of welcoming the intrepid American, who gives every appearance of succeeding where Nungesser, Fonck, St. Romain, and other famous aces have failed.

He is expected there this evening.

No news was heard of Lindbergh from the time he passed over St. John's, Newfoundland, about 2.30 this morning British time, until he was sighted 200 miles off the South-West Coast of Ireland at 11.30 this morning. The 'plane carried no wireless apparatus.

From St. John's, it was reported that a high wind, almost approaching a gale, was blowing at the back of the aeroplane, and this would account for the high speed of over 200 miles an hour at which the Atlantic was crossed.

M. Raymond Orteig, who has offered a prize of 25,000 dollars to the first man to fly between Paris and New York non-stop, has left Pau for Paris. He declared he wanted to be in the capital for the arrival of Captain Lindbergh.

Cat Left Behind.

Captain Lindbergh's daring trans-Atlantic venture claims headings right across the front pages of this morning's New York newspapers, while two or three supplements are filled with biographical details and descriptions of the 'plane with plenitude of illustrations.

All the papers publish Washington despatches with official expressions of goodwill from President Coolidge, Mr. Mellon, the American flying authorities and others, and many devote leading articles to the flight. The "New York World" publishes a cartoon representing an aeroplane in triumphant flight across the sea towards the splendour of the rising sun, and underneath is the inscription "The spirit of St. Louis," followed by the exclamation, "The spirit of youth."

The intrepid airman finally decided to leave his cat mascot behind out of consideration for the cat's possible discomfort during the flight.

Chamberlin Delays.

Hundreds of people visited Roosevelt Field, New York, this morning, in the expectation of seeing Mr. Clarence Chamberlin, with some, at present unknown, airman as a partner, in the Bellanca aeroplane, Columbia, emulate the example of Captain Lindbergh and start for Paris.

They were, however, disappointed.

Mr. Levine, the backer of this flight, had announced that as a sporting proposition the Bellanca aeroplane would start immediately.

Mr. Chamberlin, however, did not like the weather reports, indicating north-west cross winds for the first 1,000 miles of the journey.

Commander Byrd's Fokker aeroplane has still to undergo her final load test, and her owners have announced that she will not start until word has been received that Captain Lindbergh is safe.

BOARD'S ACTION.

Ashby Miners to be Prosecuted for Loans.

Ashby Guardians to-day adopted a resolution, proposed by a special committee, to deal with loans to miners during the industrial struggle, to prosecute in certain cases and warn in others where no repayments had been made.

About £28,000 was loaned to miners during the trouble.

It was stated that as a result of only a few days being worked by many miners, not much headway had been made in reducing the loan.

WORKHOUSE TRAGEDY.

A verdict of "Accidental death" was recorded at an inquest on Louise Weal, aged 61, an inmate of the Billesdon Workhouse.

John Henry Carl, a porter, said he heard a shout on the landing against the women's dormitory, and found that the woman had fallen down a step.

MIDLAND LABOUR PROTEST.

A special meeting of the Midland Council of the Independent Labour Party, in Leicester, this afternoon, passed a resolution protesting against the "continued delay of the Government in affording the country any excuse or justification for its deliberate violation of the immunities conferred by the trade agreement of 1921 by the raid on the premises of the Russian Trade Delegation."

CATCH OF THE SEASON.—A Palace artiste excels in the field against the Leicester Co-operative cricketers.

BRAVE DEED BY ACTRESS.

Children Saved From Blazing Car.

Miss Julia Neilson, the famous actress, and wife of Mr. Fred Terry, performed an heroic act when her motor-car caught fire as she was driving home after her performance late last night.

Miss Neilson, who has been playing at Richmond, was driving back to London, when she collided with another car at St. John's Wood.

The actress's car immediately burst into flames, and Miss Neilson managed to jump clear in time to avert injury.

Dashing back to the car, however, she lifted out two children, who were travelling with her, at great risk to herself.

MISS JULIA NEILSON

She handed them to the chauffeur, who got out safely, though he had a narrow escape.

The fire brigade was called, but the back of the car was burnt out before they arrived.

Miss Neilson, none the worse for her experience, went on to London in another car.

BOY OF SIX KILLED.

Knocked Down by Car in Leicester.

A fatal accident occurred at the corner of Avenue-road Extension and Welford-road, Leicester, the victim being George Ball, aged six, of 27, Herrick-road, Leicester, who was crossing the road when he was knocked down by a motor-car.

He was picked up by a private car and taken in an unconscious state to the Royal Infirmary, where he was found to be suffering from very bad concussion.

He died there shortly afterwards.

FOUR IN CRASH.

Woman Killed and Three Hurt Near Grantham.

Mr. Rowland Chantry, who was injured in a motor-cycle accident on Friday night on the Harlaxton-road, Grantham, was stated to-day to be in a very serious condition. His wife was killed.

Two Croxton Kerrial (near Melton) ironstone labourers were travelling home from Grantham, one driving a motor-cycle and his companion riding pillion, when on the Harlaxton-road they came into collision with Mr. and Mrs. Rowland Chantry, who were crossing the road.

It was found that the husband had sustained fractures of both legs. One of the motor-cycle riders was suffering from severe concussion and was also badly cut. The second man had slight concussion and wounds on the arm and knee.

CENSURE MOTION.

Conservative M.P. Gives Shock to Government.

Something of a sensation has been caused in political circles by the motion put down by one of the Government's most prominent supporters, Sir George Courthope, M.P., calling upon the Government to extend the Safeguarding of Industries Act to the agricultural industry.

Sir George Courthope is Chairman of the Unionist Agricultural Committee, which has 300 members, but it is understood that he has made it clear that he has put down the motion as an individual and not as Chairman of the committee.

In some quarters the motion has been interpreted as a vote of censure on the Government for the "inadequacy" of its agricultural policy, and immediate steps are to be taken by the Minister of Agriculture to make clear his attitude towards the question.

THRILLING FIGHT WITH BANDITS IN MEXICO.

ENGLISH TOURISTS IN A TRAIN WRECKING EPISODE.

60 PEOPLE KILLED.

"MERCURY" CORRESPONDENT.

Liverpool, To-day.

An English tourist and his wife, who arrived in Liverpool to-day, told a vivid story of a pitched battle between 300 Mexican bandits and the passengers of the train on which they were travelling from Mexico City. The train was wrecked, riddled with bullets, and then set on fire. Sixty people were killed. The couple managed to escape with the aid of bribes and cajolery.

THE couple were Mr. and Mrs. T. H. Watson, who were travelling in America with their daughter, whose home is in Derbyshire.

When they reached Liverpool to-day on the Canadian Pacific steamer Minnedosa, they appeared none the worse for the experience, and chatted freely.

They were staying with a family named Dock at Guadalajara, which is about 100 miles from Mexico City.

They left this place by the evening train, and were seated comfortably enjoying their supper whe nthe alarm was given.

"My wife and daughter and I were in the drawing room of the Pullman car when we found the train crossing two bridges which were burning.

Danger Point.

"Then there came a terrible crash, and the train came to a sudden standstill.

"The engine had crashed into an obstruction and had become derailed. None of the passengers were hurt in what we thought was an ordinary rail mishap, and we were just beginning to congratulate one another when shots were fired.

"Bullets began to splinter the train, glass was shattered, punctures appeared in the walls of the compartments, and the alarm was given by the train attendants "lie down!"

"We were being attacked from both sides at once.

"This cross-firing by a force of bandits estimated at 300 was enough to paralyse the nerves of the strongest. We were all laying flat on the floor and hoping for the best, and had to suffer this agonising experience for an hour while the sides of the train were being steadily pounded with lead.

Soldiers' Surrender.

"The object of [illegible] firing was to dispose of the military guard of 60 soldiers who were on the train, and at the end of our terrible hour the hoarse voices of the bandits could be heard calling the soldiers to surrender. These men showed no courage, and at the first invitation capitulated, and they met the fate of the cowards.

"The bandits swarmed round the wrecked train and gleefully witnessed the summary execution of these wretched soldiers.

"We were called to our feet and compelled to hol dour hands up. Every gun was pointed at us while we were called upon to deliver our personal goods—watches, money and jewelery—were handed over or snatched. We had to exercise the greatest tact and show the most abject submissiveness as we could.

"Our friend, Mr. Dock, who was accompanying us was a brick, and being able to speak Mexican he employed diplomacy, which probably saved our lives.

"By this time it was 10 o'clock at night and without a thing except what we stood up in, we were driven like so many sheep out on to the prairie, miles from anywhere.

"A sudden explosion and a burst of flame beneath thetrain told us what they had been doing. They were destroying all trace of the butchery by burying our train.

"We then heard the throbbing of a railway engine. We heard among our company the joyful words, 'A relief train.'

(Continued in Next Column).

KNOCKED DOWN BY TRAIN.

Aged Man's Escape in Leicester.

While crossing the rails near the London and North Eastern Cattle Docks, Leicester, to-day, an old employe of the company named Harry Smith (72), who lives at 77, Luther-street, Leicester, was knocked down by a goods train.

Fortunately, he was flung clear of the train, but he received injuries to his left arm and a compound fracture of the left leg.

How Smith happened to be on the permanent way is not known, but it is believed that he must have used it as a short cut to his garden, which is situated on the other side of the docks.

He was conveyed to the Royal Infirmary, where his condition is stated to be not very serious.

Obstacle race at Ald. Newton's Girls' sports.

WHITE LINES MOVE.

Leicester Surveyor Considering New Proposals.

The need for white lines on the main roads of Leicester as safety devices is daily finding more and more advocates. Mr. J. E. Lester, the secretary of the Leicester Road Improvement Association, in an interview with a "Mercury" representative, pointed out that he was constantly receiving testimony of the growing public opinion on this matter.

He said that the Road Improvement Association and the Leicestershire Automobile Association had been discussing this matter for some time, and had pressed the Highway Committee to receive a deputation, but that body had so far refused.

The latest step was that he had put certain suggestions before the City Surveyor, who, he understood, was considering them.

TALE OF A COAT.

Sydney Barton Smith, of the B Battalion Royal Horse Artillery, stationed at Aldershot, was charged at Loughborough with stealing a coat and vest value 20s, the property of Walter Poole, at Rothley.

Sergeant Smith stated that Poole had taken off his coat and waistcoat while at work, and later missed them. When arrested Smith was wearing the two garments, having discarded his uniform.

He was remanded for a week.

"It was a train filled with soldiers who were a braver lot than those who had accompanied us. As the train drew up these men leaped from the coaches and immediately commenced an attack on the bandits.

"The latter, however, mounted their horses and dispersed [illegible] and were soon hidden to view by the prairie bushes.

"We received friendly aid and were supplied with garments of all kinds so that was some compensation, but little did we dream when we started our [illegible] miles tour that we were to have such a thrilling adventure."

passengers and loud bursts of cheering followed. Policemen for the time being took no notice of the traffic blocks. They too were eager to learn that the stoppage had ended.'

Due to the loyalty of many of the staff and their willingness to assist in unaccustomed roles, the Mercury was published throughout the Strike, though in an abbreviated form. It was one of the few whose publication was not interrupted.

It was in the spring of 1927 that the 'Mercury Walk,' a walking race through the city and part of the county, began. It was to become one of Leicester's major annual sporting events and attracted many of the best-known athletes in the country. On June 11, it was won by T Lloyd Johnson of Leicester. Other sports also received encouragement from the Mercury. Silver cups, bowls or other trophies were presented for annual competition in football, golf, lawn tennis, bowls, rowing, billiards and chess. A silver bowl was also given to the organisers of the annual music festival.

It was becoming increasingly obvious at the Leicester Mercury that progress could not continue at the same rate on the present issued capital of £70,000. On December 29, 1927, therefore, F Hewitt & Son Ltd became

1925

◆ A children's club, which eventually was to have 184,000 members was started in 1925 and continued until the outbreak of the second world war. The Oozoos Club was run by journalist Mrs W M Goddard.

1928

◆ Memories of the Mercury at this time include one from Mrs Emma Norris of Gaddesby Avenue in Leicester. She has fond memories and can vividly remember as a girl of 14, in 1928, passing by the offices in Albion Street each evening, stopping to look at the 'news photos,' with flashes of news and sports personalities, which were always kept up to date.

a public company under the style of F Hewitt & Son (1927) Ltd, with a capital of £335,000, divided into 200,000 8% Cumulative Preference Shares of £1; 132,500 10% Cumulative Preferred Ordinary Shares of £1 and 2,500 Deferred Ordinary Shares of £1.

The shareholders of the old company, who were all members of the Hewitt family, were given 20 Preference Shares in the new company for every seven held in the old company and 53 Preferred Ordinary Shares for every 28 old shares. Mr Hewitt retired from the managing directorship and was given 2,493 Deferred Ordinary Shares as compensation for loss of office.

By agreement, all the 200,000 Preference Shares were then sold, at 20 shillings each less nine and a half per cent commission to Myers and Co, of London and transferred to trustees for sale to the public. It had been arranged that members of the staff might obtain Shares at 19/9d and about 40 took advantage of this.

Mr Vernon Hewitt became the first chairman of the new company and Mr W J Basford and Mr C T Barton were appointed managing directors. Mr Barton had joined from London as an accountant in 1919 and after acting as an assistant to Mr Hewitt and then Mr Basford, he became assistant general manager. Under the Articles of Association of the new Company, the holders of the 10% Preferred Ordinary Shares were given the right to appoint three of the maximum of six directors. The three other directors were Mr J A Hopps, Mr John Parsons and Mr T S Rowley. Mr Hopps, a partner in the accountants' firm of Hopps & Bankart, had known all three generations of the Hewitt family and for long had audited the accounts of their newspapers. He was the liquidator when F Hewitt & Son became a public company and his active association with the Hewitt concern was to extend over a period

of more than half a century, until he died in 1951 at the age of 88. Mr Parsons was a partner in the firm of solicitors acting for the company and Mr Rowley a director of a local firm of hosiery manufacturers. Both had been closely associated with the Hewitt family for many years.

The first secretary of the company was Mr A W Peake, a Leicester man, who came as a clerk in 1923. He was to hold the position for 20 years, undertaking much responsibility.

CLEMENT T. BARTON
Chairman 1954-1963

Early in 1928 and with the new company only two months' old, an offer was made to the Mercury to buy the Leicester Evening Mail. It came from a member of the Mail Board, Sir Arthur Wheeler, who had been a director of the Mail since 1923. It was another concern in which Sir Wheeler was interested that took up the greater part of an issue of new capital made by the Mail to assist them in developing the site opposite the London Road railway station, which they purchased in 1924.

The chairman of the Mail at this time was Sir Arthur Faire, who had held office since the death of Sir Herbert Marshall on August 21, 1918, aged 67. When Sir Arthur Faire died in 1929, he was succeeded by Lieut-Col C F (later Sir Frederick) Oliver.

The Hewitt Board told Sir Wheeler that they were not interested in his proposition. In reality, they had no wish to take over what was admittedly a sinking ship.

Near left: Managing Director C T Barton.

Far left: Managing Director A W Peake.

Chapter 6
Unemployment and Newspaper Wars
1930 – 40

The next decade was dramatic. It was the era of dictators with Hitler, Mussolini and Franco putting their jackboots into democracies' attempts to establish a lasting peace in a climate of mounting economic problems which produced the Wall Street crash of 1930 and the fall of the 1929 Labour Government to be replaced by a National Government led by the Labour Prime Minister Ramsay MacDonald with Tory Stanley Baldwin as his deputy.

These were the times that raised unemployment in Britain to two and a half million, produced the notorious Means Test, the Jarrow marchers and developed the much criticised policy of appeasement.

Mr Searson Thompson of Terrace Road, Aberdovey, Gwynned, has written, informing me that he was with the Leicester Mercury from 1927 to 1947. He started as the first motorcyclist depatch rider, or 'flyer,' with the circulation department run by Joe Berridge and Fred Smith.

He writes: 'We were also responsible for any big event where the Leicester Mercury was to be prominent, more prominent than the opposition, the *Leicester Evening Mail*. We were a favoured department and received many perks than other departments. My brother and I were keen motorcyclists, belonging to the Leicester and District Motor Club and the Leicester Query Club. We were champion trails riders, representing our club and Leicestershire in the big ACU events, grass track, road racers, at places like Syston Park and Donington Park. In one year alone we won over 150 awards.

One day we were asked if we would like to earn a little money in our spare time by despatch riding for the Mercury. The job entailed delivering the Sports Mercury to the district offices, Coalville, Market Harborough, Rugby and Hinckley. They needed to arrive before the Evening Mail sports edition. In those days there were no speed limits on the roads, other than a 30mph limit on commercial vehicles. It was often night driving and lighting was by acetylene gas lamps at the start. The job turned out to be very successful and very lucrative and eventually we were able to buy a better machine for the job with electric lighting and full mod cons. Searson became very much in favour with the heads of departments, by delivering other jobs quickly, like press plates for the photographers, when they were photographing special events in other towns. Eventually I became a full-time despatch rider and attached to the much coveted 'Organising' Staff of Joe Berridge and Fred Smith. They bought me a brand new 350cc camshaft Norton that the best money could buy and fitted me out with special water-proof clothing, boots, breeches, in fact anything I wanted. The machine eventually blew up because of poor maintenance and a new 350cc overhead camshaft Velocette was bought. It was still in use by the time the Second World War broke out. I also had to deliver 30 or 40 quires in a satchel on my back to Skegness at holiday times. It was 84 miles from office to office and I became expected to do this in one and a quarter hours!

Leicester City were playing a cup-tie at West Bromwich one Saturday and my brother and I and another rider were called upon to rush pictures back so they could be published in the same day's Mercury. Unbeknown to us, on Monday, the photographic department published a photograph of all three of us with a headline: This Is How We Did It.'

Searson spent the war years with the RAF No. 5 Bomber Group at Scampton during the Battle of Britain and was later posted overseas to Africa. He was demobbed early but found it difficult to settle down. The Organising Department had lost all its glamour, so he resigned and started up his own business, later joining Bell Woodworking and became a managing director, before retiring to Aberdovy in 1973.

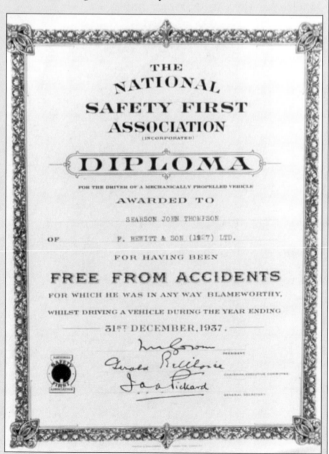

THE NATIONAL SAFETY FIRST ASSOCIATION (INCORPORATED)

DIPLOMA

FOR THE DRIVER OF A MECHANICALLY PROPELLED VEHICLE

AWARDED TO

SEARSON JOHN THOMPSON

OF P. HEWITT & SON (1927) LTD.

FOR HAVING BEEN

FREE FROM ACCIDENTS

FOR WHICH HE WAS IN ANY WAY BLAMEWORTHY, WHILST DRIVING A VEHICLE DURING THE YEAR ENDING

31ST DECEMBER, 1937.

Above: Mr Searson J Thompson, 'Flyer' with the Circulation Department.

Stoney Stanton lost one of its best-known and highly respected residents with the death of Mr David White on April 21, 1930. Granddaughter Mrs Margaret Cox of Edward Avenue, Braunstone, tells me he was a man of many parts and had been correspondent for the Leicester Daily Post, the Leicester Mercury and Leicester Advertiser for over 40 years, whilst for many years he wrote under the name of 'Rambler' for the Hinckley Times.

Mr Stan Allen, of Narborough Road South, Leicester, worked in the Mercury machine room for 42 years and retired in December 1972. His last year was spent in the display advertising department.

Mr C E Herbert, of Empire Road, Leicester, says he and his friend worked Saturdays during the pre-war years, 1937-38, and in lieu received Thursday afternoons. Very often during that time they both accompanied the van-driver taking the Leicester Mercury 4pm edition to the Rugby branch. The racing results were rubber-stamped in the stop press column with a John Bull child-like hand printing outfit.

Mr Percy Davis Kemp was associated with the Loughborough Monitor and the Loughborough office of the Mercury for 41 years, managing sales and circulation there until his retirement in 1946. Throughout his career he never drove a car and often preferred to walk to visit his customers and agents no matter how far. He died, aged 93, in January 1973.

Gwen West, of Iris Avenue, Birstall, remembers as a small child she used to read the Children's Page, which had features such as Auntie Susie, Uncle Bob, Percy the Parrot and Winkie the Cat. She entered a drawing and colouring competition and won a packet of assorted flower seeds. She used to wear her Oozoo Badge with pride. Her brother-in-law, Burnett Stevens of Belgrave, had strong connections with the Sports Mercury and used to report on football and cricket matches. By trade he was a compositor and she believes he worked for the Mercury at one time. His son Michael and grandson continued to phone local football results to the office after he retired.

The Mail had continued for three years, but then, in 1931, went into voluntary liquidation. It was immediately acquired by Midland Newspapers Ltd, a Northcliffe Newspapers Ltd subsidiary formed two years previously. Northcliffe Newspapers Ltd was a London group which embarked, on behalf of the first Lord Rothermere, on a gigantic

1930

◆ The maiden voyage of the airship R101 to India plunged to ruin in France on October 5, 1930. It was a Sunday and Mercury staff came out of their churches and off the golf courses to produce a special edition. Mr Ernest Hall, of Grange Drive, Melton Mowbray, remembers the tragedy well and remembers selling copies of the special edition in the town on the Sunday.

1930

◆ When the population 'transferred' itself to Skegness for the August holiday, steps were taken to get the Mercury there too. In 1930 an aeroplane was used for the first time, taking papers from Leicester to Skegness every afternoon in the holiday week, so that they could be read one and a half hours after publication.

campaign for power in the provinces. Leicester, Bristol and Newcastle felt the main impact of this.

A future chairman, the late Mr F Brian Thompson, grandson of Francis Hewitt, came to Leicester as a junior reporter at 10 shillings (50p) a week in 1931. His early education was at home under governess Enid Blyton, whose first children's book was dedicated to his three brothers and himself. He became a rugby football correspondent for six years until the outbreak of war in 1939.

Towards the end of May, 1931, a letter from Sir Robert Donald arrived at the Mercury offices. It was an offer from Northcliffe Newspapers to acquire a 51 per cent interest (£60,000) in the copyright and goodwill of the Hewitt company. The Hewitts would be left in possession of all present assets and to have a 49 per cent interest in and representation on the Board of a new holding company. Accompanying the offer was a sinister reference to the alternative to acceptance – there would be a period of intense competition and it was thought that Northcliffe Newspapers had put aside 'at least £300,000' for the first stage of their campaign.

The Hewitt directors gave the same reply to this offer as they had done three years earlier to the other suggestion.

The business was growing. All efforts were being given to sales promotion. A branch office had been bought for £600 in Coalville and greater prominence to news from that region was given in the columns of all papers. The company now owned offices in Loughborough and Coalville and very

Above: Copies of the Leicester Mercury being loaded onto a plane to fly to Skegness in August, 1930.

Right: The Mercury fleet before the Second World War – the majority of vans are ASYC Bedford 8 cwts and the seven larger ones at the back are BYC Bedford 12 cwts.

soon they rented premises in Market Harborough, Melton Mowbray and Hinckley. They also had staff men in Ashby-de-la-Zouch and Burton-on-Trent. From these branches, the collection of news and distribution of papers in the outlying parts of the county and over the boundaries into neighbouring counties became easier and the Mercury appeal widened.

Since the formation of F Hewitt & Son (1927) Ltd, at the end of 1927, the Mercury sale was 70,000 copies a night. Eighteen months later it was 77,000, by June 1930 it was 83,000 and it first passed the 90,000 mark in June 1931.

In order to increase the popularity of the already-popular Sports Mercury, a football competition was started at the beginning of the 1929-30 season and a more ambitious one, named Buff Jumbles, the following season, with the prize for an all-correct solution of £500. It had been printed on buff newsprint since May 1928. The legality of the competition came into question in 1935 and the Sports Mercury at once instituted its own Football Pools, which proved very popular. Coupons were distributed each week to 35,000 clients in all parts of the country. On one occasion an entry was received with a stake of two shillings, bearing the address of St James's Palace. It proved to be a bad debt! A court case brought during the Second World War to test the Betting and Lotteries Act, 1934, finally declared newspaper pools illegal. A Meteor press bought to print colour coupons was eventually used to print the company's own stationery.

The first signs of the Mail's onslaught against the Mercury was the use by the Mail in October 1931 of their 'green seals'. Each copy of the paper sold for one penny carried a green seal which could be exchanged at certain shops for one penny worth of goods. The effect was bad news for the Mercury. Sales saw a gradual reduction to just below 76,000.

Not to be outdone, the Mercury management remained on the attack. In June 1932 a page of pictures was introduced into the paper for the first time and a year later the Board considered the eventual arrival of colour and began to formulate plans; 32-page papers were frequently being brought out and

Top: New 8 cwt Bedford ASYC vans touring the city streets in 1936.

Bottom: Circulation and Garage staff.

to ease the burden on machines and staff further linotypes were bought and an extension was made to one of the presses. In order to maintain the high pitch of efficiency attained by the delivery side of the business, an arrangement was reached whereby the whole fleet of vans was exchanged every two years for new vehicles.

Work began in 1931 on a new machine room just beneath ground level on the Wellington Street side of the buildings and a line of three new presses were ordered. By the end of 1932, this extension was in full operation, having cost nearly £30,000.

The editorial staff also showed enterprise. The editor, Mr H W Bourne, and his staff were ever on the alert for news which their competitors had missed and where an item could not be exclusive every attempt would be made to publish it first. Occasionally a special event was created. A new toy, the yo-yo, was becoming the craze and each member of staff was given one in order to publicise it and then a championship

Below: Alexander Betts and colleagues in 1937-38, working in the composing room.

of Leicestershire was organised, with the finals attended by 2,500 people in the De Montfort Hall.

When Miss Mercedes Gleitze attempted to swim the English Channel in the opposite direction to her first successful one, a Mercury reporter was in the support boat, the only Press-man there, and Leicester had the first news of her abandonment when four miles from her goal.

Northcliffe Newspapers went into liquidation in 1932 and Associated Newspapers Ltd took it over. The Leicester Evening Mail could rely on the assistance and resources of the London Daily Mail for coverage of events in the Royal Family. It was no easy task for the Mercury to compete against such a set-up when it came to events in London, but for the Jubilee of George V and Queen Mary, the funeral of George V, the Coronation of George VI and Queen Elizabeth and the marriage of the Duke of Kent and Princess Marina of Greece, the Mercury sent a member of the editorial staff to London to obtain the earliest photographs, to send one set off to Leicester by specially-chartered aeroplane and to bring the second set himself by train in case disaster overtook the plane.

The reply from the Evening Mail to all this was first to intensify the 'green seal' campaign, then to start a free insurance scheme with benefits exceeding those obtainable through the Mercury.

An unusual offer for the business came, not from the Evening Mail, but from an individual associated more with specialist types of journalism. He offered 'up to' £250,000. The answer was just the same: 'Not interested.'

By the autumn of 1934, the Mercury sale had risen again to over 80,000 copies a night. The management of the Mail realised that something must be done. In October, they came up with a free-gift scheme. At first, anyone registering for 12 weeks was given five shillings; later it was tea-sets, dinner services, mangles and garden implements.

Mrs M Jebbett of Brailsford Road, Wigston, remembers she used to live on Kimberley Road, in fact next door to the then Editor of the Mercury, Mr Harry Bourne.

Mr Walter Cockshaw, of Shropshire Road, Leicester, whose great-great uncle Albert Cockshaw published the first Leicestershire Mercury in July 1836, left school in 1934 and joined the Mercury as copy-boy in the proof-reading department with a starting wage of ten shillings (50p) a week with a promise of a half a crown rise in the future, although he cannot remember ever getting it. The name 'department' was a misnomer, as it was a small area on the top floor of the building in Albion Street and it was partitioned off from all the Linotype machines that covered the rest of the floor. The furnishing was Dickensian in style, with high desks and tall stools, with a grey wooden floor. His main duty was to read the script, which was usually hand-written, to the proof reader, who had to check the printed proof for any mistakes, then each reader would sign the proof in case of any problems after publication, so the person could be identified. He remembers some of the reporters' handwriting was atrocious and the abbreviations they used often confused him when he started, but after a while he got used to the meanings of the dashes and scribbles that formed part of their English language. Each day's copy was put on a spike and then filed away for any future reference.

His working hours were from 8am to 6pm from Monday to Friday with the exception of one half day per week that he was allowed to take when it was convenient, but it was unusual to take the half day towards the end of the week as this was the time for the other papers to be published. Bank holidays were not really recognised and the only two days apart from Sundays and Christmas Day, when the paper was not published, were Good Friday and Boxing Day. The latter was known as the Wazegoose day.

The main proof reading staff of that period were the Rawsons, father and son. He believes Mr Rawson senior was a Freeman of

Above: Alexander Betts working on a Linotype machine in 1940.

Left: Alexander Betts on the stone in the Composing Room in 1952.

1934

◆ One of the most boring jobs was to check columns of horse racing form. Walter Cockshaw would often carry on reading only to discover the person who was supposed to be checking the proofs had nodded off to sleep, so they had to start all over again. The form had to be ready for the early publication of the next day's issue of the Mercury Mid-day which catered for the local horse-racing fraternity. Staff made their own tea from a large boiler in the corner of the room and Walter had to collect pennies from the staff to buy the milk from a small shop in Chatham Street. His predecessor apparently used to supplement his spending money by watering down the milk. The majority of Linotype operators used snuff and another of his duties was to make periodic visits to Youngs in Belvoir Street to obtain the various types they asked for. During the fishing season, he also had to get some red dye to colour their maggots.

the city as he had an allotment on Freeman's Common. His son later became the landlord of a public house in Blaby. Another colourful character was Nathanial Hands, known to everyone as Nat and one of Walter's duties was to fetch him a lunchtime pie from a pub in Wellington Street known as the King's Head. There was also a Mr Sharp, who lived in Medway Street, a kindly soul, who gave Walter quite a few of his old school books.

Life was never dull. Men in the department nick-named Walter 'Snowy' because of his batch of fair hair and they tried to send him on futile errands to buy them rubber nails and pints of pigeon milk.

Separate printing presses were located in premises on Chatham Street that were used to print the weekly papers, but during the summer they were also used to produce the Skegness edition. Walter had to run from Albion Street to Chatham Street with the latest news column. He had a great thrill when he entered the building, shouting 'Box..Box' over the noise of the presses and the machines would roll to a halt for the stop press to be fitted.

He remembers Mr Bourne as Editor; Rita Wakefield, who had a daily column; a Mr Mogford, who was a keen cricketer; Mr Trevethic, a stone hand, who could read the reversed print like a book when setting up a page; two top executives, Mr Basford, who was feared in the proof reading room, as he would send for the proof reader who had allowed a serious mistake to slip through, and Mr Barton, who was an officer in the Territorial Army, the same unit Walter entered later.

The Mail's gift scheme scattered doom and gloom amongst the Mercury staff. Some older members of the staff retired and the young members were told that their expectations of permanent employment could not be guaranteed, so Walter took the hint and moved on.

1934 saw the Mercury involvement in another family's service to the newspaper industry. Mr Alec Betts, senior, joined the Mercury at that time, having worked for the Sheffield Independent, several other papers, and then, from 1914, the Leicester Mail in Belvoir Street, which was under the ownership of Sir Arthur Wheeler. His father-in-law Fred Nicholson also worked in the composing room of the Mail. He retired in 1951 at the age of 68. During the 1930s, his son, Eric, started as an apprentice. Alec Betts, junior, started at the Mail in January, 1930 and was to join the Mercury in 1946.

With these events in the background, the Mercury celebrated its Diamond Jubilee with a dinner for the staff at the Grand Hotel on January 2, 1935. At the dinner, Mr Hewitt referred to the newspaper war:

'For many years before the war the Mercury enjoyed competition with other newspapers, including perhaps the best known, the Leicester Evening News, which was launched by the late Sir Arthur Pearson. This paper ceased publication after three uneventful years. Another period of competition followed which was also enjoyable and a friendly spirit was maintained between both papers. I may say that this competition was carried on business-like lines. Today, we have as a competitor here in Leicester a paper purchased recently by Northcliffe Newspapers. Now, however, we find that newspaper competition assumes more novel lines and many tempting offers are made by certain newspapers to increase their circulations. But, in spite of enormous expenditure, and other inducements to our readers by outside interests, we find that the net sale of the Leicester Mercury has reached a record high level. For our part we intend to let our gift to the public be in the presentation of a complete newspaper with news and pictures, for which our citizens will, we feel sure, be willing to pay their penny.'

The dinner was attended by the Lord Lieutenant of Leicestershire (Sir Arthur Hazlerigg), the Lord Mayor, the chairman of the Leicester and County Chamber of Commerce, and, representing the provincial Press, the President of the Newspaper Society. The menu and toast list had, as an outer cover, a photographic reproduction of the first Leicester Daily Mercury. Inside were some historical facts, showing the staff had grown in 60 years from 25 to 250, circulation from 5,000 to 80,000 and vehicles from two hand-carts to 38 motor vehicles. Before the dinner ended, staff and guests were given a special edition of the Mercury containing a full report and pictures of the dinner! A skeleton staff of volunteers had left the function early in order to bring out this souvenir-production.

Considerable progress was made in the 1930s on the social side of life at Albion Street. As part of a vigorous staff Social Club, there were extremely active cricket, golf, tennis and dramatic sections, while every now and again a team was arranged for an Association or Rugby football match. The cricket club won the Spicer Cup, competed for among the printing and associated trades in the county, in 1936. They beat Adam Brothers and Shardlow in the semi-final and then the Co-op Printers in the final. Ken Smith, of Paignton, remembers the team, particularly Tom Pope and Norman Jones. Mrs Eden, of Thurlow Road, Clarendon Park, started working for the Mercury around this time on the front advertising desk and remembers two of her work-mates, who played in the team – Frank Bailey and Norman Jones. Her other workmates were Wilf Brown, Dan Gould, Ted Haylett, Alan and Edith Veasey, Mr Smith (Advertising Manager), Rita Merry, Doris Billington and Peggy Lippitt. The dramatic society performed short plays and mimes, usually composed by their own members, for the benefit of staff and public.

Edward VIII was proclaimed King on January 21 1936 and his romance with Mrs Simpson, while being discussed freely in America and France for weeks, had been kept from people in Britain while negotiations went on behind the scenes to find a solution to the King's insistence that he should marry the woman of his choice, even though she had been previously married twice. The story broke on a startled nation on December 4 and the Mercury ran a special morning edition to announce 'A constitutional crisis.' For six days there was no lack of 'full information' and the Mercury columns overflowed with the story of the King who was prepared to give up his throne for love and which saw Winston Churchill and Stanley Baldwin on opposite sides as King's champion and anti-champion. On December 10, Edward renounced the throne and as Duke of Windsor departed for foreign shores, while his brother, the Duke of York, stepped up to the throne as King George VI.

Mrs C M Voss, of Tetuan Road, Leicester, was on the editorial staff of the Mercury at the time. She was an assistant librarian and, in her words, 'general dogsbody.' Archie Hackett was the librarian and her memories of him were sitting mending many books, chewing his fingers and suffering from asthma. May Pearson (Rita's Diary) also had a desk in the library. Cartoonist R B Davies was in the adjoining office. Her job consisted of collecting picture blocks of people of note, filing them for future reference, along with anything of interest that appeared in the paper. A shorthand-typist, she also used to type the Editor's letters. Sometimes she was called on to type copy telephoned in. She also remembers being given a free flight when Sir Alan Cobham brought his flying circus to Leicester. She was married in 1934 and in those days married ladies were asked to leave, but she was the first to ask Mr Barton for permission to stay on – it was granted. At the time of Edward VIII's abdication, Archie Hackett was off work with a severe asthma attack and a staff car took her to see him to make sure she had given the Editor all the information the library had. On arriving back at the office, she told them she had done so and the story went to press.

The 'tempting offers' referred to by Mr Hewitt were such that circulation figures again dropped and continued to do so, until, in August 1936, they hit the low mark of 65,346. It proved to be the turning point. August is always a bad month in any case, but by the following April the 70,000 figure had been passed again.

Meanwhile, the Leicester Evening Mail claimed a sale 'in excess of' 64,000 and had been trying to force the Mercury to make their figures public. The Mercury claimed

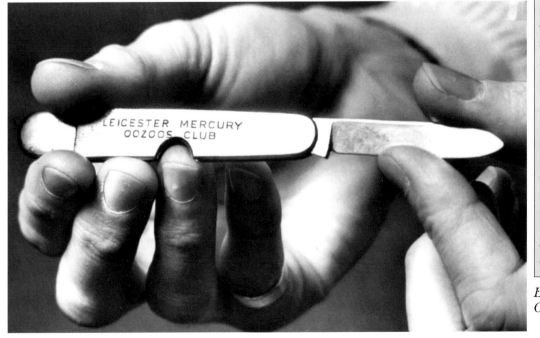

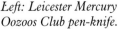

Left: Leicester Mercury Oozoos Club pen-knife.

THE LEICESTER MERCURY, THURSDAY, 10th DECEMBER, 1936.

Leicester Mercury

LARGEST NET READER SALE   6 O'CLOCK EDITION

Your *LOCAL* Evening Newspaper—The Paper Everybody Reads

Estab. 1874 (*Registered as a Newspaper*)   THURSDAY, 10th DECEMBER, 1936.   ONE PENNY

THE KING ABDICATES

Duke Of York To Become The Sovereign

MR. BALDWIN TELLS THE WHOLE STORY

'I Am Going To Marry Mrs. Simpson And I Am Prepared To Go'

—THE KING

PRICE MONARCH MUST PAY

THE SPEAKER ANNOUNCED IN THE HOUSE OF COMMONS THIS AFTERNOON THE ABDICATION OF THE KING. THE DUKE OF YORK IS TO SUCCEED HIM.

The decision was conveyed in a message in which the King announced that he would renounce the Throne. The King said: " My mind is made up."

Mr. Baldwin, in his speech, told the secret history of the crisis in dramatic and moving terms. How, on November 16th, the question of the marriage was mentioned ; how he told the King that this particular marriage was not one which would meet with the approbation of the country ; and how the King said : " I am going to marry Mrs. Simpson, and I am prepared to go."

Mr. Baldwin said that during this conversation he pointed out the difference between a King's marriage and an ordinary marriage, and this he called " the price a King must pay . . . ."

One of Mr. Baldwin's statements was this : " The House must remember, and it is difficult to realise, his Majesty is not a boy. He looks so young we all think of him as our Prince. He is a mature man of wide and great experience of life and of the world."

Mr. Baldwin produced what he said was a pencilled note sent to him by his Majesty this morning.

The Note said that the Duke of York and the King "have always been on the best of terms as brothers, and the King is confident the Duke deserves and will receive the support of the whole Empire."

Mr. Baldwin said that yesterday morning the Cabinet received the King's final and definite answer officially. The House was suspended till 6 o'clock. "At a later stage to-day I shall ask you to bring in the necessary Bill, which will be ready to-night," said Mr. Baldwin.

The King's Message

THE KING'S MESSAGE BEGAN: "AFTER LONG AND ANXIOUS CONSIDERATION I HAVE DETERMINED TO RENOUNCE THE THRONE TO WHICH I SUCCEEDED ON THE DEATH OF MY FATHER, AND I AM NOW COMMUNICATING THIS MY FINAL AND IRREVOCABLE DECISION.

"REALISING, as I do, the gravity of this step, I can only hope that I shall have the understanding of my peoples in the decision I have taken, and the reasons which have led me to take it.

" I will not enter into my private feelings, but I would beg that it should be remembered that the burden which constantly rests on the shoulders of a sovereign is so heavy that it can only be borne in circumstances different from those in which I now find myself.

The Public Interest

" I conceive that I am not overlooking the duty that rests on me to place in the forefront the public interest when I declare that I am conscious that I can no longer discharge this heavy task with efficiency or with satisfaction to myself,

" I have accordingly this morning executed an instrument of abdication in the terms following:

" I, Edward the Eighth of Great Britain, Ireland, and the British Dominions beyond the seas, King Emperor of India, do hereby declare my irrevocable determination to renounce the throne for myself and for my descendants, and my desire that effect should be given to this instrument of abdication immediately.

" In token whereof I have here unto set my hand this tenth day of December, 1936, in the presence of the witnesses whose signatures are subscribed.

(Signed) EDWARD R.I.
(CONTINUED ON PAGE TWELVE.)

KING EDWARD

THE NEW KING AND QUEEN
The Duke and Duchess and the Princesses, an illustration by studio Lisa from " Our Princesses and Their Dogs," a charming intimate story, profusely illustrated, of the Royal children, just published by John Murray.

THE NEW KING

The career of the new King, the Duke of York, is on centre pages.

Shortest Reign For 453 Years

THE King had, on December 10th, 1936, reigned for 10 months and 21 days, having acceded to the throne on the death of his father, King George, on January 20, 1936.

There has been only one shorter reign of a Monarch of Great Britain since the Norman Conquest—that of Edward V., who became King on April 9, 1483, and occupied the throne for little more than two months, being murdered, together with his brother, the Duke of York, in the Tower of London on June 23, 1483.

Lady Jane Grey has been termed the " Nine Day's Queen."

Edward VI., who died on July 6, 1553, had, it is stated, been persuaded by the Duke of Northumberland, Lady Jane's father-in-law, to make a settlement of the Crown on Lady Jane, who was proclaimed Queen on July 10.

Nine days later, however, Mary was proclaimed Queen by the Lord Mayor of London, and Lady Jane was told that she must relinquish the position.

This she did willingly. In the following November she and her husband were beheaded.

LOCAL FOG

Late afternoon forecast: Weather will be mainly cloudy, with local fog. It will be rather cold.

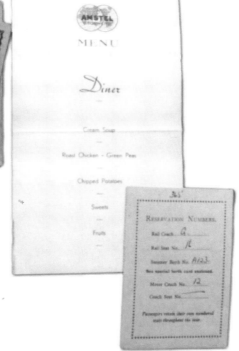

Opposite page: The Leicester Mercury reports the Abdication on the day it was announced, Thursday December 10, 1936.

Left: A selection of Leicester Mercury Excursions.

Below: Leicester Mercury free insurance certificate, made available to regular subscribers who registered for the scheme.

Bottom: Tickets for excursions run by the rival Leicester Evening Mail (belonging to Mr N Bird of Thurnby Lodge).

that comparison should not be made between a reader sale and one assisted by the offer of free gifts and declined to do so until May 1937, when they published a certificate showing a sale exceeding 70,000. The Mail replied to this by publishing an outspoken comment on this certificate, making certain allegations, and by printing under their title-heading each evening 'Largest Certified Net Sale,' a claim also being made by the Mercury.

F Hewitt & Son (1927) Ltd issued a writ against Midland Newspapers Ltd, asking for an injunction to prevent the Mail publishing their claim to have the larger sale and also claiming damages. The case was to be heard at Leicester Assizes in October 1938, but was settled on payment by the Mail of damages and the issue of a written apology.

The result of it all was the formation, on January 29 1939, of a holding company to control both newspapers and, of course, the Mercury's associated publications.

The new company was named News Holdings Ltd, with a capital of £100,000 in Ordinary Shares of £1. This company acquired 2,494 of the Deferred Ordinary Shares in F Hewitt & Son (1927) Ltd from Mr Hewitt and the whole of the Share Capital of Midland Newspapers Ltd from Associated Newspapers Ltd.

Mr Hewitt was allotted 60,000 of the News Holdings shares and Associated Newspapers the remaining 40,000. Under the Articles, Mr Hewitt became chairman for life and had the right to appoint two of the

Left: Happy Birthday from the Oozoos Club and Auntie Susie.

◆ The Leicester Mercury continued to expand. The new Loughborough office was built, premises were rented and an office opened at Rugby and in Leicester efforts were being made to 'centralise.' The Granby Street property was sold in 1937 for £36,500. The Advertiser offices in Chatham Street, the process engraving department in South Albion Street and the photographic department in York Street were all moved into 12 Albion Street, on which a lease had been obtained. In addition, land, including a street (Park Street), was bought on the other side of Wellington Street for £4,425 and a garage built, so that shortly all vehicles were able to move from Brazil Street garage, which became merely a newsprint store. The Midland Holiday Bureau moved to Bowling Green Street.

directors. He appointed Mr Basford and Mr Barton. Mr Peake became the new company's first secretary.

Therefore, News Holdings obtained ownership of the Mail and control of the Mercury, and Mr Hewitt, as the majority shareholder, control of every newspaper published in Leicester.

Between the date of the sales certificate in May 1937 and the incorporation of News Holdings in January 1939, the Mercury sale increased by nearly 10,000 copies a day. Such was the demand for advertising space, that every now and again a 40-page paper was produced (much to the annoyance of newsvendors, who complained that it was too heavy to hold in quantity) and 32-page papers were published regularly.

For the weeklies, however, the position was less happy. The Chronicle sale, which had been about 14,000 in 1927 had been dropping gradually until, by the end of 1939, it was under 4,000. Consideration was given to the possibility of merging the Chronicle with the Advertiser, but no such step was taken.

The first target for the directors of News Holdings was to cut out wasteful competition and try to put the Mail on its feet without restricting the progress of the Mercury. They were convinced there was room for two evening newspapers in Leicester to pay their way. No longer would canvassers shadow their competitors, motor bicycles or cars race each other to get first to strategic points or towns or villages, or money be spent in countless other ways on out-performing the opposition merely for the sake of being 'on

top.' On the other hand, news services for each paper owed it to their readers to try to get the best and the earliest news and to present it in a way which it thought best. One van might deliver both papers, but news stories would invariably be covered by representatives from each paper.

The new situation worked well and both the papers and the public benefited. Though the 'inducements' stopped and meant a drop in sales at first, the Mail circulation soon settled. The Mercury sale had reached 86,000, the highest figure for over seven years, when the Second World War broke out in September 1939.

The war began on a Sunday with Neville Chamberlain's radio message to the nation that a state of war existed because Hitler had not complied with specific requests. There is no Mercury record of the historic radio announcement – events had overtaken it. The front page of Monday, September 4, was given over almost entirely to the first act of war – the sinking by a German submarine of the liner Athenia. It occurred when the ship was 200 miles west of the Hebrides outward-bound for Canada with 1,400 passengers and crew on board, 75 per cent of whom were women and children, including some 300 Americans on their way home from Belfast, Liverpool and Glasgow. Norwegian and Swedish steamers in the area reported picking up 1,000 of the passengers from the sinking ship. This news contrasted with a heading on the same page which said: 'Hitler does not want to start first' over a message from neutral correspondents in Berlin saying that Hitler was determined that Britain and France should fire the first shots and that Germany would 'react but not provoke.' Germany was, of course, militarily pre-occupied with the conquest of Poland in which the techniques of blitzkrieg practised in the Spanish civil war were perfected in readiness for use on the Allies.

Mr Barton, a Territorial Army officer, and several members of staff went into uniform. Mr Hewitt, who had lived in the Eastbourne area since 1927, returned to Leicester to help in the first few months of readjustment. It was decided that no special inducements must be held out to readers and in October 1939 the Mercury free insurance scheme was discontinued.

Chapter 7

War and Peace
1940 – 1950

Newsprint again proved to be a major problem. Before the war, it cost £9 to £10 a ton and plentiful. However, the German occupied Scandinavia in 1940 and submarines were threatening sea routes from Canada, even if merchant ships were available and they were not. The commodity was to become very scarce and the price to rise almost threefold. This time the Ministry of Supply approved a plan, in which the proprietors of London and provincial papers were to assume full responsibility for buying (under Board of Trade licence) and distributing newsprint. This they undertook through a new organisation called the Newsprint Supply Co Ltd. Therefore every newspaper throughout the land, large or small, weekly or daily, had a fair share of the amount of newsprint available and at a non-competitive price. No restriction was yet to be placed on sales, but careful conservation of supplies was necessary. The Newsprint Supply Co imposed a limit on the size of newspapers very early in the war.

In order to make the best use of the reduced space, the width of each column was reduced in May 1940 to allow six columns instead of five per page. At the same time, it was found, with the cost of newsprint standing at £17 a ton and with less space for advertisements, that the price of the paper was to rise to one and a half pence. This naturally had the effect of a fall in sales. Within four months, sales plummeted from 89,000 copies a day to below 77,000 and it was not until September 1943 that the loss was recovered.

This was to be a very different kind of war to the first, because of aerial attacks. Leicester and Leicestershire people did not need to be told about German night bombers. The county was part of a Bomb Alley, the flight path from the Continental night bomber stations to the war factories of the Midlands, with the Cropston, Swithland and Thornton reservoirs providing a navigational signpost. The nightly drone of Dorniers and Junkers with their off-beat rhythm was as familiar as the warning air raid siren. They knew when they came and they knew when they departed and they sheltered accordingly.

It was not very long before the youngest and fittest members of the Mercury staff in all departments had left for the various theatres of war. Others had to shoulder extra responsibilities – sub-editors and feature writers had to turn their hand again to reporting and some of the sales organisers assisted with the accounts. A rota of fire-watchers had to be arranged to do duty at

1940

◆ Arrangements were made for the papers to be printed elsewhere in the event of the premises being bombed. If the Mercury buildings were bombed and the Mail remained untouched, both papers were to be published by the Mail; otherwise the Mercury would be printed by the Nottingham Guardian. The Mercury also undertook to print, with its depleted staff, nearly 750,000 copies of the Daily Herald each night and nearly 2 million copies of The People on Sundays in the event of their own London premises being put out of commission. The contract with Odhams Press Ltd was a very lucrative one. An incendiary bomb did fall on the Daily Herald's premises and they asked for a trial run in Leicester, which was most successful. But unfortunately the full emergency for which everyone was prepared never arose. After the war, the directors of the Daily Herald and The People presented a silver cigarette case to Mr A W Peake in appreciation.

Left: Mercury photographer James Mapham.

D-Day picture by JAMES MAPHAM, former Leicester Mercury Chief Photographer, who was Field Marshal Montgomery's personal photographer.

Above: James Mapham's D-Day picture.

Right: Wartime picture by James Mapham.

Wartime picture by JAMES MAPHAM, former Leicester Mercury photographer

the office throughout the night. Air Raid Precaution and Decontamination Squads were also formed, trained and equipped.

A small paper was published for the benefit of staff away in the Forces and those at home. It was called the Mercurian and was edited by Mr A Pratt, chief sub-editor of the Mercury since 1923. A copy was sent to every member of staff, in whatever part of the world he or she might be. Letters came back from the far corners telling grim and happy stories, which were usually published and were of great interest. Staff were kept reasonably well in touch.

The Leicesters, it seemed, were everywhere. The 2/5th Battalion had been shipped to North Norway to join the fight against Germany invading Denmark and Norway; the surrender of Singapore; in Burma with General Slim's 14th Army, which eventually began to contain the Japanese swarm; part of the Chindits who operated behind the Japanese supply lines; after El Alamein they took part in the great drive through Italy and, when the conquest of Germany finally began, they were at Montgomery's elbow for the surrender near Lunesburg Heath.

◆ The Mercury, like all other newspapers, had to work strictly within censorship rules and had to send all material and pictures, which might convey information to an enemy agent, to the censors operating within the Ministry of Information in London. The weather became completely taboo and when the great snows of 1940 fell it became tricky to report the consequences. On February 1st, the front page was only able to say: 'Thousands walked to work in Leicester today. Few buses: none from neighbouring towns. Villages cut off for days: schools closed.' The story told of villages cut off, buses marooned and factories and schools closing through lack of fuel. The Mercury was not allowed to say why, although any enemy agent or reconnaissance plane must have seen the effects of several days' snow, which blocked the roads, the railways and brought the country to a temporary standstill. From then, newspapers were not allowed to mention even the consequences of the weather.

Left: The Mercurian, sent to staff members in the Forces during the Second World War.

Above: Audrey Timms and Peggy Driver spring cleaning the Library at the Mercury in 1945.

Opposite page: The Leicester Mercury front page for May 8, 1945, announcing the end of the War in Europe.

The Editor, Mr H W Bourne, was elected to the Board of directors in February 1941. He replaced Mr T S Rowley, who had died in 1937. In September of the same year, Mr John Parsons also died, soon after he had been given the Freedom of the City. His place was taken by Secretary Mr Peake in June 1942. The other directors were Mr Hewitt, Mr Basford, Mr Barton and Mr Hopps.

The big news of April 30, 1945, was the report that Hitler was dead, killed by his own hand in his Berlin bunker. This was followed by successive reports that large numbers of German troops were surrendering, Hitler's successors were seeking peace and Churchill himself was announcing VE Day – a day of national holiday to celebrate Victory in Europe – even the newspapers rejoiced by not even publishing. The war in the East still had to be resolved, but what looked like being a long war of attrition ended dramatically with the first atom bombs on Hiroshima and Nagasaki, with its consequent devastation and the unconditional surrender of the Japanese on August 14 to give another opportunity for national rejoicing as VJ Day, August 15.

So, after five long years, readers of the Mercury could look forward to their nightly reading without fear of what the headlines would say, without thought for blackout precautions and without keeping an eye on the clock with firewatching, Civil Defence or Home Guard duties in mind.

At the end of September 1945, Mr Basford retired, having spent 62 years with the Hewitt concern. A dinner held in his honour heard many deserved tributes paid to him by Mr Hewitt and others. Mr C T Barton became senior managing director and was joined by Mr Peake as the other managing director. Mr Peake replaced Mr Basford on the board of News Holdings Ltd. Mr Basford was the first of a number of long-service men to retire about this time. Five who had served under Mr Basford had completed over half-a-century with the firm: Sam Berridge (66 years), his brother Joe (59), for many years circulation manager; G F Maskell and J Kettle (54) and A H Hackett (53), son of a former editor. Others who had completed 40 years' service were C T Wainwright (58), J T Hodgkin (57), E R Whitwell (51), E H Pick (49), A Chamberlain (49), N J Hand (49), H T Mercy (44), H Turner (43) and W Gimson (41).

Circulation figures improved, once the reaction to the price rise was over, to 100,000 for the first time in June 1944. The weeklies also increased. By April 1945, the Chronicle reached 10,000 for the first time since November 1932.

Members of the Forces were returning in 1946 (incidentally, the year the author was born) and younger men were moved up into the places vacated by those who had retired and positions which had remained unfilled during the war found new occupants. Efforts to help the Mercury march forward were, however, frustrated. Newsprint now cost £28 a ton and still rising, in common with all other materials, and the maximum size for the Mercury was still only eight pages.

In September 1946, however, came the first concession. The Mercury was able to print an average of ten pages a day, with appropriate increases for the weeklies too. Circulation at once began to climb and in six months, it was over 120,000 copies a day. When sales again became 'pegged' in the middle of 1947 and a return had to be made to eight pages, the sale was 125,000. The Chronicle rose from 11,000 to just under 30,000 in a short period of 'free sale' and a souvenir edition following the visit of King George VI and Queen Elizabeth to Leicester in November 1946 comprised no fewer than 98,950 copies.

A great reunion was held at a dinner at the Grand Hotel in Leicester towards the end of 1946, to which the heads of every department were invited, along with pensioners.

THE LEICESTER MERCURY, TUESDAY, MAY 8th, 1945.

Leicester Mercury

VE EDITION

★ LARGEST CERTIFIED NET SALE ★

Estab. 1874 *(Registered as a Newspaper)*   TUESDAY, MAY 8th, 1945   Three-Half-Pence

Hostilities To Cease Officially At 12.1 a.m. Tomorrow

CHURCHILL ANNOUNCES THE END

Churchill At Buckingham Palace

LONDON had great rejoicings to-day.

From an early hour, people assembled in the vicinity of Buckingham Palace — t h r e e young women had been there all night, having missed their last train home—and by 11.30 p.m. several thousands of people, including scores of American soldiers and bluejackets, were congregated there.

First big thrill of the day for the waiting crowds outside Buckingham Palace came when an open car drove through the Palace Gates from the Mall.

In it, in a black civilian suit, was the Prime Minister.

King And Queen On Balcony

He was on his way to lunch with the King and Queen; his first meeting with his Sovereign since the war ended.

The crowd, cheering and waving, closed in round the Premier's car, and Palace police had difficulty in keeping a narrow passage open for it.

Smiling and radiantly happy, Mr. Churchill gave the V sign time and time again to the crowd as he drove into the Palace.

Mr. Churchill lunched with the King and Queen.

The King and Queen appeared on the balcony of Buckingham Palace with the two Princesses at 11 minutes past three to-day, and waved to the cheering crowd for three minutes.

Whitehall Crowds

Thousands of people lined Whitehall waiting for Mr. Churchill, who was expected to appear on the balcony of the Ministry of Health this evening.

It is possible that in response to the ovation he is certain to get from the huge crowd, he may make a short speech.

Service men and women marched arm-in-arm singing lustily, their caps covered with flags, their uniforms festooned with ribbons and flowers.

Buses were packed. Many conductresses abandoned all hope of taking fares.

St. Paul's Cathedral was packed for the noon victory thanksgiving service.

People stood in a solid mass in the aisles, and at the back of the cathedral.

Many, unable to get in, remained on the cathedral steps.

WEATHER NEWS AGAIN

For the first time since the war began, it is possible to tell the world what weather Britain is having while it is having it.

To-day, all restrictions were removed by the censors, and the Straits of Dover's exclusive priority in up-to-date weather news was ended.

The first weather forecast since the outbreak of war was issued by the Air Ministry early this afternoon. It covered the period until 9 a.m. to-morrow morning. For London, South-East England, East England, E. Midlands and W. Midlands the forecast was:

Light or moderate, variable or easterly winds, mainly fine at first, scattered thunderstorms and thundery rain later to-day and tonight; warm.

A section of the vast crowd that assembled at Leicester's VE Day Service in the Town Hall Square.

Berlin Ratification Of Agreement

THUNDERSTORM FOR VE DAY SERVICE

At about 11 o'clock this morning, when the crowd was assembling for the service of thanksgiving in the Town Hall Square, Leicester, there was a hailstorm, followed by a torrential downpour.

Then came thunder and lightning and still heavier rain and people were forced to find whatever shelter they could.

For a time there was not a single person to be seen in the centre of the city. Later, however, there was a considerable improvement in the weather, and a great crowd thronged the Town Hall Square in the afternoon to listen to martial and other airs played by the "Specials'" Brass Band.

Scores of street teas for children were arranged in all parts of Leicester, but the break in the weather caused alterations in the programme, the celebrations in many cases being transferred to schoolrooms.

[LEICESTER VE DAY SERVICE AND SCENES ARE REPORTED ON PAGE SIX.]

TERMS OF SURRENDER OF GERMAN NAVY

THE Admiralty announce that the following orders have been issued for the surrender of the German Fleet:

"All German and German-controlled warships, auxiliaries, merchant ships and other craft at sea are being ordered to report their position in plain language to the nearest Allied wireless telegraph station and are being given orders to proceed to such Allied ports as directed.

"All warships, auxiliaries, merchant ships and other craft in harbour are being ordered to remain in harbour.

"U-boats at sea are being ordered to surface, to fly a black flag or pennant and to report their position in plain language to nearest Allied wireless, telegraph station. They will then proceed on the surface to such port as they may be directed.

"All warships and merchant ships, whether in port or at sea, are being instructed to train all weapons fore and aft. Breech blocks will be removed from guns and torpedo tubes will be unloaded.

"In harbour all ammunition explosives, torpedo war-heads and all portable weapons will be landed.

"Minesweeping vessels and salvage vessels, though similarly disarmed, will be instructed to complete with fuel, if necessary, and to prepare themselves immediately for minesweeping or salvage service as directed."

AFTER BIG BEN HAD STRUCK THREE THIS AFTERNOON, MR. CHURCHILL CAME TO THE MICROPHONE AND BROADCAST THAT THE WAR IN EUROPE ENDS OFFICIALLY AT 12.1 a.m. TO-MORROW, ALTHOUGH THE CEASE FIRE ORDER WAS GIVEN YESTERDAY.

The agreement will be ratified and confirmed in Berlin to-day.

MR. CHURCHILL CONCCLUDED HIS BROADCAST WITH THE WORDS: "ADVANCE BRITANNIA," AFTER GIVING THE WARNING THAT WE HAD NOW TO FINISH THE WAR AGAINST JAPAN.

Mr. Churchill said: Yesterday morning, at 2.41 a.m., at General Eisenhower's headquarters, General Jodl, the representative of the German High Command and of Grand Admiral Doenitz, designated head of the German State, signed the act of unconditional surrender of German land, sea and air forces in Europe to the Allied Expeditionary Force and simultaneously to the Soviet High Command.

General Bedell Smith, Chief of Staff of the United States Army, and General Francois Sevez, signed the document on behalf of the Supreme Commander of the Allied Expeditionary Forces, and General Suslaparov signed on behalf of the Russian High Command.

Ratification To-day

To-day this agreement will be ratified and confirmed at Berlin, where Air Chief Marshal Tedder, Deputy Supreme Commander of the Allied Expeditionary Force, and General Tassigny will sign on behalf of General Eisenhower.

General Zhukov will sign on behalf of the Soviet High Command.

The German representatives will be Field-Marshal Keitel, chief of the High Command, and commanders in chief of the German Army, Navy and Air Force.

Hostilities will end officially at one minute after midnight to-night (Tuesday, 8th May), but in the interests of saving lives, the cease fire began yesterday, to be sounded all along the front, and our dear Channel Islands are also to be freed to-day.

(Continued On Back Page).

Leicester Mercury

In common with other evening newspapers the "Leicester Mercury" will not publish to-morrow. This is in accordance with the expressed desire of the Government that workers generally should enjoy a day's holiday following the announcement of the cessation of hostilities in Europe.

VE Day With British Second Army

With the British Second Army, Tuesday.

VE DAY was celebrated by over 100,000 British troops in Germany with bonfires, Verey lights of a dozen different colours, and festivities in every mess and billet from the Weser to the Rhine, from the Elbe, and from the Baltic to Brussels.

Lights blazed from unshuttered windows, and headlights were dazzling. There were toasts to " Those who have fallen " and to "Lasting Peace." There were prayers in stables, in tents in the fields, and in German homes.

There was peace on German soil last night.

Some sang popular songs to the accompaniment of mouth-organ bagpipes and accordions.

No German Holiday

This is VE Day in Europe, the troops had the same reveille, and the same breakfast an hour later. Each man will get a bit with his dinner.

VE Day was no German. More than 60,000,000 cooped in compounds, bread queues, wandering and living aimlessly, but controlled.

Special cinema programme arranged.—Reuter.

1947

◆ New linotype machines and new equipment for the stereotyping department were bought at the head office in Leicester, but the biggest advance was the installation of six teleprinters in 1947 to bring national and international news from the Press Association in London, replacing the Creed machines which had been in service since the First World War and used morse on tape and had to be passed through another machine to make a transcription in type. The saving on time, with an added degree of accuracy, led to teleprinters being installed at branch offices at Loughborough and Coalville in 1949 for the purpose of sending news into head office.

1949

◆ On July 22, 1949, charge-hand Mr Harry Turner retired after 54 years' association with the Mercury. Mr Barton said he thought only one member of the firm had been employed longer. Mr Turner, of Gwendolen Road, Leicester, was presented with an electric clock.

Since Mr Basford's retirement, Mr Peake had combined the joint managing directorship with the secretaryship, but on January 1st, 1947, he relinquished the latter appointment after a reign of 20 years and was succeeded by Mr Francis Brian Thompson. He, like Mr Vernon Hewitt, was a grandson of the first Francis Hewitt and had been given his grandfather's Christian name. His mother was a daughter of Francis Hewitt by his second wife; Mr Vernon Hewitt's father a son by his first wife. On release from the Services early in 1946, he understudied the secretaryship.

Another change which came about on the first day of 1947 was the retirement of Mr C J Tonsley from the editorship of the Chronicle after 30 years, with 43 years on the Hewitt staff altogether. He was succeeded by Mr E J F Fortune, who had joined the reporting staff of the Mercury in 1929 and after war service in the Royal Air Force had returned in 1946 to become art editor. The Chronicle became remodelled. Pictorial features of general interest appeared, rather than merely local photographs of events which had been already reported fully in the evening papers.

Within two and a half years, all five of the Hewitt titles had a new editor. Mr Halls retired from the Leicester Advertiser to be succeeded by Mr H O Ledbrooke, a Mercury staff member for 20 years, mostly as deputy chief sub-editor. Towards the end of 1948, Mr H W Bourne stood down as Editor of the Mercury, a post he held for 22 years and his place was taken by Mr John Fortune. The Chronicle was entrusted to Mr Douglas Goodlad. In 1949, the founder Editor of the Sports Mercury, Mr T G Whitton, retired and Mr I W Smith resigned from the editorial chair of the Monitor. In their places were appointed Mr W G Smith and Mr Ralph F Lowings. Mr Smith handed over the editorship of the Sports Mercury to Mr D Johnson in 1950.

Mr H W Bourne had had an association of over 38 years with the paper. During his editorship, the stamp of his character was reflected in all he did and in every word he wrote. In the course of his work and his interest in the affairs of Leicester and the county he had always made friends, for he had placed human relationships high in his scale of values. He began his journalistic career at Dover and after experience in Essex, Sussex and London, joined the Mercury staff in March, 1910. He was successively reporter and sub-editor. For some ten seasons he reported the matches of the old Fosse Club and later the Leicester City Football Club under the pen name 'Albion.' In the summer he followed the Leicestershire Cricket Club and had remained a keen supporter of Leicester football and county cricket. He had completed 50 years as a journalist and was appointed editor in September, 1926. In 1941 he joined the board of directors of the firm. He was a member of the Guild of British Newspaper Editors and treasurer of the East Midland Region of the organisation.

Mr John Fortune became editor on October 1, 1948. He had joined the Mercury staff in October, 1929 and in 1938 had become Trade Commissioner. During the war, he was commanding officer of an RAF Air-Sea Rescue Unit and on his return to the paper was appointed Art Editor, before becoming editor of the Illustrated Leicester Chronicle in January, 1947.

Conditions in Albion Street were considered too cramped. A site in Granby Street had been bought and later sold again. Now, in March 1947, came another hope. The premises next door, 17-23 Albion Street, which had been gutted in a fire in 1945 and had also damaged the composing room and swept across the road to do considerable damage to the process engraving department at 12 Albion Street, came on the market and was purchased for £3,400. Plans were prepared for an imposing new building, taking in this new site, building over the machine room in Wellington Street and extending towards Chatham Street, so that every department would come under one roof. The local authority approved the plans, but no licence was forthcoming because of the shortage of materials. In spite of frequent renewals of the application, permission to build seemed ever further away.

A first-rate site in the main street of Market Harborough was bought for £4,350 and rapidly converted into a fine modern office.

After the German surrender, Germany had been divided into zones for occupation by the various Allies and Berlin, geographically within the Russian zone, had itself been zoned. To get supplies to the British zone of Berlin, it was necessary to cross the Russian zone of Germany, but differences of opinion between the two nations led to a blockade by the Russians of British traffic to Berlin. Britain's alternative was to send supplies by air and, after the air-lift had been running for some time, an opportunity was given to editors of the principal British national and provincial papers to travel to Berlin on the 'lift' and see what was being done. In December 1948, Mr Fortune flew to Berlin on this mission and his story was wired to Leicester from the German capital. On his return, he was elected to succeed Mr Bourne, who had retired, as a member of the Board of directors.

Chapter 8
Mr Hewitt Sells Control
1950 – 1960

By the middle of 1948 there were certain signs that the newsprint situation was getting easier and the future of newspapers looked brighter than for a decade. The cost of newsprint, which had been rising since the outbreak of war nine years previously, reached the peak of £45 a ton in May and then, in June, began to drop. The price went down gradually to £23 within the next 18 months: in January 1949, the Mercury was permitted alternate eight and 12 pages, instead of eight daily; in April 12 daily and in January 1950 alternate 12 and 16 with no limit on sales – in fact, tonnage rationing, at long last, was ended.

Sales soared. Circulation went to 130,000 daily for the first time in April 1949 and 134,000 a year later (double what it had been during the height of the newspaper 'war' in 1936). The Sports Mercury exceeded 50,000 copies each Saturday night, the Chronicle 30,000 weekly and the Advertiser and Monitor not far short of 8,000 and 6,000.

All hopes, all planning for advancement in the near future were however dashed when, in October 1950, tonnage rationing of newsprint was reimposed. Only ten months of freedom had been enjoyed. The Government had caused contracts made between the Newsprint Supply Co and the Canadian suppliers to be broken on three occasions, had insisted on the export to Australia of newsprint urgently required at home and had, in fact, so juggled with the newsprint problem that stocks were getting dangerously low. The result was that the Scandinavian suppliers, knowing that they had cornered the British market, raised the price. The Mercury returned to 12 pages and, along with all the weeklies, had not merely to call a halt to rising sales but actually reduce the figure now reached. At the same time, the price of newsprint started to rise again and within 10 months it had reached the phenomenal height of £65 per ton – six times the pre-war cost.

Inflation set in. A new press, ordered in 1946 at three times the pre-war cost, was quoted in 1951 at six times and still not delivered. Staff wages were increased, often several times in a year. Something had to be done if these additional burdens were to be met and, on May 7, 1951, the price of the Mercury was increased to 2d. The cost of producing a copy of the Mercury was 1.04d in 1939; in 1950 it was 1.32d, an increase of 27 per cent, and still rising.

In the summer of 1951, the Mercury lost one of its oldest friends. Mr J A Hopps had known the three Hewitt generations well, both socially and in his professional capacity as an accountant and was a member of the Board. He died in his 89th year.

Mr Thompson was elected in his place on the Board as one of the Preferred Ordinary Shareholders' representatives.

A new office at Melton Mowbray was bought in 1951, one at Hinckley in 1953 and in 1957 the new building at Albion Street was completed and occupied by the staff of Chatham Street and 12 Albion Street, plus some overflow from the advertisement department. Work on putting down a new double width press, equipped for colour, started in 1954 and when, it came into operation the following year, it had cost about £90,000. Teletypesetters were bought for speeding up production in the composing room.

The Mercury came out in 1952 with its first 24-page issue since 1940 and when rationing by paging had gone by 1957 there appeared the first 32-page papers since 1938. Turnover exceeded £750,000 for the first time in 1955.

Early headlines in this decade were of austerity, of belt-tightening, exhortations to work harder. There was full employment – Leicester's unemployment register had only a handful of names on it – but there was not much to buy with the wages the promised prosperity brought to Leicester.

This was the era of Stafford Cripps, Nye Bevan, Ernie Bevan and Herbert Morrison. From them came a stream of nationalisation measures: railways, coal-mines, electricity, gas, steel and road transport. Out too came the national health service and the national hospital service – all accomplished on a tight shoe string, with equally tight rationing of clothing, food and such essentials as petrol.

This austerity survived one general election in 1950, but floundered in 1951, when the Tories took control and retained it until 1964, when the election of the Harold Wilson Government put an end to a 13-year period of legislation stage-managed by four Conservative Prime Ministers (Churchill,

Above: Caricatures of the staff in 1938.

Below: A yellow and black Austin A40 van.

Before the Coronation, however, the Mercury was called upon to report on the East Coast floods caused by high tides and gales on January 31, 1953. It caused great loss of life and immense damage to property.

In January, 1954, the Mercury added eight new A40 commercial vans to its delivery fleet. They were not the first of the A40 range to wear the Leicester Mercury colours. Others had already been in service for up to two years and even after 40,000 miles they were still giving a highly satisfactory return for the care that was lavished on them.

The most important historical event of the time for all Leicester's newspapers was the passing of control from Mr Hewitt to Associated Newspapers Ltd on April 1, 1954. Mr Hewitt's capital was tied up in his six newspapers and the crippling rate of death tax (maximum 80%), coupled with the 1940 Finance Act provisions relating to the valuation of assets of a private company for death duty purposes, made it essential for him to part with control. This could be done only by selling his 60 per cent interest in News Holdings. Its Articles of Association required that if either Mr Hewitt or Associated Newspapers wished to sell, he must first offer his shares to the other.

So Associated Newspapers became owners of the whole of the capital of News Holdings Ltd and thereby owners of the Leicester Evening Mail again and controllers of the Mercury, Chronicle, Advertiser, Monitor and Sports Mercury.

The news was made known to staff in a special letter from Mr Hewitt and to the public in an announcement in the Mercury front page on March 3, 1954, which read:

'In a letter to shareholders today, Mr F Vernon Hewitt, Chairman of F Hewitt and Son (1927) Ltd, announces his intention to dispose of his controlling interest in News Holdings Ltd to Associated Newspapers Ltd.

News Holdings Ltd is the parent company controlling F Hewitt and Son (1927) Ltd, which owns the Leicester Mercury and other newspapers. It also controls Midland Newspapers Ltd, which publishes the Leicester Evening Mail. The share capital of News Holdings Ltd is held by Mr Hewitt and Associated Newspapers Ltd in the proportion of 60% and 40% respectively.

Mr Hewitt's arrangements with Associated Newspaper is conditional on certain alterations to the memorandum and articles of

Eden, Macmillan and Douglas Home) who let the world know that the British 'had never had it so good.'

It was also the start of the second Elizabethan age. It began with the death in his sleep of King George VI at Sandringham in February 1952 without the usual preamble of illness bulletins and it caught the young Princess Elizabeth and her husband far away in Kenya.

association of F Hewitt and Son (1927) Ltd being passed by the shareholders at meetings for which notices were issued yesterday. These alterations are desired by Mr Hewitt and Associated Newspapers Ltd to preserve the independent and local character of newspapers published by the company and their freedom from control by any political party or trade association.

In a statement issued today, Mr Hewitt explains that the disposal of his interest is rendered necessary to provide for death duties. He intends to remain Chairman of News Holdings Ltd and will thus retain his close interest in the newspapers published by its subsidiary companies. In a letter to staff, Mr Hewitt announces the provision of a non-contributory pension scheme for the benefit of all employees.

Mr Hewitt's arrangement with Associated Newspapers Ltd also provides for continuity of present

1953

◆ The Coronation in June 1953 brought television into its heritage as part of the British way of life and there was much rejoicing which provided emotional chapters for the Mercury. It was marked by a Leicestershire Village Competition run by the Leicester Advertiser. Prizes were offered for the Loveliest Village and the Best Kept Village. The judges, under the chairmanship of Lord Hungarton, awarded the prizes to Horninghold and East Langton respectively. The BBC filmed, for television, the winning villages and the presentation of prizes. Both places subsequently decided to use some of the prize money to erect a sign to perpetuate the occasion – and the Advertiser's name.

The Queen looks out smiling as the State Coach leaves Buckingham Palace for Westminster Abbey.

Left: Leicester Mercury for June 2, 1953, the day of the Coronation of Queen Elizabeth II.

Right: The Mercury's fleet of Austin A40 vans were a distinctive sight throughout the 1950s.

1953

◆ Mr Leicester's News and Notes on May 11, 1953, recorded the fact that May 12 of that year was the 200th anniversary of an occasion that was of considerable significance to Leicester. It was on May 12, 1753, that Leicester's first newspaper under the title of the Leicester and Nottingham Journal appeared. It was published by J Gregory in the Market Place, had four pages eleven inches by sixteen and a half inches and its price was two and a half pennies.

◆ In December, 1953, the Leicester Mercury appealed to the people of Leicester and Leicestershire for £800 to save the railway horses of Leicester. The Blue Cross section of Our Dumb Friends League had set a target of £2,000 to buy the Leicester British Railways horses which will become redundant through mechanisation early in 1954. Some £1,200 had already been raised. On December 14, 1953, it was reported £1,067/17/6d had been reached.

management of F Hewitt and Son (1927) Ltd, for Mr C T Barton to succeed Mr Hewitt as Chairman and remain managing director, and for the board to include Mr A W Peake, managing director, Mr E J F Fortune and Mr F B Thompson, who have served the company as directors for some years past. In addition the arrangement provides for Mr A S Fuller, Mr Gerald Sanger and Mr Grenville Beckett (directors of Associated Newspapers Ltd), Mr John Thomson and Mr C L W Chant (directors of Northcliffe Newspapers Group Ltd) to join the Board. F Hewitt and Son (1927) Ltd are the publishers of the Leicester Mercury, Illustrated Leicester Chronicle, Leicester Advertiser, Sports Mercury, Mercury Mid-Day and Loughborough Monitor. Mr Crane will continue to act as the London Advertising Agent.'

A sad event for all connected with the paper, for although Mr Hewitt was to continue as chairman of News Holdings, it was impossible to escape the fact that a concern which had been in his family for 80 years had passed into the hands of others. For those who remembered the struggle of the 1930s, there was, perhaps, a little sadness in the realisation that the vanquished of that battle were now their lords and masters.

There had, however, been many changes in the opposing camp over the past 20 years; for 15 years Mr Hewitt and Associated Newspapers had worked side by side most amicably in News Holdings and the new

directors nominated by Associated included Mr Fuller and Mr Thomson, for some years directors of News Holdings, two men most highly respected by the Mercury management. In addition, Lord Rothermere, Chairman of Associated Newspapers since 1951, gave Mr Hewitt a personal assurance that his intention was that the Leicester papers should continue just as before. The staff and public very soon forgot that there had been any changes at the top.

By the new Articles, the holders of the 10% Preferred Ordinary Shares, all members of the Hewitt family or directors, became custodians of the Mercury's independence of character and the position of all preference shareholders was strengthened in a number of ways.

Mr Barton became the first non-Hewitt chairman of the company. He and Mr Peake remained managing directors, with Mr Fortune and Mr Thompson combining their directorships with the editorship and secretaryship respectively. Mr John Thomson, as managing director of Northcliffe Newspapers Group Ltd, became the chief liaison between Leicester and London. Mr Fuller was vice-chairman to Lord Rothermere of Associated Newspapers, on whose Board also were Mr Sanger and Mr Beckett. The fifth newcomer, Mr Chant, was general manager and a director of Northcliffe Newspapers Group, the Associated subsidiary charged with the care of its provincial interests.

The Mercury delivery fleet of vans was boosted with the addition of four new Anglias in March, 1954. The model was making its debut in international rallies and was found to be mechanically sturdy, with independent coil spring front suspension.

Mr H A Hackett, who retired ten years previous after 53 years' service with the Leicester Mercury, died in September 1957. He was the son of the late Mr Harry Hackett, a former editor of the Leicester Mercury. Mr H A Hackett, known to his many friends as Archie, entered the business in May 1894 as a copy boy in the readers' room. He was responsible to the founding of the editorial library as a self-contained department.

The Loughborough Monitor reached its centenary in October 1957 and the editor sent a loyal message to the Queen at Balmoral. In reply, Her Majesty's Private Secretary wrote:

> 'The Queen has commanded me to thank you for your letter of September 16.
> Her Majesty has received with pleasure the greetings from the Loughborough Monitor sent on the occasion of the centenary of its foundation and commands me to convey to you and to all concerned with the production of the newspaper her congratulations and good wishes.'

Mr Ralph Lowings had been in the editorial chair since 1949, but left for an appointment as assistant editor with the Leicester Mercury in 1959 and was succeeded by Mr Frank Smith.

The inflationary trend which had beset the national economy since the war gathered momentum about this time and the cost of living rose steadily. Inevitably the result of higher prices was felt by the newspaper industry as much as by any other. Expenditure on wages, newsprint and distribution grew. By the start of 1958, it was necessary once more to raise the price of the Leicester Mercury – to two and a half pence. The effect on sales was fortunately small and, by the end of the year, the daily average was again firmly established above 150,000.

In 1959, three unions, the Typographical Association, the National Society of Operative Printers and Assistants and the National Society of Electrotypers and Stereotypers, went on strike throughout the Provinces in support of a claim for a 10% wage increase and shorter hours. The company's own men were already working a shorter week than was being asked for and, although they loyally entered their Union's campaign at the start, they were far from wholeheartedly behind the strike action when this loomed up.

However, after three weeks' withdrawal of overtime, 120 employees from the composing, machine and stereotyping departments went on strike on June 22, along with their fellows from newspapers throughout the Provinces.

The morning Racing Edition and all the weekly papers had to be discontinued, but, with the loyalty and enthusiasm of the overseers and a few others remaining in these departments and of those normally on other work, publication of the Mercury went on, one of only a handful of evening papers which continued to print.

There was staff enough, the overseer and his two deputies, to man only one press, but by trebling plates it was found possible to print 24 pages, containing three complete 8-page papers and so maintain full sale and a sizeable profit. Occasionally, a 12-page paper was produced by printing two in one. Newsagents co-operated by taking triplicate or duplicate copies and separating them before delivery. Ink and newsprint supplies were maintained, despite difficulties. Only one of three newsprint mills would supply in view of threats to their lorry drivers and ink had to be obtained from Holland and Scandinavia and delivered with the utmost secrecy.

Settlement was eventually reached. A wage increase of only 4.5% was agreed. But the TA and NSES declined to observe the no-victimisation clause in the Return-to-Work Agreement in respect of those of their members who had helped to produce the Mercury during the strike. The Mercury management refused to permit the return to work of those Union members who went on strike. NATSOPA, however, returned after six weeks. The battle with the dissentient Unions was fierce and prolonged. The Mercury became TV and national newspaper headline news. After a further nine weeks, the TA agreed not to victimise those who had remained at work and four weeks later, on November 9, the NSES agreed also.

The outcome was widely acclaimed by the industry and the general public. None had watched with greater interest than those newspapers who had taken their men back and then had to watch victimisation in operation while they themselves had discarded their last weapon of self-defence.

As a result of the strike and its aftermath, the Loughborough Monitor was out of circulation for 6 weeks and the Illustrated Chronicle, Leicester Advertiser and Mercury Racing Edition for 15. It was an uphill struggle for many months to regain the pre-Strike sale. The Mercury trading profit was 10% higher than the previous year and the largest ever.

1955

◆ In August, 1955, Mr William Gimson, an advertising representative, of Oadby Hill Drive, Oadby, retired after 55 years with the paper. He was first employed as an office boy in the publishing department and became a member of the outside advertising staff in 1919.

◆ Mr Sydney Carr, of Craighill Road, Knighton, retired after 53 years' service with the Mercury and allied papers. He transferred to the Mercury from the Leicester Advertiser in 1921 and worked as a linotype operator. For the last 15 years before retirement, he had been in charge of the copy desk.

◆ Mr Fuller died in 1959 after five years on the Hewitt Board and twelve as Associated Newspapers' nominee on the Board of News Holdings.

◆ A report published in November, 1959, recognised the vital importance of files of local newspapers to people engaged on historical research. The city reference library had made arrangements to obtain microfilm copies of early editions of the Leicester Mercury.

Chapter 9

Momentous Years
1960 – 1970

Further board and editorial changes took place at the begin of the decade. Mr Chant, general manager and director of Northcliffe Newspapers Group, resigned on being moved to the West Country from the Group's headquarters in London – he had been a director for seven years. Mr Robert Russell replaced Mr Frank Smith as editor of the Loughborough Monitor in 1961. Ill-health forced the retirement of Mr H O Ledbrooke from the editorial chair of the Leicester Advertiser and Mr Les Wilkes, a Mercury sub-editor, took his place.

Some property came on to the market in 1960 and with it the dream of a new building with all departments under one roof, with newsprint going in at one end and the printed paper out at the other. The attraction of this site, which was a timber merchant's factory and warehouse, was not only its closeness to the city centre, but also the fact that the property between it and Carlton Street would fall to the buyer because a ring road was planned for Carlton Street.

Below: The site of proposed new offices in Welford Road.

The main site was purchased at auction for £45,000 and the existing buildings demolished. Most of the other properties close-by were bought, bringing the total cost to nearly £70,000. Orders were placed for a new twelve-unit Goss printing press with its ancillary equipment and motors to the cost of nearly £400,000. But the company met with planning difficulties. It seemed the last straw, when, in 1962, the City's planners decided against going ahead with the ring road scheme and it became obvious that the vital last few properties would become so expensive to acquire, making the project beyond sound reasoning, while the vision of a ring road frontage had disappeared.

Around the beginning of 1960, Mrs Eileen A Malcolm (nee Cooke) joined the staff as subscription/photograph clerk – proof-reading was also added to her job description. She worked in a small back corridor behind the main counter in Albion Street. 'It was a very close-knit circle and a very enjoyable working atmosphere as well as

sociable, after-work friendliness. I remember winning the Darts Tournament in 1960 and received 1 doz nylon stockings as my prize. In September 1961, I was married and the Leicester Mercury took my wedding photographs as a gift from the management. I was unfortunately taken ill soon after I was married and was unable to continue work after April 1962. In November 1965, together with my husband and two children, I emigrated to Edmonton, Canada and again the Mercury recorded the event with a photograph and a write-up. During the following years we lived in Vancouver, but kept very much in touch with Leicester as our families were still here and we visited at least every other year. In 1991, my husband and I left Canada to travel to Indonesia where my husband worked as a Forest Products Consultant and from there we went to the Philippines. After six years in the Far East I returned to Leicestershire and made my base in Old Dalby, where I have become involved in the Millennium Committee, the Village Hall Committee and Co-ordinator of the Restoration Committee for our Church, which is in danger of being closed down.'

Mr A J Stephens (Jimmy Stephens), whose name was known to thousands of sports fans for his coverage of soccer and cricket in the Leicester Mercury and Sports Mercury, died in October, 1960. He was 66.

Mr Philip Thornton, of Bonnington Road, Leicester, was employed as a publisher by the Circulation Department for three years during the early 1960s. 'In those days, the Mercury premises were in Albion Street, where the National Youth Agency is now, with the glass-roofed basements that contained the gigantic presses leading through to Wellington Street. In addition, there was a machine room in nearby York Street. The sports edition was printed there on Saturday afternoons. The Black Boy was (and still is) a public house on the corner of Albion Street and Chatham Street. It was the haunt of newspapermen. I was soon to learn that if anyone was sought in the event of an emergency, this pub was the first place to look! A publisher's wage was around £14 a week, which was regarded as good pay 30-odd years ago. For this we worked a five-day week from 9am to 6pm, including Saturdays. Every other week, because of my specialised duties, I worked until about 7.30pm. I had a weekday off in lieu: Thursdays. One of my first tasks was to assist in the preparation of wrappers in the publishing room. Under the direction of Bert Harding, we labelled sheets of plain white paper (cut to size beforehand by an ex-sailor, whose name, I think, was Jack Allen) with the names of newsagents and the quantities of newspapers in dozens, using black wax crayon. The number of wrappers depended on the anticipated size of each parcel, which in turn depended on the planned thickness of the day" edition. The Mercury was quite small in those days: 40-pagers were just coming into being for the first time since the war. Newsprint was still rationed. Another of my jobs was to assist with the print run. This took place in the afternoon, beginning at about 2.30pm with the early out-of-town editions, then building up to the main edition, which commenced at 3.30pm approximately and lasted for at least an hour. Bill Mann was our plump, perspiring foreman during a frantic period when the presses below spewed newspapers up to the publishing room remorselessly, sometimes depositing them in piles several feet high if the publishers were not quick enough to dispose of them. On those occasions it was necessary for all hands to be quick and nimble in their movements. Occasionally, we were set an example by Jim Lee, the Circulation Manager, himself. Years of experience in the rough-and-tumble newspaper business had made him more active than many younger men. The responsibilities of the publishers on the print run included counting newspapers into appropriate sized parcels (they came off the machines in two-dozen packs), checking, wrapping, or tying the bundles and tossing them down chutes where they were loaded on to queuing vans under the supervision of Bill Stretton, the assistant manager.

Newspaper production took place in the atmosphere of whirling paper dust and a pounding thunder from the presses below. The noise in the machine room was incredible. When it was necessary to take a message to the foreman there, it was almost impossible to make oneself heard. There was a deafening racket from the rollers for one thing. For another, his ears were stuffed with cotton wool to protect their drums. Communication was difficult! Every now and then we would gain a brief respite. This occurred when the cry "Break!" was heard from the machine room. It indicated that a paper roll had torn and that frantic repairs were being carried out below. Extra assistance in the afternoons, incidentally, was given by milkmen "moonlighting" from the Co-op. If they had finished their doorstep rounds early enough, they earned extra income by working part-time for the Mercury. The first vans to shoot off were those heading for the two main railway stations, which were the Midland on London Road and the old LNER in Great Central Street, plus St Margaret's and Southgates bus stations. There, small rolls of newspapers were put on trains or buses for the more remote parts of the county. Afterwards, the bulk of the city's newsagents were served by the main fleet. I remember some of those agents' names: Waring of Oadby; Wills of Allandale Road; Tailby of Egington Street.

To my dismay, after a few months I was transferred from the publishing room to the office that faced Albion Street. Disappointed, because I had rather enjoyed the pressure and comradeship up there, it took me time to settle down again. I think Jim Lee felt that my experience in dealing with the public (I was raised in a greengrocer's shop on the corner of Grasmere Street and Jarrom Street) and expertise with figures could be put to good use. He was probably right because before long I came to enjoy the work.'

He retired in July 1959 after covering Leicester City first team matches for 34 years. His longest trip with the team was to the Rumanian capital, Bucharest. Mr Stephens, who lived in Highway Road, Leicester, at one time used the name Blue Don.

The paper was compelled to increase its selling price from two and a half pence to three pence in April 1962, because of the continued rise in production costs.

In March, 1963, Mr Barton died suddenly at the age of 66. He had been with the company for 44 years, as managing director for 36 years and chairman for nine. The highest honours in the industry had been his and he had guided the company wisely and well. Not many of his friends who knew of his World War II army service realised that he was one of the few Leicester men remaining who had fought in the First World War Dardanelles campaign. He had been personal assistant to Vernon Hewitt and then to the late Mr W J Basford. Mr Peake, who had been joint managing director with Mr Barton for 18 years, became chairman of the company.

One of his first moves was to review the position of the proposed new building and it was quickly decided to look for another site with a larger ground area. Eventually, 9,950 square yards on St George Street were purchased from Leicester Corporation at £13 5s 0d a square yard. Only two-thirds were to be built on at first in case the remainder would be required for ring road purposes. By mid-1964, everything was ready for a start to be made on building.

On May 15, 1963, for the first time in its history, the Leicester Mercury was printing in colour. On pages 8 and 21, a two-page spread of Cadbury advertising appeared in 'realistic' four-colour gravure. The colour was pre-printed and fed into the Mercury machinery and overprinted. In the printing industry, this process is colloquially known as the wallpaper system.

From July 1, 1963, the Mercury went 'Royal.' The body matter of the paper was to be printed in Royal, a new type produced by Intertype. It professed to have everything – good design, sharp reproduction, grace and legibility. Extensive study and research lay behind its design. It had the essential inherent qualities necessary for the production of a crisp and clean newspaper. The complete changeover involved 100,000 matrices in 80 fonts of type. Each existing

Below: St George Street prior to 1964.

magazine had to be emptied, cleaned and the new type fed in by hand. The paper received congratulations from city printing experts. Mr Kenneth Gee, president of the Leicester Master Printers' Association, declared: 'I quite like the formation of letters. I thought it cleaned up the small advertisements considerably and it makes quite a nice page.' Mr Tom Wesley, lecturer in typographic design at Leicester's School of Graphic Design and Printing, said: 'The Leicester Mercury is to be congratulated on choosing Royal for its text. Legibility is primarily concerned in the height of the lower case letters rather than the width. Royal accomplishes this.'

Also in July 1963, a 'tele-ads' department was set up, with five girls and a classified advertisement manager. Customers were invited to telephone their small advertisements to a trained staff who would take them straight on to typewriters, after giving any advice needed. It was an instant success and within the first year the volume of classified advertising increased by a third.

At the end of June, 1963, Mr Hewitt resigned his chairmanship of News Holdings and cut his last visible link with the Mercury. He had been connected with the paper for 58 years, but advancing years persuaded him that he must no longer keep any responsibility. The Mercury was so much in his blood that he could not possibly lose interest and, in fact, the telephone lines between Leicester and his home in Eastbourne continued to be kept busy. He was always the first to congratulate staff on new ventures.

On September 6, 1963, the Oadby and Wigston Advertiser was born, under the editorship of Mr Les Wilkes, already editor of the Leicester Advertiser. At first, it was intended to be an edition of the Leicester paper, but plans were changed when two local journalists decided to bring out a separate newspaper, the Oadby and Wigston Express. The Express, however, found it an uphill struggle and at the end of the following year, it ceased publication and merged with the Oadby and Wigston Advertiser.

Perhaps the most surprising event of 1963 was the closure of the Leicester Evening Mail, after 32 years of publication. It had been losing money for a number of years. On November 11, 1963, it came out as normal, without even a hint that it was the final edition.

The staff were informed that evening and the following morning practically all who had served the paper for 15 years or more (95 per cent of all members of staff) reported to Albion Street to become members of the staff

Above: Terraced houses in St George Street, demolished in 1964.

Below: Offices of the Leicester Evening Mail, which closed in 1963.

Hilary Woods of Blackpool Road, Carleton, Poulton-le-Fylde, Lancashire, wrote: 'I worked on the newspaper from 1963 to 1966 in the photo-sales department. In fact, I was the photo-sales department, as there was only me and my other duties included cataloguing the negatives and being a general dogsbody for the photographers. My only claim to fame was that I was the first person to be allowed to continue working whilst pregnant, as it was a company rule that once a girl knew of her condition, she left and sought alternative employment, usually with a temping agency until such time that she gave up work for her confinement. I think it probably stemmed from the fact that the front counter girls who received the adverts were not allowed to advertise what they had been up to in their spare time and so, as to avoid arguments, the back office girls were included as well. Providing you got your work done, the office manager was quite lenient. Lunch hour was taken anytime between 12 noon and 3pm, sometimes that is what it took, other times I didn't take any – it all depended on the work load. One thing I do remember well was the Moors Murder trial. Obviously, a lot of information regarding the trial was received, but the photographers would never discuss it in front of me, in case it would upset me. Another of my little jobs was to type the captions to accompany the photographs that appeared in the windows. One of the conditions for the job was – Must be able to type. I couldn't, so I borrowed a typewriter and learned to type the following: The Leicester Mercury Albion Street and the quick brown fox, etc. At the interview, I was asked to demonstrate my typing skills by typing the name and address of the newspaper. Phew! I was very sad to leave, but for several years after I took my son Marcus in to see the chaps, especially when he needed a new pair of shoes, as he always came away with a fistful of two bob pieces. I handed over my reins to Linda Peck, who later became my son's godmother.'

1964

◆ Miss Mary Kathleen Sowter, Leicester Mercury librarian for 18 years, died in hospital on April 25, 1964. Miss Sowter, who lived on Uppingham Road, was the daughter of the late Mr William Sowter, shoe mercer. She had joined the Mercury in 1946, soon after the death of her father.

◆ In the autumn of 1964, the morning Racing Edition, which had been a Saturday instead of a daily publication since April 1960, was discontinued. The Mercury began a weekly 'Where's the Ball?' competition. Each week £1,000 in prizes was given away to those who came nearest to pinpointing the position of the ball on a football match picture from which the ball had been painted out. It was immediately popular and attracted more than 20,000 entries each week.

of the Mercury, with continuing pension rights. The Mercury of November 12 carried under its title the words 'Incorporating the Leicester Evening Mail.' Taking over the Mail sale lifted that of the Mercury from 166,000 to 180,000.

The contractors moved on to the St George Street site on August 3, 1964. Four streets of terraced cottages, Peel Street, Carrington Street, Baker Street and East Short Street, once stood there. Less than ten months later, on May 27, 1965, the chairman, Mr Peake, performed the 'topping-out' ceremony.

On the weekend of July 2 and 3, 1966, the move from Albion Street took place. Cranes

Above: The St George Street site on 5th August 1964, as work commences on the new building.
Opposite Page: Top and middle, panoramas of the site on 11th August 1964.
Bottom: By 3rd September 1964 excavation of the basement was well underway.

*Above: By the summer
of 1965 the new
Mercury building was
taking shape.*

*Right: The move from
Albion Street in July
1966.*

lifted all machinery, except presses, out of a hole made in the front wall of the old building and delivered it to the new. On July 4, 1966, the first Mercury was produced at St George Street.

The new Goss presses, originally ordered for Welford Road, had been in the course of erection since April and it was several months before the first began to run and printing could be gradually transferred to St George Street. In the meantime, casting and printing had to continue at Albion Street and York Street. The matrices had to be carried there from St George Street.

Printing went on at York Street until the double-width presses were dismantled, added to and re-erected at St George Street to make a third line. By the end of the year, everything else was complete – an imposing new building costing (with the land) nearly £1,000,000 and machinery, furniture and other equipment worth nearly another £1,000,000.

Supervising the whole project, liaising between the directors and the architects and contractors, was Mr John Murray, appointed production manager shortly before the start of the venture. He had joined the company in 1961 after wide experience on the production side of newspapers both in this country and abroad.

On January 11, 1967, Her Royal Highness Princess Alexandra came to Leicester especially to open the new building. She unveiled a plaque in the foyer and then for an hour and a half toured the offices and press hall with the Lord Lieutenant and Lord Mayor. She spoke to some 50 or so members of staff at their work. Afterwards she took tea in the Boardroom with the directors and their wives, architects, contractor, production manager and company secretary. On behalf of the company, Mr Peake presented the Princess with an antique Battersea enamel box, as a momento of the occasion. On her return home, she wrote a letter of appreciation and thanks in her own hand.

Many messages were received that day, including ones from the Queen and the Prime Minister, Mr Harold Wilson. The following day, a supplement was published with the Mercury, describing the new building and machinery in detail and giving a record in words and pictures of the Royal visit. It pointed out that the machinery included two Seniormatic casting machines, among the first in the country and two Monarch Intertype machines which could set type automatically from perforated tape and perform in one hour what the conventional machine took one day or so.

A champagne buffet luncheon was given to the Lord Lieutenant, Lord Mayor, High Sheriff, other city and county civic dignitaries, the Bishop of Leicester, leading personalities in industry and commerce, advertising agents and leaders in the world of sport. This was followed by a dinner for the

Below: Mr Peake accompanies Her Royal Highness Princess Alexandra into the new Mercury building.

staff, numbering nearly 500, on January 17, 1967 at the De Montfort Hall and finally a luncheon for London advertising agents.

Mr Eric Hollingworth, deputy composing room manager, proposed a toast to the company at the staff dinner. 'If the present management and staff looked as far ahead as did their predecessors, then the prosperity of the company was assured. The company had to look far ahead in answering the questions posed by the changes brought about by the advent of technology. The Leicester Mercury had gone from strength to strength during recent years, in an industry that had contracted. Many papers have closed – many men have lost jobs. We have been more fortunate. We have jobs with security on a newspaper with prospects that are immense.' He felt that the defence of the written word was a serious duty and one that was shared by every member of the Leicester Mercury team. One of the replies to the toast came from Mr John Fortune, director and editor, who cited the headline in the supplement brought out in honour of the opening of the new building: 'At Last Our Chance To Start Making A Newspaper Designed For The Future.' They now had the tools and the directors had every confidence in the staff now being able to carry on with the job and see that the paper marched with the times into the future.

Kaye Almey summed up the experience of working in the new offices in her column. 'I can scarcely

Above: Princess Alexandra reads all about Her visit in that days Leicester Mercury, hot off the press.

Right: She signs the visitors' book, watched by Mercury Chairman A W Peake.

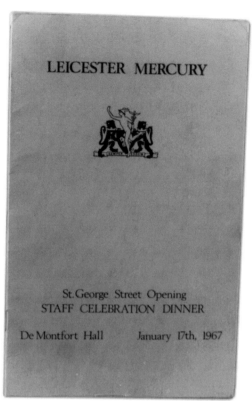

LEICESTER MERCURY

St. George Street Opening
STAFF CELEBRATION DINNER

De Montfort Hall   January 17th, 1967

believe what has happened to me. The years I've spent facing a blank wall to type this column. Always electric light. Through a bit of a window on my left I could see a reflection of sky in the windows of buildings across the (Albion) Street's narrow canyon... For me today a room with a view. And daylight. Like an emerging troglodyte, I'm so dazzled that I'm typing in sunspecs. I'm so captivated that I don't want to type on my new noiseless typewriter. I want to sit and gaze. My rooftop vista is perhaps not the most spectacular the city could offer but to a newcomer it's as stunning as a sudden wide East Anglian horizon would be to inhabitants of a railway cutting. On the skyline directly in front of me rise the creeper-clad walls of Hillcrest Hospital, two tones of emerald green. To their right the bleached finger of St Peter's Church spire tightly ringed with chimneys, slate roofs, terraced houses. If I had a telescope, I could watch picaninnies on their way to school. A hunk of dirty grey engine sheds in the middle distance displeases me but above them the onion dome of Highfield Street synagogue shines like a turquoise bead... My foreground carries a bird's eye view of Leicester and County Convalescent Homes Society's headquarters, the top decks of buses loping over Swain Street

bridge and a picture gallery of fluorescent posters. All this and a huge basinful of sky.'

John Albion's Gossip column in the Illustrated Chronicle for January 13, 1967, featured the Leicester Mercury Library – 'A library with only a few books.' It is interesting to note that, even then, the library contained 'nearly 8,000 pictures of royalty, 180,000 pictures of other people and 120,000 general scenes, landscape and buildings. It is the same story with the metal blocks (pictures on metal used for printing) – 156,000 of people and 7,000 of general scenes. In a normal week, the library staff deal with 1,000 pictures and nearly half as many blocks.' As far as cuttings are concerned, three years' city cuttings occupied one drawer in the 1940s, but in 1967 one year's city cuttings occupied two drawers.

Rising costs in the newspaper industry meant price rises – the weekly papers were increased from 3d to 4d in March 1965 and in September the Mercury from 3d to 4d. Mr H N Chambers, a chartered accountant, had arrived in 1961 to take charge of the fast-increasing accounting side of the business. In March 1965, he became secretary. Mr Thompson had held the post for 18 years.

Sales manager at the Mercury's Loughborough office, Mr Cecil Wakefield, achieved 50 years' service in November 1964. He had started in the publishing office at the age of thirteen and a half. He had, said Mr Peake, 'brought tremendous rewards to the circulation side of the paper.' He was the second longest serving employee at the time and had been sales manager at four branch offices – Loughborough, Coalville, Rugby and Market Harborough, which he had opened in the late 1920s.

Mr Hubert Neville Chambers became company secretary and accountant of F Hewitt and Son (1927) Ltd, the proprietors of the Mercury, on March 1, 1965. A Leicester man, he joined the firm as an accountant from the British United Shoe Machinery Company Ltd.

Mr Harold Taylor, who helped to put the first picture in the newspaper early in the First World War, died in March 1965. He was 71. He had worked with the paper for 44 years and retired in 1959. He had come from Preston with Mr George Wright and helped to build up the process engraving department until it handled between 250 and 300 blocks a week. For 26 years, he was manager of the department.

Mr Grenville Beckett, a member of the Board since 1954, died, aged 74, in December 1965, in Redhill, Surrey. He was one of the

Left: Staff Celebration Dinner in January, 1967.

1965

◆ The price of the Leicester Mercury increased to 4d in September 1965. It brought the paper in line with the majority of provincial evening newspapers which had been selling at 4d for some time. Costs of production had increased to such an extent as to make the new price necessary.

◆ Mr George Harold Churchill, assistant circulation manager, retired in October, 1965, after 42 years in the industry. Mr Churchill, who lived in Oadby Road, Wigston, was a founder member of the Newsvendors' Benevolent Institution's Leicester committee (Old Ben), when it was formed in 1933 and was president for the last 16 years.

◆ Also, in December, 1965, Mr Thomas Charles Griffiths, a former sports editor of the Mercury, passed away in Hall Green, Birmingham. He was 79. Tom Griffiths, as he was popularly known, came to Leicester from the Worcester Echo in 1919 and retired after 37 years with the Mercury in 1956. He covered racing under the pseudonym of 'Advocate' and was one of the foremost boxing critics in the country.

1967

◆ Robert Mark, Chief Constable of Leicester City Police, left his post to become Assistant Commissioner of the Metropolitan Police at Scotland Yard in January, 1967.

Before he left, he sent a letter to the Leicester Mercury, expressing his wish to publicly pay tribute to the way in which the Mercury had helped to found a good relationship between the police and the public. 'There has been for some years a noticeable growth of confidence and co-operation between this force and your staff, partly because each is concerned to discharge a proper obligation to the public interest and partly because neither expects nor receives any improper privilege as a result of their association with each other.'

country's leading authorities in the newsprint industry.

Mr Lawrie Simpkin was appointed news editor of the Leicester Mercury in February 1966. An experienced news and sports journalist, he began his career in Nottingham and had worked at Grantham, where he was chief reporter. Later he became editor of the Ilkeston Pioneer before returning to evening paper reporting in the sports room of the Nottingham Evening Post. He was appointed to the sports staff of the Leicester Mercury in 1960, with the special responsibility of reporting Leicester City's games. His predecessor, Mr D Robinson, news editor for the previous four years, joined the BBC.

A former editor of the Mercury, Mr Henry William Bourne, died in April 1966 at his home in Middlesex. He was 83. When he retired from the editorship in 1948, he had spent over 50 years in journalism. His patience and unflappability were two great assets and he was never afraid of his character showing through his work. A member of his staff at his retirement dinner described him as 'a true gentleman of the Press.' He became a director in 1941.

Another death this year was that of the former sports editor of the Leicester Evening Mail, Mr Noel Tarbotton. He was 69. He wrote articles on Leicester City under the pen name of 'Crusader.' Appointed sports editor in 1946, he retired in 1963, when the paper closed. He wrote From Fosse to City, a history of the local football club.

Another of those national tragedies which had so often inspired the Mercury to give aid in the past occurred shortly after the Mercury had moved into its new home. A coal-tip at Aberfan in South Wales slipped and engulfed a school, resulting in the deaths of 144 people, including 116 children. An appeal to readers was launched immediately and the response was so great that the editor himself went down to Aberfan with the Lord Mayor on November 30, 1966, to hand over a cheque for £43,544, the largest single donation Aberfan received.

Between 1967 and 1969, the Mercury sale averaged over 180,000 daily. The best year, 1969, saw the figure at 181,199. The highest monthly average was in March 1969 when the figure was 185,008.

There was every reason to be satisfied with the Mercury's position, because there were other factors than price increases which were affecting sales generally. Constant broadcasting of news on television and national radio, the tendency of the general public to take more holidays and fly off to destinations overseas, all contributed to the new situation.

An important development in radio broadcasting took place in October 1967. Britain's first local radio station was established by the BBC in Leicester. Operating first on VHF alone, it had limited coverage and research at the end of the year showed that its maximum audience at any one time was only 6 per cent of the population. Even when it could be heard later on the medium wave band, its audience remained very small.

In 1973, Professor J Halloran, giving his inaugural lecture as Director of the Centre of Mass Communication Research at Leicester University, said that the expressed aim of the BBC of rejuvenating community life through local radio stations had 'failed hopelessly,' but the Government still proclaimed it a success. The Mercury criticised the City Council for a decision to grant £104,000 over two years as a subsidy for local radio, without reference to the ratepayers.

Another University of Leicester Professor, Jack Simmons, in his 'Leicester Past and Present,' published in 1974, referred to this criticism: 'One thing, however, can be said and this weighed with a good many members of the City Council when the matter was debated: that since 1963 ... Leicester had been reduced to a single daily paper, the Mercury. It seemed to many people a good thing in itself that the purveyance of local news should not be a monopoly. This need imply no criticism of the Mercury. Indeed, towards the conclusion of a study that has been largely concerned with the last two centuries, it would be ungracious to express anything but gratitude to it and to all the newspapers that have served Leicester in succession. They enjoy one advantage that neither radio nor television can ever command: all their words are permanently recorded in print.'

Another threat to provincial newspapers in the 1960s was the 'free sheet.' This was nothing new, for several local weeklies had started in this way. But advertising was now more than ever before the life blood of a newspaper and to have some of this creamed off by a non-newspaper was a serious matter. Faced with the urgent prospect of a free sheet starting in Leicester, the Mercury instituted its own in 1969 purely as a defensive measure. It was called the Leicester Shopwindow and was distributed in four segments of the city weekly in rotation, so that each area of the 25,000 houses received one copy every four weeks. It drew a great deal of its advertising from these areas and had little or no effect on the Mercury or the weekly papers. It was printed by offset process in Leamington and delivered by professional distributors.

Sir Geoffrey Harmsworth, Bart, joined the Board of Directors in 1967. Among his many newspaper interests, he was a director of the Daily Mail and General Trust.

In January, 1968, a presentation of a stereo radio gramophone was made to the chairman and managing director, Mr A W Peake, by his fellow directors. It was to mark the part he played at the opening of the new St George Street offices and printing works by Princess Alexandra and as a momento of two service records achieved, 45 years with the company and 25 years as a director.

ARTHUR W. PEAKE
Chairman 1964-1970

Some 150 members of the Students' Union of Leicester University marched from Victoria Park to the Leicester Mercury offices at the beginning of May, 1968. A message of protest was delivered to the newspaper by Mr R N Barbor-Might, president of the Union. The protest was on two points – that the Union found obnoxious the coverage of their representation issue (student representation on management committees of the University) and of the newspaper's handling of race relations. The Editor, Mr E J F Fortune, in reply, wrote:

'The case put up by the students for representation on management committees of the University has always been fully and faithfully reported. The leader column has been outspokenly critical of the disgraceful sit-in strike which kept the Vice-Chancellor and his staff out of their own offices, caused some £300 worth of damage to the premises and certainly much more

damage to the students' own cause. We shall continue to condemn such immature behaviour. The Leicester Mercury has consistently espoused a policy of restraining further immigration until the present immigrants can be integrated, their housing needs met and adequate schooling provided for many children who cannot write English – a policy which appears to be meeting with wider support among politicians of all parties.'

Mr Charles McCann, manager of the Stereotype Department for 22 years, retired in July 1968 to become a part-time consultant for a London firm. During his career, he sailed on the maiden voyage of the liner Athenia to the United States, where he took up his duties with the Detroit News for three years. 'One reason for the rapid rise in the circulation of the Mercury has been its good production,' he remarked. Mr Sidney Turner, assistant manager for 12 years, was appointed in his place. He was a member of the Leicester Mercury '40 Club.' Mr Tim McCaffrey, an employee for eight years, was promoted to assistant manager.

Chief photographer, Mr James Mapham, whose picture of the British troops landing on the Normandy beaches on D-Day, 1944, was acclaimed by the Americans as 'the greatest photograph of the war,' died at his home on September 20, 1968. He was 59. Following the D-Day invasion, he operated among a French Resistance group and the 'Marquis' threw a party in his honour and made him an honorary member of the unit. He had been appointed Field Marshal Montgomery's official photographer and accompanied him on the great drive from El Alamein to Tripoli. He had been chief photographer at the Mercury for 20 years.

Billy Wilson, a well-known Leicester magician, who had been employed by the Mercury for 47 years in circulation and then advertising as a representative, retired in September, 1968, along with Mr John F N Smith, advertising manager of the weekly publications, who had spent 51 years in the newspaper industry in Leicester and Mr Edward A Rogers, advertising representative for the Illustrated Chronicle.

Mr Norman Jones, who had started with the paper when he left school, became advertisement manager in October 1968. The new deputy manager was Mr D Roughton.

Mr Wilfred Toone became machine room manager in December 1968, in succession to Mr E J Bishop, who had retired after 27 years' service. Mr Toone began work with the Mercury in 1935 at the age of 15.

◆ Mr Michael Beaman, of Marys Lane, Barnet, Herts, wrote saying his family had been connected with the paper from the 1880s until 1967, when his father died. His great grandfather (Edward Beaman) was employed as a compositor in the 1880s, having been apprenticed by his father, who was a compositor for a newspaper in Shrewsbury in the 1870s. He in turn apprenticed his late father (Frederick Beaman) as a compositor in 1921. Frederick remained in the newspaper's employment until his death in 1967. He received a long service award shortly before he died, from the editor Mr John Fortune.

◆ The death occurred, in hospital, of Mrs Winifred Mary Goddard, in July, 1968. She was 85. She had organised the Leicester Mercury Oozoo's Club and won herself thousands of devotees through her daily children's column. During her last years with the paper, she was librarian. 'Auntie Susie,' as she was affectionately known to all her colleagues and friends, was country-bred, at Cosby. She was for many years a resident of Cropston and was particularly devoted to Bradgate Park. One window of her home was deliberately angled to afford a fine view of Old John.

1968

◆ On April 23, 1969, the issue of the Leicester Mercury proudly announced: 'The type you are now reading has been set by the aid of a computer. The Leicester Mercury has installed one of the very latest aids to typesetting known as a Muset. It is the latest example of keeping the newspaper in the forefront of technological advance. For some years now we have been using punched tape which fed into a Linotype or Intertype machine and produced lines of type without an operator sitting at the machine. What the Muset does is to enable an operator to perforate tape without regard to the end of a line or hyphenation. This allows the operator to work twice as fast because he can produce unjustified tape. This tape, passed through the computer, is converted into justified tape – justified for each line of the newspaper column in a few seconds.' The very latest wire picture machine had also been installed.

Right: On Monday July 21st 1969 the Mercury reported the first moon landing. The main picture, as the caption explains, was taken by a staff photographer, from his own television screen. (Note also the error in the headline.)

A contributory pension scheme for the staff was introduced in 1968 and the annual lunch for former members of the staff, previously held at a hotel, could now take place on the premises. The other two annual events, dinners for members of the '40 Club' and for Editors and Managers, continued as before. The '40 Club,' for serving directors and staff with 40 years service, retained a membership of about 20 for many years. The editor, Mr John Fortune, joined the club in October 1969.

In July, 1969, a special 24-page pull-out supplement was published to celebrate Leicester's 50th anniversary as a City. It traced the events leading up to the honour and the progress and life of the city through the difficult periods after two world wars. It won praise from the Lord Mayor, Edward Marston.

Rising costs of services, wages and materials had been absorbed for as long as possible, but in September 1969 it was found inevitable that the price of the paper was to be increased to 5d.

ARMSTRONG'S HISTORIC FIRST WORDS FROM THE MOON:

One Small Step For Man But One Giant Step For Mankind

APOLLO CREW UNLOCK THE SECRETS OF A NEW WORLD

Chapter 10
Centenary Celebrations
1970 – 1980

Decimilisation came in 1971. One penny (1p) substituted the equivalent of 2.4d and the Mercury cover price was converted from 6d to two and a half new pence. Inflation raged on, until it was running at nearly 20% a year. The cost of living increased and wages fell behind so rapidly that at one time adjustments were being made every six months. Then, for a couple of years, came statutory control with a maximum permitted annual increase.

Newsprint, the other main cost factor, had for long been obtainable at a price uneconomic to the producer, which had encouraged him to turn machinery over to other uses. At the same time the raw material position had been worsening. Then came a greatly increased demand caused by an advertising explosion in 1972 and 1973, particularly for displayed situations vacant and the outcome was newsprint shortage and rocketing prices. The enormous increase in turnover (the 1973 figure was double that of the previous year) was due partly to inflation but more to the advertising upsurge. The advertisement rate went up by three stages in eight years and the cover price four.

Mr George Farrin retired in January, 1970, after 45 years with the Leicester Mercury circulation department. He had won an award from the Royal Society for the Prevention of Accidents for driving for 28 years without a blameworthy accident.

In April, Mr Brian West joined the Mercury as Deputy Editor. He came from the Surrey Comet, a London suburban bi-weekly paper, for which he was an editor for six years. Mr Simeon Garner, who has been assistant editor for the last 20 years, was to continue in that position. Mr Roy Harris, who had begun his career as a 16-year-old office boy with the Evening Mail, became Advertisement Manager-in-Chief of all departments. Mr Eric Hollingworth, who had spent his entire career with the Mercury, starting as a composing room apprentice, became Assistant Production Manager.

In April, it was reported that the former premises of the Leicester Evening Mail with its tower will soon disappear from the London Road skyline. Allied Carpets, of Birmingham, had bought it and planned to demolish it and erect a two-storey shop and office block on the site.

Left: Mr Brett Chambers.

Two new appointments were made to the Board of Directors in May, 1970: Mr H N Chambers, who had joined the Mercury as an accountant in 1961 and became company secretary in 1965; Mr John Murray, who had joined the Mercury group of newspapers in 1961 after a wide experience both in this country and abroad.

The Mercury began to print radio and television programmes for the early part of the following day from June 1970 and many readers decided they had no further need for a national daily newspaper. Indeed, a strike threat had been affecting all national daily papers published in London and Manchester that month. The Mercury also produced a special parliamentary election results edition at 8am on June 19.

Mr John Thomas Sharpe, a compositor for nearly 38 years with the Mercury, died in August 1970. He was apprenticed in London before moving to Leicester in May 1920 and had held office in the Typographical Association for many years.

Mr A W Peake, Chairman and Managing Director, retired at the end of September, 1970 and a dinner was held in his honour at the Top Rank Suite, Leicester, on October 7. He had joined the newspaper as a junior clerk in 1923. He had taken an increasing part in

1970

◆ The Mercury went to great lengths in October, 1970, to explain that it thought it was time the council workers' dispute was settled and normal living standards returned to the people. The strike was entering its third week and its by-products could be seen in the spreading nausea of the Leicester refuse compounds, a nausea created by scavenging dogs and rats. 'The Leicester Mercury believes that a continuance of the strike and likely extensions of it is against the interests of good government and against the welfare of the people of Leicester. An immediate settlement of it on the men's terms would have the substantial backing of the people of Leicester, who will have to pay the ultimate bill. So we say to Leicester City Council and their negotiators: End this strike now.'

Above right: Mr John Fortune, Chairman.

Below right: Mr Brian West, appointed editor in 1970.

management during the years of fierce newspaper competition with the Leicester Evening Mail and was behind a number of enterprises such as the Holiday Bureau, Continental holiday tours, the Leicester Mercury free insurance scheme for readers and the Sports Mercury Football Pools. He became a director in 1942 and was made joint managing director with Mr C T Barton in 1945. On the death of Mr Barton in 1963, he became Chairman and Managing Director. It was his vision and knowledge of the needs of the paper of the future that led to the acquisition and opening of the St George Street site. He was to continue to serve the company on the board of directors. At the dinner, Mr Fortune proposed the toast to Mr Peake. He mentioned the four qualities he would identify with Mr Peake: loyalty, determination, courage and kindness. He also made the company's presentation of an inscribed silver salver, signed by all the directors. Mr Brian Thompson made the supporting speech and made a presentation of a gold necklace and bracelet to Mrs Peake. Mr Peter Jackson, a member of the composing staff, presented him with a pair of inscribed binoculars and thanked him for the unpublicised help and support he gave to employees who were ill or in adversity. On behalf of the pensioners, Mr John Sharvell, a former composing room manager, presented him with a pair of gold cuff-links. The directors had also previously given him a silver stirrup cup.

Mr Peake became president of the Newspaper Society in May 1972. He spoke of his faith in the printed word and his unshakeable belief in the freedom and continued success of provincial newspapers. He was the third president of the society from the Leicester Mercury. His predecessors were Mr Francis Hewitt (1892-93) and Mr C T Barton (1957-58).

Mr Peake was succeeded by Mr John Fortune, Editor and director of the Mercury for the previous 22 years. He had started his long career in 1929 as a reporter. After war-time service as an officer with the RAF Air Sea Rescue Service, he became editor of the Leicester Chronicle, then known as the Illustrated Leicester Chronicle. Two years later he was appointed editor of the Leicester Mercury and within three months was elected to the board of directors. He succeeded the late Mr H W Bourne as editor.

Mr F Brian Thompson was appointed director and general manager in October, 1970. He joined as a reporter in 1931 and was elected to the board in 1951.

Mr Raymond Beddows, who had worked for the paper for 39 years, died in October,

JOHN FORTUNE
Chairman 1970-1974

1970. After a short spell as a junior in the publishing department, he transferred to the stereotyping department.

Mr Brian West was appointed Editor of the Leicester Mercury in November 1970, after joining the paper in March. He was a member of the Guild of British Newspaper Editors and of the Young Newspapermen's Association. He also lectured and examined for the Training of Journalists.

Mr William Regester retired in the same month, after 39 years' work in the composing room. He had joined on April 5, 1931. 'I won't forget that date,' he said. 'The following year I backed a horse called April 5th for the

83

Derby – and it won.' He had served as a member of the Leicester City Council for eight years.

One of Leicester's best known newsvendors, Mr Harry Carvell, of Didsbury Street, Braunstone, died at the end of November at the age of 54. For 40 years, he had stood on the Humberstone Gate side of the Clock Tower and during this time had become a familiar figure to thousands of Leicester people.

The Mercury ran a nostalgia piece on former employees in January 1971, especially those who had left former other media. Michael Barratt, BBC television's Nationwide anchor man, and Sam Leitch, a key figure in the Corporation's sports service,

were both former employees. Nearer home, it seems Leicester Mercury reporters had taken a commanding hold over Radio Nottingham. In 1968, former Leicester Mercury reporter Mr Gerald Nethercot was appointed station manager when Radio Nottingham first went on air. He planned to retire in the spring of 1971 and former Loughborough Monitor reporter, Colin St John Walters, was to take over. His appointment made him the youngest station manager in the country.

Agricultural correspondent of the Leicester Mercury for five years, Mrs Margaret McNeill, won a top award for her work in January 1971. A travel scholarship, worth £250, was presented to her by Lord J T Netherthorpe, chairman of Fisons Ltd, the

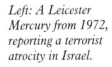

1971

◆ As a reminder of the campaign launched by the Leicester Mercury when the new maternity unit at the Leicester Royal Infirmary was threatened with postponement and of the outstanding support given by readers at the time, the Leicester Mercury decided to present christening cups to the first boy and to the first girl born at the hospital. They were replicas of a 1700 design known as the Sloane cup. The first boy was Clinton Hurst, son of Mr and Mrs Robert Hurst, of Canal Street, Wigston. He was named after Clint Eastwood, because his parents liked his films and they thought it was a good name for a son. The first girl was Rita Laraine Hayes, second daughter of Mr and Mrs Richard Hayes, of Bale Road, Northfields, Leicester.

Left: A Leicester Mercury from 1972, reporting a terrorist atrocity in Israel.

◆ A touring exhibition showing how the Mercury was produced was inaugurated at Mountsorrel library in November 1971. Present were Mr Peter Oldroyd (principal librarian for north Leicestershire), who arranged the exhibition, Mrs Patricia West, Editor Mr Brian West and County Librarian Mr Geoffrey Smith. The layout was devised by the Editor in conjunction with the Deputy Picture Editor, Mr Eric Taylor. It was intended to be 'on the road' for two years.

below: The touring exhibition: Mr Peter Oldroyd, Mrs Patricia West, Mr Brian West and County Librarian Mr Geoffrey Smith.

sponsors. The citation mentioned her capacity for interpreting the world of agriculture to the non-farming public.

Mr Wilfrid Brown, head of Leicester Mercury's pricing department, was presented with an inscribed silver dish in February 1971 to mark his 50 years' service with the firm. He was due to retire in September.

In March, Mr Douglas Johnson, Editor of the Sports Mercury and Sports Editor of the Leicester Mercury for the previous 21 years, died suddenly. He had come to Leicester from the North in 1950 to assume the two appointments at the Mercury. He left a wife, Ella, and two children. His son, Ian, was Editor of the Sports Argus, Birmingham. His successor was Mr Michael Wood, the former boxing and rugby correspondent. Mr Alfred Perkins was to continue as deputy Sports Editor. Mike Wood left three years later for other fields and handed over to Mr David Welch. Mr Welch joined the sports staff in 1969 after graduating in physical education at Loughborough College of Education. He had become an acknowledged expert on racing.

Compositor Mr Maurice Dare retired in May, 1971, after 50 years' service with the firm. He was presented with a barometer and a 400-day clock by Mr A W Peake, director. He was one of the Mercury team that captured the Spicer Cricket Cup in 1936.

Another retirement saw Linotype operator Mr Harold Curtis leaving after 50 years' service. He had started work with the Leicester Evening Mail in 1920 at the age of fourteen.

Glenn Barker, women's page editor, wrote her last feature in July 1971. She was succeeded by Miss Olive Nelson, who was born in Southern Ireland and brought up in Yorkshire. She had tried quite a number of other jobs before joining the staff, such as waitress, goat-keeper, temporary secretary, door-to-door saleswoman and hairdresser. She came from the Cambridge Evening News, where she was women's page editor and film critic, papers in Newcastle and then from the assistant editorship of Housewives' Circle, a Birmingham Evening Mail publication.

Former deputy garage manager, Mr Allan Kirton, died in August 1971. He had worked for the firm for 45 years and had received several safe driving awards. The death also occurred in October of Mr Wilfred Riley, who had worked for the firm for 44 years. He was 73 and had been branch manager of the circulation department at Loughborough between 1950 to 1955. The next month, Mr Herbert Norton, the Mercury's cricket correspondent, died aged 59. He had joined the Evening Mail as a

young man in 1926 and was deeply interested in racing. For many years up until the war, he was the Evening Mail's racing correspondent, writing under the name of 'Friar.'

Mr Jack Smith, a senior member of the staff in the Mercury's stereo department, retired in January 1972 after working for newspapers since 1924. Also in January 1972 Mr Oliver E Satchell, a sub-editor with the Leicester Advertiser, retired after a career in the newspaper industry that began 51 years previously and included service under 15 editors. He sadly died six months later.

This was a period of changing readership trends. The frequent increase in cover-price of all newspapers and magazines saw the end of the two and three daily newspaper habit. In future it was more inclined to be one only. In the Leicester Mercury's circulation area it ultimately became apparent that 25% of households were no longer taking a morning paper at all and in the city and surrounding built-up area this figure was over 40%. Realising the new circumstances, the management made gradual change in the content of the Mercury, giving it more national and international news and something nearer to a 24-hour coverage. The publishing time of the main edition was brought forward to 3pm because of a tendency for factories to close earlier as a result of a shorter working week. In the 1930s, this edition was printed at 4.45pm.

These moves doubtless helped to save the Mercury from the fall in sales experienced by most newspapers. The combined circulation of evening papers in the 150,000 to 190,000 a day bracket fell during the ten-year period to 1973 by 10.3%. The Mercury sale actually rose by 540 copies a night, namely 0.3%, in this decade – all it had lost, in fact, was the size of its former growth of 1.5% yearly. The weekly papers on the other hand suffered an overall drop of more than 25%, the individual figures ranging from 33% with the Advertiser to 4% in the case of the Oadby and Wigston Advertiser.

The price of the Mercury rose to 3p in August 1972 due to heavy increases in wages and materials, particularly in the cost of newsprint. It had been two years since the previous price rise.

Local commercial radio was first introduced into the country in 1972 and Leicester was scheduled to have a station in early 1974. But it did not come.

At the half-yearly meeting of the Newspaper Society in November 1972, Mr Peake forecast that over the next ten years the provincial Press would face new forms of competition and would have to work harder

to overcome them. He said the BBC intended to have local TV stations eventually and local commercial radio was now getting under way. When commercial TV started it did grave damage to the national press and also had affected advertisement revenue of papers in the provinces. 'We must consistently examine our style and content of our newspapers, to ensure that our advertisement salesmen are properly selected and trained – yes, and properly rewarded – so that they, too, will sell systematically and aggressively.'

A Nottingham undertaking decided to come into Leicester under the title of Leicester Trader. Immediately Leicester Shopwindow jumped into attack, doubled its coverage by dividing the city into two halves and going into each half fortnightly with upwards of 50,000 copies a time. The opposition remained apparently undaunted, but they made little impression.

Mr John Thomson retired in 1972 after 18 years on the Hewitt Board and 22 on that of News Holdings, having made a notable contribution throughout the years of change from Hewitt control to Associated Newspapers and later absorption of the Leicester Evening Mail. He had been joined on both Boards a year earlier by Mr J S Wallwork, his successor as Managing Director of the Northcliffe Newspapers Group. Mr Thomson died in 1974. Mr Sanger also left both Boards in 1972 after 18 years' service.

After 20 years of carrying out the duties of the Mercury's theatre correspondent in addition to his main work as a sub-editor, Mr Denis Downes decided to take a rest. The Stage Page was to take a break until a successor was found.

Exactly 50 years to the day since office manager Mr Harry Edwin (Ted) Haylett joined the Leicester Mercury, he was presented with a set of goblets on an inscribed tray by Mr John Fortune. He retired in March 1973, although he continued to show groups around the building.

Mr Harry Heath, Mercury staff photographer for the previous 26 years, retired in March 1973. 'Jock' left with many memories – in his time he photographed every British monarch since King George V, Haile Selassie, King Hussein, Bebe and Ben Lyon and Edward Everett Horton (the film star).

Mercury photographer Richard Elliott was runner-up for the title of Midland Press Photographer of 1973 and received his award from Mr Enoch Powell in May 1973.

Mr George Graham was appointed features editor in April 1973 in succession to Mr O K Smith, who joined East Midlands

Gas as press officer. Mr Graham joined the former Leicester Evening Mail in 1954 from a journalist career in Glasgow.

Preparations began early in 1973 for the centenary of the Leicester Mercury, which was to fall on January 31, 1974. It would have been a great occasion for Mr Vernon Hewitt, but he was seriously ill at his Eastbourne home and he died a few months before the event, in June, at the age of 85. He was chairman from 1927 until his retirement in 1954 and before that managing director from 1911. He succeeded his father and grandfather and their combined service at the head of the company spanned 80 years.

The Mercury welcomed a new Women's Page writer in September 1973. Joan Stephens was already known through her Coffee Break programmes on Radio Leicester.

The next month saw Mr H H Mogford, a journalist with the company, retire after 45 years. For the previous 10 years, he was responsible for the news coverage for the Oadby and Wigston Advertiser.

A dispute between the National Union of Journalists and the Newspaper Society over a new national agreement on pay, hours and conditions presented considerable difficulties for the production of the paper in November. Editorial executives continued to produce full size editions and only slightly curtailed issues of the weekly papers. Readers would notice a reduction in the amount of editorial material, but were assured that executives would give them just as much of the news and regular features that it was possible to handle.

Mr W Leslie Putt was presented with a clock on the completion of 50 years' service as a compositor by Mr John Fortune in January 1974.

The first centenary event was a schools project which was launched a few months before the day. Children in different age groups were required to portray some features running through the last 100 years. It attracted numerous entries from all over the county and resulted in a display of winning entries at Leicester Museum.

For a fortnight before, a commemorative postal cover bearing a facsimile of the front page of the first Leicester Daily Mercury was on sale to the public. Copies were issued free to the staff. All 7,600 covers were posted to carry the special postmark of January 31, 1974. All mail posted in the Mercury's circulation area carried a special slogan: LEICESTER MERCURY CENTENARY – 1874-1974.

A '100 years of News' exhibition opened in the foyer of the new Haymarket Theatre with a civic cocktail party the week before. It comprised 60 photographs of pages from the Mercury showing the outstanding events of the century. It subsequently made a year's

Opposite page: Leicester Mercury on its centenary, January 31, 1974

Below: Centenary First Day Cover, which included a facimile of the first Leicester Daily Mercury front page.

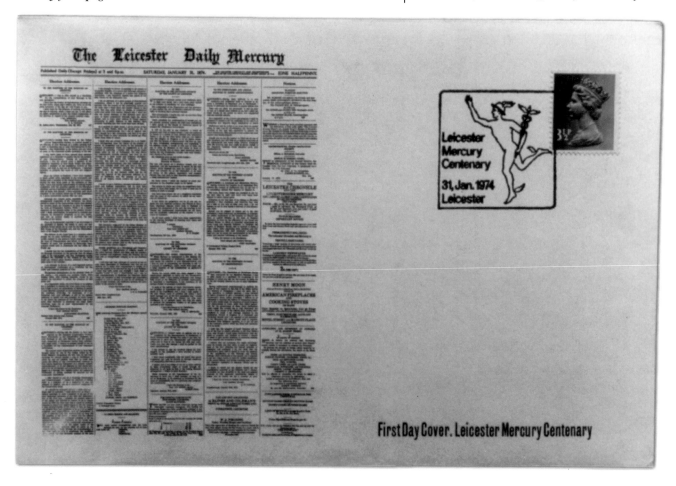

100 YEARS TODAY
LAST NEWS

Leicester Mercury

Established 1874   THURSDAY, JANUARY 31, 1974   3p

BALLOT BEGINS: MASSIVE 'YES' SAY OFFICIALS

THE STRIKE BALLOT of Britain's 260,000 miners was in full swing today —amid claims by union officials that a massive "Yes" vote was being registered.

The day of decision started in the Leicestershire coalfield at a minute past midnight when voting stations were set up at the pitheads. Voting was going on round the clock, to catch the men on the three shifts.

Miners are being asked on their ballot paper to say yes or no on the question of whether their national executive committee should be given authority to call an all out strike to further their wage claim.

At the moment industrial action in the pits is limited to the overtime ban, which in turn has led to restrictions on the use of power and the three-day week.

'Move soon on relativities' — Heath

THE PRIME MINISTER, Mr. Heath, told the Commons today that the Government hoped to move forward soon on the basis of the Pay Board's report on relativities.

But, said Leader of the Opposition, Harold Wilson, proposals in the Pay Board's report had medium and long term implications and did not provide an answer to the coal dispute.

Mr. Wilson said that neither of the Prime Minister's own proposals met the situation either.

Mr. Wilson: "Will you consider the problem of providing the possibility of serious, negotiations after the ballot, if it gives the Executive authority, and before the beginning of any strike."

Mr. Heath said the right way to proceed was to ask the CBI and TUC to agree on principles and then to set up machinery.

To Conservative cheers, Mr Heath asked if it was too much that the miners should accept a Stage Three offer "rather than plunge the nation into a national strike."

TERRIBLE CHOICE

When all the votes are in, the papers will be sent in sealed containers to the Electoral Reform Society, who will be responsible for the count and the result will be known next Tuesday.

The president of the Miners' Council, Mr. Jack Jones, said today: "For the men it is an awesome and terrible choice to have to make, as they have responsibilities to consider.

"But pressure through the ballot box is the only real way to make the view of the men known."

Mr. Jones was speaking from his desk in the offices of the headquarters of the union at Coalville, where he is doing temporary administrative duties during the absence of Mr. Frank Smith, the union secretary, on sick leave.

HARDENED

Polling in the Nottinghamshire coalfield was reported to be "pretty heavy", Mr. Len Martin, the Nottinghamshire miners' secretary, said he was confident of a 75 to 80 per cent vote in favour of a strike.

At Woolley Colliery in the heart of Yorkshire, Mr. Alvin Phillips the union secretary at

the pit, said: "I think we will get about 80 per cent in favour."

He added: "We are usually a moderate pit but the longer this has gone on the more the attitudes of the men have hardened."

At the Agecroft Colliery near Manchester a branch official said almost all the votes had been in favour of a strike.

CRASH PLANE BURNS: 91 ABOARD

A Pan American airliner carrying 91 passengers and crew crashed and burned in Pago Pago in the South Pacific today, an airline spokesman said in New York.

The spokesman said there was no immediate word on survivors or casualties. The Boeing 707 crashed and burned as it came in to land. Weather conditions were bad with heavy rain squalls as the airliner approached the runway.

Sam Goldwyn dies

Hollywood pioneer, Sam Goldwyn died today, aged 91. His film productions included such classics of the silent and talkie eras as "All Quiet On The Western Front," and "Wuthering Heights."

Classrooms ransacked

Vandals broke into Christ the King Roman Catholic School in Glenfield Road, Leicester, last night and ransacked classrooms and stole a small amount of confectionery.

TOMORROW'S WEATHER

Leicester, East Midlands: Becoming cloudy, with rain tonight and tomorrow. Mild. Max 9C (48F).

Outlook: Squally showers and sunny intervals. Windy generally. Temperatures near normal.

Lighting-up: 5.20 p.m. to 7.21 a.m.

Mr. Edwin Lowesby, of the Leicester post office staff, carefully hand stamps the thousands of commemorative covers which are being despatched today to mark the Leicester Mercury's centenary.

Dealings halted in Horizon Midlands

DEALINGS in the shares of Horizon Midlands, the Birmingham-based package tour company, were suspended on the London Stock Exchange today.

The company asked for suspension, pending the result of talks over the future of its parent company, Horizon Holidays.

Travel agencies in and around Leicester were continuing to deal with Horizon Midlands

Mr. Vladimir Raitz is chairman of both companies. He is having discussions with Court Line, the aviation company which already owns Clarksons, the big package tour group.

Horizon Holidays, whose shares are not quoted on the Stock Exchange, is said to be in a loss-making position.

A spokesman for Horizon Midlands stressed today that the company's current position was "very sound indeed."

Horizon Midlands had "always been an entirely autonomous company, both financially and operationally."

It was expected that its profit for the year ending November 30 would repeat the previous year's £473,000. The cash position was "strongly liquid", he added.

Horizon Midlands' bookings, like other operators, have been slower this year than last. But with the current position only some 23 percent to 30 percent down on 1973 it is thought to be faring better than some of its rivals.

Figures issued today show that in 1972 Horizon Midland made the highest profit of any tour company — £473,000 on a turnover of about £6 million.

Early closing

Readers and advertisers are asked to note that, due to the centenary celebrations, the Leicester Mercury offices and the tele-ads department will close half an hour early, at 5 p.m. tomorrow.

Our 100th birthday

The Leicester Mercury is 100 today.

It was on Saturday, January 31, 1874, that the paper's founder, Mr. James Thompson, published the few thousand copies of the first four-page Leicester Daily Mercury.

Today with every one of more than 180,000 copies of the paper is issued a free 40-page souvenir supplement which records the growth of the paper and of the city and county it has served for the past 100 years.

On page 20 today can be found congratulatory messages from the Queen, the Prime Minister, the Leader of the Opposition, and the Leader of the Liberal Party and a special leading article.

A selection of other messages is on page 21. On page 11 there is a reproduction of page one of the first Mercury.

News of the centenary will be carried all over the world today in the mail— by thousands of commemorative covers, bearing a special hand stamp.

Tonight civic leaders, MPs and other public figures will attend a centenary dinner at the Grand Hotel and tomorrow over 1,100 members of the paper's staff and their guests will attend a ball at the De Montfort Hall.

Miners' lodge officials Mr. Albert Robinson (left) and Mr. Roy Rowe, hand strike ballot forms to Mr. John Watson, a banksman, and Mr. Frank Edenbeck (right), a belt fitter, at Snibston Colliery today.

tour of the newspaper's circulation area, showing at libraries, museums and at a number of schools and hospitals.

On the day of Thursday, January 31, there appeared a special 40-page centenary supplement issued with the Mercury and a centenary dinner was held at the Grand Hotel in the evening. The supplement was printed on the newspaper's own presses and traced the history of the Mercury and the development of Leicester generally over the period. The front and back pages and centre spread were in full colour. The main paper contained messages of congratulation from the Queen and the Prime Minister.

The Centenary Dinner was attended by the Lord Lieutenants and High Sheriffs of Leicestershire and Rutland, the Lord Bishop, Vice-Chancellor of the University, the Lord Mayor, the Mayors of Loughborough and Rugby, leaders of all urban and rural districts in the area, members of both Houses of Parliament and representatives of industry and commerce, education, the arts, sport, advertising and newsagents. As Mr Thompson said, when proposing the toast of the guests, it was the most distinguished gathering Leicester had seen in 100 years.

A feature of the dinner, attended by 200 people, was the menu card in the form of a newsboy. Under his arm he carried a miniature measuring three and a half by five inches of the front and back pages of that same night's paper published only a few hours earlier. In the newsboy's bag were six complete miniature newspapers selected

Above: Menu Card featuring a cartoon newsboy, with a miniature Leicester Mercury for January 31, 1974.

Right and opposite page: The Centenary Celebration Dinner.

from the 100 years of the Mercury's life and a small magnifying glass.

The staff were given a champagne lunch in the canteen that day and the following evening there was a buffet supper-dance at the De Montfort Hall for 1,000 people, staff, their guests and pensioners. Each person attending was handed a gilt tie pin or brooch in the form of the god Mercury.

Very shortly after the celebrations, Mr Brian West left for a public relations post with the Littlewoods Organisation in Liverpool. Mr West had taken a particular interest in editorial promotions and introduced the Slimming Sprees and Cook of the Year competitions for women readers. He also devised and organised the Schools Projects Competition, which was part of the paper's centenary celebrations. He was succeeded by Mr Neville Stack, then Editor of the Stockport Advertiser group. He had been a reporter on local papers in the north of England and then a reporter in Fleet Street on the Daily Mirror. He was promoted to northern news editor successively of the People, Daily Herald and, after working on the launch, of IPC's popular-serious broadsheet The Sun (no kin to the present Murdoch product). He had launched a major group of free newspapers in the Manchester area and then joined the Daily Express as senior sub-editor, becoming in charge of photonews. Mr Stack became editor-in-chief

Mercury gifts to the community were announced by the chairman and managing director, Mr John Fortune, at the dinner to mark the centenary.

◆ A cheque for £1,170 to pay for the laundry equipment for the village of CARE (Shangton), a new productive farming community where mentally handicapped boys and girls live and work in a farm community. It was the inspiration of Mr Jack Townsend who put 30 acres of his farm into the establishment of the new village.

◆ A mini bus for the Leicester Social Services Department to be used to transport housebound elderly people for day care. This new experiment, to reverse the tendency for such people to withdraw from life, had been seriously hampered by lack of suitable transport. It was hoped the acquisition of a mini bus will be an important milestone in the development of this personal social service to the city.

◆ A mini bus for the Leicester and District Spastics Society to transport children to the Spastics Day centre, Aylestone, where splendid work was being done in training these children, sometimes for normal schooling. £1,000 to the Leicester Lions Club for the provision of a flatlet in the extension to Lions Lodge, the second home made for old people by the club.

◆ £1,000 to the Leicester Education Committee as an emergency fund to assist city boys and girls at university, whose circumstances suddenly change and who cannot swiftly obtain supplementary payments from any other sources. £1,000 to the Trustees of Bradgate Park for the audio/visual equipment to be installed in the proposed Charnwood Centre for Interpretation at the entrance to Bradgate Park. The centre was being provided to give historial and geological background and information of the fauna and flora of the area.

◆ £1,000 to the Haymarket Theatre to start a fund for the completion of the Studio Theatre. The Haymarket ran out of funds to finish the seating and lighting of the Studio Theatre used for rehearsals, lunch-time and late shows. £1,000 to the Leicestershire Rural Community Council for the supply of public seats in villages and rural areas. Villages and parish meetings were circularised by the Community Council who were arranging the selection and distribution.

◆ £1,000 to the Leicester Society for Handicapped Children to launch an appeal for a home to be used for short term residential care. The home is needed to allow parents of mentally handicapped children to have a holiday in the knowledge that their child was in good hands.

Near right: Mr Neville Stack.

Far right: Mr F Brian Thompson.

1974

◆ Mr Sidney Turner, a former manager of the Mercury stereotype department, died in February. He was 66. He had retired in 1972 after completing nearly 50 years. His father, the late Mr Harry Turner, gave the Leicester Mercury 54 years unbroken service and his brother, Leslie, served 21 years with the firm. Between them they notched up a total of about 120 years.

◆ Mr William Regester, for 39 years a member of the composing room, died in April. He was a City Councillor for eight years and was on the Entertainments Committee at the time of the Coronation.

of the Mercury and its group papers. It was then Britain's tenth biggest provincial daily.

Other top executive changes followed in May 1974. Mr Fortune retired as Chairman and Managing Director, but remained a non-executive director. Glowing tributes made front page news in a special cover to mark his retirement. They came from his contemporaries in many fields and reflected the esteem and affection in which he was so widely held, both throughout the city and county and in his profession. Whenever an editorial contribution, be it picture, story or snappy headline, had caught his eye as being of special merit, he acknowledged it in his own distinctive way. The item that pleased him would be torn out of the paper, marked with a tick, alongside the letters VG and his initials and the scrap of paper was left on the contributor's desk. It was rumoured, but never actually proved, that three such slips presented to the Chief Cashier could be encashed for a £5 note! Two examples of his greatest personal involvements were the exposure of a secret plan to take part of Victoria Park for a civic centre and the prodding of the Ministry to get something done about the conditions at the Bond Street maternity home, which resulted in the magnificent new maternity facilities at the Royal Infirmary. A retirement dinner was held in his honour at the end of April 1974.

The new Chairman was Mr F Brian Thompson, the fourth member of the Hewitt family to hold the post. He relinquished the position of General Manager.

Mr R J R Tyldesley was appointed Managing Director. He had joined the company nine months earlier from the

Newcastle Chronicle and Journal, where he was Assistant Managing Director, responsible for marketing, circulation and advertising sales for the Evening Chronicle, Journal and Sunday Sun.

Mr Leslie Putt retired early in May 1974 after more than 50 years in the printing industry. He had started work as an apprentice compositor with the Evening Mail in 1923, when he was 14.

A stained glass window in Leicester Cathedral in memory of Mr James Thompson, founder of the Mercury, was smashed by vandals in May, 1974. Car wing mirrors had been thrown through the window in the north aisle, leaving hefty holes. The window depicts the Parable of the Talents and has the inscription that was given by Frances Mary Cooper in memory of her brother, the historian James Thompson, FRHS, FSA, who died on May 20, 1877. It had been installed by a London firm of ecclesiastical glaziers in 1880 at a cost of £100.

Mr Vic Soames, chief teletype operator, retired in October after 41 years' service. He was apprenticed to the Blackfiars Press in the days when the printing works were next door to the Mercury offices in Albion Street. He joined the paper as a linotype operator in 1933

Further increases in the cover-charge and advertisement rates became necessary. The price of all newspapers was raised to 4p and the main advertisement rate for the Mercury became £1.60 per single column centimetre (approximately £4 per single column inch). The cost of newsprint rose to nearly £150 per tonne and for the first time a Mercury with 64 pages was published. Successive governments failed to curb inflation and the cover price of all papers had doubled to 8p by 1978 and by the following year the advertisement rate of the Mercury was more than doubled too, at £3.50 per single column centimetre.

Turnover at £10 million and trading profit £2.5 million in 1979 were also twice what they were in 1973. The wage bill was up by 160% on a staff of similar size, some of the increase being due to payment for extra skills introduced with computerisation. The price of newsprint rose from £150 to £256.

Editor Mr Neville Stack seized upon his first campaign in July 1974 when Mrs Irene Pollard mentioned cleaning up Leicester in her mayor-making speech. He invited readers to have a hand in Leicester's Big Clean Up. Readers could actually help direct council workmen to black spots which disfigured the city. The aim was to establish a partnership which should regain for Leicester her proud pre-war title of the cleanest city in the Midlands.

It was becoming increasingly obvious that readers wanted to be even more involved in their local newspaper. To nurture that feeling a number of things were done in the 1970s. More trophies were offered, notably for sailing and indoor cricket; an annual tailor-made de-luxe holiday for readers was run, to North America and the Far East initially; a yearly Leicester Mercury lecture on a communications subject formed part of the programme of the prestigious Leicester Literary and Philosophical Society. In 1975 a small monthly luncheon in the boardroom was started at which the directors and editor were hosts to important people from throughout the circulation area, men and women representative of local and national government, industry and commerce, the church, the trade unions, sport, education and the arts. The annual visit to lunch by the Lord Mayor and Lady Mayoress, started a few years earlier, continued.

The paper was selected by the Central Office of Information as the most appropriate provincial newspaper to be visited by representatives of Governments overseas, particularly from the Third World, who came to Britain from time to time to study public relations and the media.

The paper organised a referendum on a plan to spend more than £6 million on buying, adapting and equipping a new Civic Centre. When the poll was announced, the ruling Labour Party on the City Council, the sponsors of the scheme, poured cold water on the referendum, saying that only opponents would bother to vote. It was thought particularly significant that more people voted than supported any single party in the

Left: Mr Douglas Goodlad.

election which put the present City Council in office. The 97 per cent rejection of the scheme was a crystal clear indication to all who held political office that whether the scheme was a bargain or not, it was one they did not want to afford at a time of financial restraint. The Labour Group decided however to go ahead with the plan.

Leicester Mercury compositor-stonehand Mr Andrew Spriggs retired in June 1975 after a printing career spanning 51 years, 39 years with the Evening Mail and Mercury. He was presented with a dome clock.

Conservative leader Mrs Margaret Thatcher visited the newspaper offices on December 1, 1975, where she was received by the Chairman, Mr F Brian Thompson, the Managing Director, Mr R J R Tyldesley and the Editor, Mr Neville Stack. She toured the editorial and production departments and discussed local matters with members of the staff.

Mr F Brian Thompson presented a pair of inscribed silver goblets to Mr Allan Veasey, who was in charge of the company's purchase accounts department, to mark his completion of 50 years with the company. He had been organist and choirmaster at St Deny's Church, Evington, where the author had been a member of the choir, for the previous 21 years.

After joining the paper 48 years previously as an office boy, Mr Frank Bailey, chief scrutineer, retired in December 1975. He was presented with a portable radio. Under his captaincy of the Mercury cricket team, the team twice won both the second

1974

◆ A presentation was made to Mr Douglas Goodlad at a ceremony at the Grand Hotel in October to mark his 25 years' editorship of the Leicester Chronicle. It took the form of an inscribed silver salver. Mr Malcolm McIntosh was his assistant editor.

◆ It was in 1974 that the first real steps were taken towards comprehensive computerisation. Teletypesetter operators had punched unjustified tape since 1968 and this tape had then passed through a computer, more accurately called the Muset tape justifier. Then in 1973 the first photo-composing machines were installed, gradually added to and the hot metal process began to be phased out. Plastic pattern-plates followed in 1974 to cut out block making from photo-composed material.

◆ A Derby organisation began publishing the Loughborough and Coalville Trader and the Mercury management immediately responded with a Loughborough Shopwindow.

THE CRUNCH ELECTION RESULTS EXTRA

Leicester Mercury

Established 1874   FRIDAY, OCTOBER 11, 1974   4p

LABOUR SCRAPE IN

HOW THE PARTIES STAND

	SEATS WON	GAINS	LOSSES
LAB.	319	20	1
CONS.	275	2	22
LIB.	9	1	3
OTHERS	20	5	2

Last Parliament: Labour 301, Conservatives 296, Liberals 14, Scottish Nat. Party 7, Ulster Unionists 10, Others 7.

A marginal seat gives Wilson his overall majority

MR. HAROLD WILSON is back in No. 10—and that's official. The result that took him over the top came from Gloucestershire West this afternoon when Labour held the marginal constituency by 409 votes.

This was the 318th Labour seat—the magic figure for the barest overall majority. The computer-based prediction was a Labour majority of three.

It will be the eighth Labour Government in Britain—and Mr. Wilson has headed four of them. He has served more terms than any Prime Minister since Gladstone.

The election result has been a bitter blow for Mr. Edward Heath who has now lost three of the four electoral campaigns he has waged since becoming Conservative leader.

It has also been disappointing for Mr. Jeremy Thorpe's Liberals, mounting their strongest challenge from Labour's postwar challenge. They now seem likely to have fewer MPs than in the last Parliament.

The fourth biggest party in terms of candidates — the National Front — has a dismal showing. It was a story of one lost deposit after another.

But the nationalist parties of Scotland and Wales fared remarkably well. Both had net

Mr. Wilson said Labour would carry out its policies — even with a small overall majority.

Only twice since the war has a government — both times Labour — been returned with a single figure majority.

In 1950 they had a margin of eight, and in 1964 only four; and neither lasted more than half its term.

Liberals lost two seats, including Woolwich East once held by Labour defector Mr. Christopher Mayhew, who failed to capture Bath.

Mr. Mayhew, who pushed the Liberal vote in Bath to 16,348—the highest Liberal poll for at least 50 years — but failed to take the seat from the Tories, said today he was ready to fight there again.

Liberals fulfilled their expec-

★ Continued on Page 25

FIRST CITY MP TO BE DEFEATED SINCE 1945

IN LABOUR'S victory hat-trick in Leicester, Mr. Tom Boardman, Conservative MP for the past seven years, became the first city Member of Parliament to be defeated since the historic Labour landslide of 1945.

All the previous changes in Leicester since the last war have been due to either electoral boundary changes or voluntary retirements.

Man responsible for this historic electoral landmark in South Leicester is 34-year-old Leicester Polytechnic lecturer Mr. Jim Marshall, who describes himself as a "moderate Socialist".

Mr. Marshall, who is Leicester City Council's leader, had a narrow majority of 1,133 over Mr. Boardman, a former Minister of Industry and Chief Secretary to the Treasury.

Second attempt

Leicester South was a cliff-hanger right through the count, but a smiling Mr. Marshall finally emerged as victor at his second attempt.

In West Leicester, Labour's Greville Janner, as expected, cruised safely home with an increased majority.

And over in East Leicester, Mr. Tom Bradley made it three for Labour by comfortably holding his seat.

All the Liberal and National Front candidates in the three city divisions had low polls and lost their deposits.

Farr in

Mr. John Farr held Harborough for the Conservatives with an increased majority of 13,289 despite polling fewer votes than in February.

Dr. Norman Reynolds, who took

Liberals to second place last time, just succeeded in holding off a strong challenge from Labour's Mr. Bob Briant by about 600 votes.

But the Liberal's share of the vote was down by nearly 3,000.

Mr. Briant, despite taking third place in a three-cornered fight, was the only candidate to increase his party's vote.

The total poll was substantially down—by about nine per cent—on last February.

Mr. Farr said: "In a low poll, I am very pleased to have increased my majority. It's a good reward for all the efforts of my workers."

HARBOROUGH
(Feb. Con. 12,473).

J. A. Farr (C)	......	25,776
N. G. Reynolds (L)	......	12,567
R. L. W. Briant (Lab.)	......	11,934
	Majority	13,289

£10,000 BET GOES DOWN

AINTREE racecourse owner, Mr. Bill Davies is a disappointed man today—he had a £10,000 bet on a Tory victory.

At odds of 6-4 with Ladbrokes, that would have made about £25,000, which the chairman of the Walton Group of companies in Liverpool planned to give to blind children and battered babies.

"I'm mainly disappointed for the children," he said today.

"It probably would have been better to give them the £10,000 outright, but that is after the event.

"We will try to make it up to the children somehow.

Man held in 'hijacked taxi' case

A MAN was detained by Leicestershire police last night following the alleged hi-jacking of a taxi in Nottingham's Market Square.

The taxi driver alleges that a man got into his car and told him to drive to Strelley village on the outskirts of Nottingham, but then changed his mind and forced him to drive to Leicester at gun point.

The car travelled on the M.1 to the Leicester Forest East exit, and from there to Glen Parva, where the taxi driver was forced to get out. The gunman drove on towards the city centre where the car was later stopped by police.

Nottinghamshire CID officers were waiting this morning for the man, who is believed to have been carrying a shotgun, to be brought from Leicester for questioning.

No further details of the case are being released until further investigations have been completed.

Kenneth Lewis coasts home in Rutland

MR. KENNETH LEWIS romped home with a 6,000 majority to retain Rutland and Stamford for the Conservatives.

ELECTION— on other PAGES

● Tories hold Blaby and Melton—Page 5.
● How the city voted—Page 7.
● Party M.P. sets record—Page 17.
● Nail-biting atmosphere held

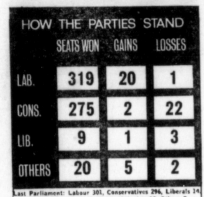

HAROLD WILSON

gains with only a few results still to come.

The Prime Minister arrived at 10 Downing Street at lunchtime. He said there would be a "victory" party at Transport House this afternoon.

Mr. Wilson's confidence in the survival of his new Government is based on his belief that the Opposition will not want to provoke another general election in the near future.

Chief Whip Mr. Bob Mellish said on television that with a majority of just five "I would expect the party to battle on much longer than in 1964."

TORIES HOLD BOSWORTH

MR. ADAM BUTLER (Conservative) retained Bosworth with a majority of

division and the first division of the printing trades' Spicer League. It also won the League's knockout cup.

Mr George Nunney, greyhound racing correspondent and sporting 'jack-of-all-trades,' retired from the sports room in January 1976, after more than 50 years's service. A native of Leicester, he was the highly successful 'Advocate' – the paper's No. 1 racing tipster.

Talking of racing tipsters, sports editor David Welch was presented with a tankard in March 1976 to commemorate his achievement in going 'through the card' at Doncaster races. His six winners paid accumulative odds of 503-1!

In March 1976, the Mercury supported local store Lewis's when they celebrated their 40th anniversary. The paper reproduced the front page of March 20, 1936, to show the turbulent times that prevailed when Lewis's opening ceremony took place. In fact, the ceremony was relayed from the wireless tower (the tower which still survives after city centre development) to other stores in Liverpool, Birmingham, Manchester, Leeds and Glasgow – quite a feat in 1936.

Mr Alec Eves, who had been in charge of the industrial desk for the previous 25 years, retired in May 1976. Hosiery manufacturers and representatives of the hosiery unions with whom Mr Eves had been associated for many years gave a reception in his honour and a silver goblet was presented to him by Mr Stephen Cook, sales director of D Byford and Co Ltd.

51-year-old Mr David W Partridge, deputy news editor, collapsed and died at work on May 22, 1976. He was well-known throughout Leicestershire, in newspaper offices all over England and in armed forces units all over the world – units he visited in his capacity as military correspondent for the newspaper. News editor Lawrie Simpkin wrote:

'It was typical of David Partridge that the office was tidy and set up for another busy day, when colleagues found him. Although he was at times an outrageous extrovert, David was also a master of detail and a meticulous administrator whose knowledge of Leicester people no reference library will ever replace. He was most of all, a devoted husband and father, a good friend and a man whose middle name should have been loyalty. He was always willing, as well as able, to overlook faults in the young and to recognise talent – although not one who suffered fools and humbugs easily. A 24-hours-a-day journalist,

he had no time for anything less and defended with vigour any erosion of his own high personal standards. The Leicester Mercury editorial floor will never be the same. And it is a tremendous loss to all privileged to list David Partridge as a friend.'

A new service for readers began on June 1, 1976. On the centre page, with the other weather statistics, appeared the local pollen count, compiled by experts at a Derby laboratory. It was to appear daily during the hay fever seasons.

The inaugural rally of the Mercury Editorial Department Cycling Club took place in July 1976. Reporters were reputedly a lazy lot, wont to shun all forms of exercise and more likely to get out the car to ride down to the corner shop for a packet of fags than risk the tiring walk. So, it will be understood that when our staffmen – and girls – formed a cycling club it was an event demanding some attention and meant, above all, that the humble bike's return to popularity was definitely established. For the record, it can be said that the club's initial run was an 18-miler to Cropston. Having nursed their aching limbs back to near normality, the pedalling scribblers planned to set off next to Ashby Folville where, on arrival – as at Cropston – the local brew was to be liberally sampled!

Two former journalists shared the limelight when BBC TV's programme, Midlands Today, went on the air on July 30, 1976. Tony Francis had been introducing the programme while the regular 'anchor man,' Tom Coyne, was on holiday, and was joined by Peter Windows, who, with Tony Francis, worked on the Leicester Mercury in 1969 and 1970.

The head of the purchase accounts department, who had worked his way up from starting as an office boy, retired in July 1976 after 50 years' service. Mr Allan Veasey had a great interest in music and had been organist and choirmaster at St Deny's Church, Evington, since 1955. He was presented with a car radio and an LP by Mercury chairman, Mr Brian Thompson.

The author of the book 90 Minutes at Entebbe, which was published and was on sale less than a month after the Israelis' daring rescue of hostages from Uganda, was a member of the reporting staff of the Mercury. William Stevenson joined just after the war and then left to join Fleet Street. In 1976, he was based in New York and had become a familiar face on Canadian television. His previous best-seller was A Man Called Intrepid.

◆ Mr Steve Kenny wrote from The Chase in East Goscote. His first full-time job at the age of 16 was with the Leicester Mercury in 1969. He served six years apprenticeship as a compositor – all the type was assembled by hand or machine in a room of approximately 50-60 people. He was one of the first apprentices to be trained on the new computerised photo-typesetting machines. He clearly remembers what an occasion it was when the Mercury celebrated its 100th birthday, with a huge party held for all its employees. He has fond memories of his time spent at the Mercury up to 1975 as he met his wife, Susan, there – she worked in the canteen. 'I can still remember the lads I worked with asking if I was going for a quick nibble when I went to the canteen!' They have now been married for nearly 24 years with two grown-up sons. He is still employed in the printing trade, having run his own business for the past ten years – 'the Mercury taught me well!'

Opposite page: Leicester Mercury of Friday October 11, 1974 following Labour's election victory.

Overleaf: Front page from July 1, 1976.

EXTRA

Leicester Mercury

Established 1874 THURSDAY, JULY 1, 1976 5p

BELVOIR RICH IN COAL
—NOW BATTLE LOOMS

Hijackers say 'We'll kill the Israelis'

Drifting race yacht riddle

A YACHT competing in the Royal Western Observer single-handed trans-Atlantic race has been found with no-one on board, the race organisers reported in London today.

An announcement said the Galloping Gael was found at sea by the S.S. Nisna 34 hours ago. It was boarded and personal possessions were identified.

The yacht, which was crewed by Canadian Mike Hasagan, was taken in tow, but later broke away in fog and could not be retrieved.

MOTORISTS trying to beat the heat are making themselves ill. Drivers of some estate cars have been opening the large window at the back in a bid to keep cool — but the move means exhaust fumes are sucked straight into the car.

POLICE cadet Andrew Gedge, who was treated with ice yesterday in a desperate attempt to bring his temperature down after collapsing from heat stroke was "slightly improved" this morning in Aberystwyth General Hospital.

ABOUT a thousand British Airways passengers spent the night in hotels near the airport after a heat-wave walkout by ticket staff at Heathrow last night, caused by hot tempers.

THE Jamaican government has banned Young England cricketers who played in South Africa from playing in Jamaica when the side starts a Caribbean tour next month.

POLISH newspaper Trybuna Ludu reported that two men were killed and 75 policemen injured during last week's riots against projected food price increases.

June temperatures highest on record

THE average daily temperatures recorded at Watnall weather centre last month were the highest since records began in 1941.

The average daily maximum temperature was 22.7C (72.9F) and on five consecutive days the temperature reached 30C (86F) which was the longest such spell in the Watnall records.

June was the fifteenth successive month of rainfall shortage with only 18.00 mms (0.71ins.) compared with the normal average of 53 mms (2.09ins).

LEICESTER - BY - THE - SEA — that's the Skegness area during the next few weeks.

Thousands of Leicester and county families will be going to the popular East Coast resorts for their get-away-from-it-all break. It's tradition and it's good fun to boot.

Getting away does not mean missing out on the local news for the Leicester Mercury is again mounting this novel — a special edition will be available at Skegness Mablethorpe and other resorts from Monday.

If you went down to the woods — at Swithland yesterday afternoon — you might have met five-year-old Jane Wilkins and her teddy bear, because she was there with her friends from the village school at a Teddy Bears' Picnic. (See centre page).

Neilson guilty of murder

DONALD NEILSON was found guilty today of murdering the 17-year-old Shropshire heiress, Lesley Whittle.

The jury at Oxford Crown Court took 1 hour 55 minutes to reach its unanimous verdict.

Neilson, standing in the dock and staring straight ahead, showed no reaction when the foreman announced that the jury of 10 men and two women had found him guilty of murder — a verdict which brought gasps and a short burst of applause from some people in the public gallery.

Neilson, a 39-year-old joiner from Grangefield Avenue, Thornbury, Bradford, has admitted kid-napping, Lesley in January last year from her home at Highley and demanding a £50,000 ransom from her mother.

Mr. Justice Mars Jones told him: "I do not propose to pass sentence on you, Donald Neilson. There are certain outstanding matters which I must deal with first."

The judge said that when he had done that, he would hear counsel and pass "such sentences as I think proper" on the kidnap and ransom charges.

ONE OF BRITAIN'S largest ever finds of coal is almost certain to be mined from beneath the lush green pastures of the Vale of Belvoir within the next ten years.

That is the clear impression gained yesterday after the Coal Board announced that known reserves in the Vale amount to a vast 360 million tons — equivalent to the largest oil find in the 40s field and bigger than the giant Selby coalfield in Yorkshire.

Although the board will not make a final decision about the Vale for at least six months, it seems highly unlikely that they would turn their backs on such a rich harvest of black gold.

A revealing comment from Mr. Donald Davies, director of the South Nottinghamshire area of the National Coal Board, was: "I cannt believe this nation doesn't want 360 million tons of coal."

Any plans to sink a mine in the Vale, which boasts areas of outstanding beauty, is bound to arouse opposition.

The Duke of Rutland, whose Belvoir Castle home towers over the area, questioned the need for a mine in the area when the country would be getting millions of extra tons of coal from Selby and also had available resources of oil and gas.

Speaking as the county councillor for the Vale of Belvoir the Duke said: "Large areas of this country have already been destroyed by the industrial revolution. Is it really necessary that the Vale should be seriously affected when the requirements for energy in the future appear uncertain.

He said that if coal mining operations got underway it would be impossible to correct the damage which would be caused to the character of the Vale.

'SORT OUT POLICY'

He added that he and the people of the area accepted that there were large deposits of coal, but he thought it should be kept as a reserve for the future or if it was necessary to mine, then the operations should be carried out from the nearby existing colliery at Cotgrave, just over the Nottinghamshire border.

The Duke was fearful of the great harm that could be caused to the area by the development of a mine and considered that the structure of the development which would be 225 foot high would be a blot on the landscape.

He claimed that it would be a difficult task to deal with the spoil from the mine and whatever the Coal Board did in the way of landscaping it would take years to even attempt to correct the impact on the visual amenities.

He also thought that a mine

★ Continued on Page 21
See leading article, Battle for Belvoir — page 22.

Heatwave means sweated labour for some

WORK for foundrymen, laundry cleaners and bakers in this current heatwave is sweated labour.

Temporary measures introduced to cope with the stifling conditions have been an earlier start to the working day for foundry workers at Russell and Sons Ltd, in Bath Lane and for laundry cleaners at Sketchley branches.

Mr. W. A. Chambers, the general manager of Squires and Kintons, bakers, said although the modern ovens are insulated they do generate some heat and one problem is keeping the water and flour cool for the baking processes.

Mr. Chambers said the doughmakers and the oven men were working in conditions of 150°F and there was little they could do to cool them, because fans would make the bread stale.

Mr. Barry Taylor, the district manager of Sketchley's said they may introduce air conditioning in their branches. Employees were starting at 6.30 a.m. instead of 8.00 a.m. and were given several breaks.

Foundry workers at Russell and Sons have sweated it out. Windows and doors have been opened at their Bath Lane premises to cool down the heat. Mr. David Hughes, the company's personnel officer, said the 300 men have been working in 108°F temperatures.

The problems in Leicester General Hospital's kitchens are being sorted out. Staff last week threatened to walk out, because of lack of ventilation. The windows have been taken out.

THE pro-Palestinian hijackers at Uganda's Entebbe Airport said today they had decided to kill all the Israelis among their more than 200 hostages if their demands were not met, diplomatic sources in Kampala said today.

They are demanding the release of 53 prisoners held in five countries.

Later Uganda Radio today broadcast a statement by the Popular Front for the Liberation of Palestine (PFLP) saying it had agreed to free all hostages except Israelis and those carrying dual nationality.

The statement said the deadline for killing the remaining hostages had been extended from 1200 GMT today until 1100 GMT (1200 BST) on Sunday.

Special Cabinet

In Tel Aviv, Prime Minister Yitzhak Rabin called a special session of his cabinet to consider the hijackers' demand.

The Cabinet met as a ministerial defence committee, a legal move to prevent information being leaked, and followed a meeting between Mr. Rabin and three ministers dealing with the affair.

Israel has offered to negotiate with the terrorists and is prepared to release "a certain number" of Palestinian prisoners, the Israeli Embassy said in Paris.

There are believed to be 83 Israelis among the hostages. Previously there have been conflicting reports on their number. Uganda Radio, quoting President Idi Amin, has said there are 145 Israelis or Jews among the hostages. Reports from Tel Aviv have said more than 70 Israelis are involved.

WEATHER FORECAST

Leicester and East Midlands: Mostly sunny and dry, very hot. max. temp. 31C (88F).
Outlook: Hot and sunny.
Light-up: 10.08 p.m. - 4.10 a.m.

Read the Mercury by the sea

July 5, until Saturday, July 31. (See page 30 for the selling points.)

It will be in a different form from normal editions, containing outside pages with the latest news, pictures, race card and TV and radio programmes, and inside that part of the previous day's Leicester Mercury we send while on the East Coast.

Your holiday will be made all the happier by keeping up to date with the home news.

And this, of course, applies to all Leicester Mercury readers wherever they go. The Leicester Mercury can be posted anywhere to your holiday address.

All you have to do is to tele-phone Leicester 50055 at any time up to 9.0 p.m. today or tomorrow and on Saturday up to 12 noon and state your name and home address and telephone number, your holiday address and the dates on which you want the Mercury sent.

The cost is £1 a week including postage of 19p a day. You will be invoiced later.

One of Leicester's best-known journalists, Mrs Madge Castle, died in October 1976, aged 78. Before she joined the Leicester Chronicle in 1946, she had written for women's magazines. She wrote for the Mercury when deputising for her friend Kaye Almey and her last work was for the Leicester Advertiser and its Oadby and Wigston associate.

The Lord Mayor of Leicester, Mr Bernard Toft, spoke at a luncheon he gave to the printing industry of Leicester to mark the Quincentenary of William Caxton in October, 1976. 'For millions of people, even in this television era, there is nothing to replace a good story unfolded in the printed page.' Mr Brian Thompson presented a limited edition Caxton commemorative plate to the Lord Mayor on behalf of guests at the luncheon.

The Mercury advertising rates in 1975 were the second lowest of all evening newspapers in the British Isles, it was revealed in a 1976 survey conducted by the Evening Newspaper Advertising Bureau. Mr R J F Tyldesley, managing director, commented: 'Despite the pressures of inflation, this confirms our success in achieving the lowest possible cost service to the benefit of all concerned.'

Employee fans of the freckle-faced teenager Lena Zavaroni were delighted that she was able to tour the Mercury offices in December 1976. She was due to appear at the Lorraine Charity annual ball the next day.

Eddie Lakin, the Mercury's senior photographer, found himself in front of the camera on December 21, 1976, when he retired after more than 30 years with the paper. It was fitting that his last job was to visit Leicester fishing tackle shop proprietor, Mr Tommy Wadsworth, who, like Mr Lakin, is retiring after 30 years in his occupation.

David Icke, who began a career in journalism with the Leicester Advertiser, later transferring to the Mercury, landed a lucrative two-year contract working with Jimmy Hill's soccer mission in Saudi Arabia at the end of 1976. He was to help set up a framework of soccer leagues and coaching in the oil-rich Middle East.

Journalist Mac Cherry, Coalville's 'Mr News' for 31 years, retired after a career spanning 50 years. He received sets of spanners and sockets for car maintenance work from the Editor, Mr Neville Stack. He also received a miniature miners' lamp from Mr Martin Ryan, Leicestershire miners' president, when he went to cover a presentation to retiring employees of Desford Colliery.

The first Celebrity Authors' Lunch took place in the autumn of 1977. It was held twice a year and within 18 months had become so popular that it was heavily over-subscribed. Book publishers rated it one of the top three literary lunches held and the best of the small number run by newspapers. The Bishop of Leicester described it as an important contribution to the cultural life of Leicester. The first authors were Margaret Powell, Paul Jennings and E W Swanton.

In Loughborough, it was decided to merge the Monitor and Shopwindow in October 1977 with the new title Loughborough News and it was to be delivered free to 32,000 homes in the area. Mr Alec Strachan of Loughborough wrote fearing the freedom of the press in the Loughborough area would suffer a serious blow with the demise of the Monitor after 120 years.

Mr John Stone was appointed Industrial Editor in November 1977. He had joined the staff in 1971 after previously being Press Officer of the Aero Engine Division of Rolls-Royce.

Mr Jim Wheeler, composing department manager, retired in February 1978 after more than 50 years in the newspaper industry. For the previous 12 months he had been concentrating on the changeover to the new computerised production techniques. He joined the Leicester Mail as an apprentice in the composing room in 1927.

Cartoonist RAP also retired at the beginning of 1978. Ralph Pugsley joined the publishers of the Leicester Mercury as a young reporter with the Loughborough Monitor. After the war, he was appointed the Mercury's official cartoonist, in succession to another set of initials, RBD.

The Mercury installed a new digital clock on top of its building in St George Street in May 1978. Mr James Brett, of Hird Brown of Bolton, the electronics engineers who made the quartz crystal clock, said: 'Basically it's an ordinary digital clock, but instead of being the size of a mantelpiece clock, it has been extended and the power level increased.' The face is composed of a series of 40-watt lamps, with 35 lamps to each 24 inches light digit. If there is a power failure, a special battery back-up means that the moment the clock lights up again, it will give the correct time. The temperature is measured at fixed intervals by an electronic probe.

A reception in honour of the Leicester Mercury's retiring chairman, Mr F Brian Thompson, was held on May 16, 1978, at the Lord Mayor's Rooms in Leicester. It was given by the Lord Mayor, Mr Bert Baker, and

1978

◆ From March 1978, the Leicester Mercury roof was the site of the newspaper's own climatological station. Weather figures were to be taken from the station by a member of the newsroom every morning. Previously, the figures came partly from Watnall in Nottinghamshire and partly from a local expert, Mr Jonathan Wilshere, on the outskirts of Evington.

◆ In May 1978, Miss May Pearson, a well-known personality in Leicester before and during the war years, died at the age of 86. For 19 years, she wrote the Mercury's women's page diary, under the pen-name of Rita Wakefield. She became a household name in the thirties and was in great demand as a visitor to and speaker at women's organisations in the city and county. Her sister, Monica, also a journalist, was a member of the editorial staff for a time until she moved to London.

◆ The following month, Mrs Elfreda Barton, wife of the late Mr C T Barton, former chairman and joint managing director, died aged 79. Mrs Barton served during and after the war with the Leicestershire branch of the Red Cross. Mr Barton died in March 1963.

Above right: Mr J S Wallwork.

Opposite page: Leicester Mercury from Monday August 27, 1979.

many distinguished personalities were among the guests. Mr Baker said:

'I am pleased to be able to say thank you to you for all that you have done towards the welfare of Leicester over the long number of years that you have served the Leicester Mercury. It would be unusual for us to be always entirely satisfied with the contents of your newspaper, but I think it is true to say that the people of Leicester do enjoy their Mercury and while it has a very large circulation nevertheless I am pleased to say that it has retained over the years those essentials which are so necessary if a newspaper is to be termed 'local'.'

Mr Thompson said:

'Any success the Mercury has achieved has always been the result of teamwork. And I believe it now has as good a team as it has ever had; one that has brought it safely during the past years into the electronic age which Fleet Street still strives for. More than ten per cent of the current staff have exceeded 25 years service and we have many staff with 40 years or more service. The Leicester Mercury has always campaigned and criticised and it has always been prepared to accept criticism. I hope we have been a thriving and integral part of Leicester. The Mercury will never claim to be always right, but I know it will always be sincere.' On May 25, 1978, Mr George Farnham, chairman of Leicestershire County Council, paid a special tribute to Mr Thompson. He hosted a retirement dinner for him at County Hall and said: 'Brian Thompson, you have brought to the chairmanship of the Leicester Mercury an involvement in the life of Leicestershire which has extended far beyond the realms of journalism. The philanthropic and social work with which you have long been associated will, we hope, continue.'

Mr Thompson actually retired on June 2, 1978, after a career which spanned 47 years and began as a trainee reporter. Although he himself was born in Surrey and educated privately by Miss Enid Blyton, at that time a nursery governess, his mother was a native of Leicester. She was the daughter of Mr Francis Hewitt, who bought the Leicester Mercury from Mr James Thompson three years after it was founded in 1874. His departure marked the end of the Hewitt family's involvement extending over 105

years. The Editor, Mr Neville Stack, was appointed to the Board.

The new elected chairman was Mr J S Wallwork, a director since 1971. As managing director of Northcliffe Newspapers Group, he was involved in a wide range of newspaper activity in many parts of the country. He was also a director of radio and publishing companies.

News Holdings Ltd, already the owners of a small part of Hewitt's 10% Preferred Ordinary Shares, made a bid for the remainder. Their offer of 145p per share was accepted. At the same time it was decided by News Holdings to make an offer of 94p per share for the publicly-owned 8% Preference Shares. This too was accepted and so, on June 30, 1978, F Hewitt & Son (1927) Ltd ceased being a public company after 50 years and became a wholly-owned subsidiary of News Holdings Ltd, itself a wholly-owned subsidiary of Associated Newspapers Group Ltd.

In June, 1978, columnist Joan Stephens had been arguing strongly for the introduction of a 'well woman's clinic' in Leicester. She had interviewed experts as well as ordinary women and had travelled to London to try for herself the benefits of what she advocates. Hundreds of women turned up at a rally at De Montfort Hall organised by the community health council to demonstrate the interest that was aroused by her forceful campaign.

Mr William Bagworth retired in July, 1978, after 51 years with the Mercury. For the previous 16 years he had worked in the reading room checking proofs of the day's stories.

Leicester Mercury

EXTRA

Established 1874 — MONDAY, AUGUST 27, 1979 — 8p

MOUNTBATTEN KILLED IN BOAT EXPLOSION

EARL MOUNTBATTEN

EARL MOUNTBATTEN OF BURMA, uncle of the Queen and the Duke of Edinburgh was killed today in an explosion in his boat off the County Sligo coast in the Irish Republic, police in Dublin reported.

Police said the explosion happened five minutes after Lord Mountbatten and his party had set off from Mullaghmore Harbour in County Sligo.

Police said that with Lord Mountbatten were Lord and Lady Brabourne and the Dowager Lady Brabourne, and, it was believed, Lord and Lady Brabourne's sons Timothy and Nicholas. It was thought boatman Paul Maxwell died in the blast.

Early unconfirmed reports indicated that one of the boys, Nicholas, was missing after the explosion.

Lord Louis Mountbatten, as he was more popularly known, was taking his usual annual holiday — boating and fishing — in the Irish Republic.

He was staying at Classiebawn Castle at Cliffony, Co. Sligo, and had been there for three weeks.

Police said the explosion happened five minutes after Lord Mountbatten (79) and his party had set off from Mullaghmore Harbour.

Earl Mountbatten was perhaps the most highly decorated man in the Western world.

His peerage was created at the end of the last war shortly before he was appointed Viceroy of India, later Governor General of the sub-continent.

He was Chief of Combined Operations for the services from 1942-43, and Supreme Allied Commander in South East Asia —the role for which he was best remembered among British troops—from 1943 to 1946.

Former Leicester Chief Constable Sir Robert Mark worked closely with Earl Mountbatten in the compiling of the Mountbatten report into prison conditions in the 1960s.

The Leicester Mercury broke the news of the Tragedy to Sir Robert at lunchtime today and he said: "I am shattered. He was a wonderful and very intelligent man."

Sir Robert was seconded from his chief constable's post by the Home Office to work with Earl Mountbatten in the compilation of the report.

"I kept in touch with him over the years and never failed to be impressed with this wonderful, wonderful man."

Lord Louis was married in 1922 to Dame Edwina Ashley, who died in 1960. He has two daughters, Lady Patricia, now Baroness Brabourne, and Lady Pamela, now married to Mr. David Nightingale Hicks.

Affectionately known as Lord Louis, Earl Mountbatten has been personal Aide-de-Camp to the Queen since her coronation in 1953, and is acknowledged as being the Royal Family's favourite uncle.

He was First Sea Lord and Chief of Naval Staff from 1955 to 1959, and Chief of Defence Staff from 1959-1965.

The Duke of Rutland said: "He was a charming man with a wonderful sense of humour. He was a very human and got along with everyone, whether important or not. Mountbatten was a great sailor and in a way a great statesman. He will be a great loss to the country."

Drivers ignored our cries for help – death crash youth

A HOUGHTON-ON-THE-HILL youth died in hospital today after the car he was driving crashed off the main A47 near the village last night.

Three of his close friends, all from Houghton, miraculously escaped from the Ford Granada car which hit a hedge at the side of the road and overturned.

The dead youth, 18-year-old Paul Timothy Simpson, of 4 Forsell's End, Houghton, was taking his friends home in his father's car after a day at the air show at Stoughton.

His father, Mr Ken Simpson, the general manager of the Leicester Able Jack DIY store, had a stall at the air show.

The others, who were discharged from Leicester Royal Infirmary today with minor injuries, were Mark Walker (17), and his brother Stephen (16), the sons of Mr. and Mrs Fred Walker of the Black Horse, Houghton, and Stephen Lowe, (15), the son of Mr. and Mrs. Martin Lowe, of 19 Northway, Houghton.

Mark Walker today criticised motorists who ignored their cries for help.

"My brother Stephen climbed out and found us and then tried to flag people down but several cars just went straight past."

"Eventually two cars stopped and one of the drivers was a radio ham who used his equipment to call the police and ambulance service.

"We don't know who he is except that he works for Cowlings. We are very grateful to him."

Paul, who formerly lived in Oadby, was a keen scout and with his three friends was a member of Houghton Venture Scouts. His mother, Mrs. Shiela Simpson, is a guider with the Houghton Girl Guides.

WEATHER

Leicester and East Midlands: Scattered showers, dry tomorrow. Rather cloudy, some bright intervals. Wind north west light. Rather cool, max. 16 to 18C (61 to 64F).

Outlook: Mostly dry with bright or sunny intervals.

Light-up: 8.41 p.m.-5.38 a.m.

Cooked meals to end in all county schools

THE PRESENT cooked school meals system will end in all Leicestershire secondary schools from January 1 next year — and in the meantime six schools will operate a pilot scheme to provide a substitute snacks service.

Negotiations are proceeding at the moment with the heads of the schools to operate the pilot scheme. For this reason, the six cannot yet be named. But they are likely to be among those schools who have already operated a successful snacks service alongside traditional meals.

In January, the snacks-only plan will be extended to all county secondary schools. Experts estimate it will save the County Council £2½ million over the next 18 months.

The decision to make the changes was taken at a private meeting of the county finance and general purposes committee and

the only obstacle appears to be a legal argument over the Education Act wording requiring schools to provide "a balanced meal."

But in a report which has not yet been made public, the County Director of Education Mr. Andrew Fairbairn says: "Following discussions with the teachers unions investigations are proceeding with a view to the introduction of a snack meal service for all secondary schools from January 1.

"It is intended to have a pilot scheme in operation in six schools during the autumn term.

★ Continued on Page 18

Bernadette Booth, of Colby Drive, Thurmaston, with her two old English sheepdogs Flash and Lisa at the City of Leicester dog show at Braunstone Park today.

Race crash won't stop PM's son

MARK THATCHER, the 25-year-old son of the Prime Minister, had a lucky escape yesterday when his car crashed into the safety barrier and burst into flames at Mallory Park.

But he has no intention of giving up motor racing, even though it is known that his mother is worried about his craze for the sport.

Hundreds of people gasped when they saw Mark's Ford Escort spin off the track at Gerard's Bend when he was travelling at more than 90 m.p.h. and challenging the leader on the 8th of the 10-lap Debenham's Escort challenge race.

STAGE COACH SETS ABBEY SHOW OFF IN STYLE

THE City of Leicester Show opened in spectacular style this morning when the Lord Mayor, Mr. Bill Scotton, arrived at Abbey Park in a stage coach.

Preceded by the City Town Crier, Mr. Norman Roberts, and a fanfare of coach horns, Mr. Scotton made his grand entrance in an 1830 London-to-Edinburgh Royal Mail coach.

Opening the show, Mr. Scotton thanked all those responsible for getting the show off the ground.

Mr. Ray Flint, chairman of the City Council recreation committee and City of Leicester Show said: "The show promises to be equal to, if not better than last year's.

"Novelty and enterprise has always been a feature of the show and we will continue this theme again this year.

The threat of rain did not deter the crowds, and show organisers were confident of breaking last year's record attendance.

Once again, the emphasis is on non-stop family entertainment, and the two-day show features the

return of last year's hit, Syd Lawrence and his Orchestra, with two concerts in the afternoon. Music was supplied throughout the day with a disco for the youngsters, and brass band concerts for the less energetic.

The showpiece is a glamorous and spectacular "fight to the death" of Roman gladiators. Caesar sits on high with his

★★ Continued on Page 18

Bride-to-be is killed

A 19-YEAR-OLD student who fell off her motorcycle on Friday night, has died in hospital only two weeks before her wedding was due to take place.

Miss Stephanie Lynne Scott, of 40 Ingarsby Drive, Evington, suffered head and internal injuries in the accident which happened at about 10.30 p.m. on Friday in Quorn.

At the time of the accident, Miss Scott, a computer science student at Warwick University, was following her fiance, Mr.

Paul Smith, of Tysoe Hill, Glenfield, from a friend's home. No other vehicle was involved.

Miss Scott was the only daughter of accountant's clerk Mr. Jason Scott and his wife Rita. They have a 16-year-old son, Nickolas.

Having recently completed her first year at university, Miss Scott was to have been married on September 8. She and Mr. Smith had already bought a house near Coventry, where Mr. Smith works.

1979

◆ A man who helped lead the battle to make the Leicester Mercury one of the strongest evening newspapers in the country, Mr Jimmy Lee, retired after 50 years' service. He was circulation manager for more than 30 years and had been in the thick of the circulation struggles of earlier years. He was being retained as a consultant with a special responsibility in connection with the company's expansion into the retail newsagency business.

◆ A brass press-button bell, which had stood on the reception counter in Albion Street and then placed in front of the cashier's screen in reception at St George Street, even though it was no longer used, was stolen in March 1979, just two days after it had been cleaned and restored to its original brilliance by cashier receptionist Mrs Nancy Wood.

Right: Mr Simeon Garner.

Viscount Rothermere, president and chairman of the Daily Mail and General Trust, died at his home in London in July. A nephew of Lord Northcliffe and a member of the Harmsworth newspaper family, the second viscount was 80. From 1932, when he was appointed Chairman of Associated Newspapers, Esmond Harmsworth had become an outstanding figure in Fleet Street in British newspapers.

Jimmy Martin, who had come to be known to readers as an authoritative commentator on all forms of sport, notably golf, soccer and rugby, retired in December, 1978. Among the highlights of his football reporting career the 1966 World Cup Finals, Leicester City's visits to Wembley for the FA Cup finals of 1961 and 1969 and City's promotion season from Division Two in 1970-71. He received a set of cut glass from his colleagues.

Senior editorial changes were announced in January, 1979. They arose because the deputy editor, Mr Simeon Garner, one of the most respected figures in provincial journalism, was due to retire in February. He had served 48 years with the company and his principal appointments had been as industrial correspondent, news editor and assistant editor. In a tribute, Mr Neville Stack, the editor-in-chief, said: 'Mr Garner will be remembered as a man of great integrity and high standards. He has been a fine example to many generations of young people in the profession whom he has helped train.' Mr Garner was presented with a gold quartz watch by the editor. He was succeeded

by Mr Lawrie Simpkin, who was promoted from assistant editor (news) and the chief sub-editor, Mr Michael Shuttlewood, became assistant editor. Mr Simpkin was a Nottingham man, who had started in journalism more than 30 years previously as a copy boy. He was a weekly paper editor at the age of 23 and joined the Leicester Mercury in 1960 as chief soccer writer, covering Leicester City's successes in the 60s. He had become news editor ten years previously. An Old Wyggestonian, Michael Shuttlewood had spent 38 years in local journalism, as reporter, sub-editor, columnist and dramatic critic. He was for 11 years deputy chief sub-editor of the Evening Mail and since 1972 had been chief sub-editor of the Leicester Mercury.

Two months later, Mr Roger De Bank became news editor and Mr Terry Dwyer became chief sub-editor. Mr De Bank transferred from the highly successful free Oadby and Wigston News. An Old Newtonian, Mr Dwyer joined the Mercury in 1951.

The first separate newsagency shop was purchased in June, 1979, at South Wigston and by the end of the year a further eight businesses had been bought, in Leicester, Whitwick, Market Harborough, Melton Mowbray, Broughton Astley, Loughborough, Syston and Kibworth.

Two new directors were appointed to the Board in August, 1979, Mr A N Dyer, General Manager of Northcliffe Newspapers Group and Mr R J Harris, Advertisement Manager-in-Chief since 1970. Mr Harris was Leicester-born and had joined the Evening Mail in 1946.

The Leicester Chronicle, which Mr D Goodlad had edited for the last 31 years of its 169 years (taking its rebirth in 1810 as its real starting date), appeared for the last time on August 31, 1979.

Plans were laid for a new Sunday newspaper for the Greater Leicester area. The Sports Mercury had closed with the edition of September 27, 1979, after a life of 60 years. The Peterborough Evening Telegraph had ended its late Saturday edition, which carried the football results and match reports, because difficulties with Saturday evening distribution. Leicester was also experiencing the same difficulties, but decided to carry on. The new Sunday paper however would have comprehensive sports coverage and the plans received a warm welcome at a reception at the Leicester City football ground for leading figures in Leicestershire sport. The editor of the new publication would be Mr David Welch, the sports editor. Mr Jim Sharlott, life vice-president of the Leicestershire and

Rutland Amateur Athletics Association said he was thoroughly in favour of the new paper. 'I have been a fan of the Sports Mercury for many years. But the replacement will reach a much wider public. I'm sure it will provide a very professional 'coverage of sport.''

The first edition of the Sunday Extra appeared on October 7, 1979. It had a circulation of 100,000, delivered principally by newsagents within the Greater Leicester area free with the national Sunday newspapers. All the following week, messages of congratulation were received from readers and advertisers for its quality. It added a new dimension to Sunday journalism, complementary to the existing range of newspapers, with a wide range of high quality sport, news and features 'for every member of the family.'

The author joined the Leicester Mercury as a Chartered Librarian in December, 1979, after leaving the Leicestershire Libraries and Information Service. He replaced June Lardner, who had been Librarian for a number of years. Deputy editor, Mr Lawrie Simpkin, had commissioned a report from the School of Librarianship at Loughborough to find out what could be achieved with the Mercury's library. The report's author, Mr Jack Hazelgrove, recommended the appointment of a Chartered Librarian and an investigation into the possibility of automating the department, which was a relatively new idea in newspaper library circles then. I knew Jack Hazelgrove from his days in Leicestershire Libraries and was pleased to see him on my interview panel. I would like to think that he recommended my appointment, for which I am eternally grateful. However, the appointment did not take place straight away. I was given a task to perform by Lawrie Simpkin. I had been honest enough to mention that I was also in the running for a new post in Leicestershire Libraries, which involved services to members of the authority. I was asked to go for that job, get it, then resign! A tall order, considering the post in question was on a salary grade the same as my current one and also considering I had been turned down for about 50 jobs within the Library Service previously! Hence the reason for a change of direction. Needless to say I was unsuccessful and I rang Lawrie Simpkin to explain why I had failed. 'That's OK,' he said. 'When can you start?' He went on to explain that he wanted me to wash local government out of my hair before I started with the Mercury! I knew I was going to be accepted at the Mercury after I had started.

One week after entering the library, I was presented with a Christmas bonus!

The library consisted of cabinets crammed full of cuttings pasted on B4 size sheets of paper, photographs and metal blocks, which were used in the production of the paper. My staff were daily indexing, cutting, sticking and filing away articles and dealing with pictures and captions, before they too were filed away for future use. Any useful metal blocks were also collected from the composing room. All the material covered the editions of the Mercury since the end of 1969, with some earlier material, which had been dutifully kept. I received some excellent help from Mrs Jean Taylor, who had been a member of the library staff for a number of years with June Lardner, especially with the routines required to keep the library running and up-to-date. Among the library staff was Mrs Ella Johnson, widow of the former Sports Mercury editor.

It was not long before I suggested compiling a library bulletin each morning, consisting of items of local interest found in the national papers and heard on the local radio. 'I wish I had that service when I was news editor,' I remember Lawrie Simpkin saying. It was also not long before the editor, Mr Neville Stack, invited me to join the early morning editorial conference. This was especially useful, as I then knew which stories the department would be concentrating on during the day and which stories I could help with by providing cuttings and pictures to assist with the writing and illustrating of those stories.

Below: The first Sunday Extra, published on October 7, 1979.

Right: Mr Roy Harris.

Chapter 11
The Arrival of Automation
1980 – 1990

In March, 1980, seven years after the installation of the first photo-composing machines, the use of hot metal came finally to an end. All setting was now computerised and printing was direct from Letterflex plates.

The same month saw a less welcome event. The non-publication of the Leicester Mercury for one day due to the withdrawal of labour by members of the National Graphical Association. They were carrying out the instructions of their national executive committee as action in support of a national pay claim. It was the first time in its 106 years' history that the Mercury had failed to publish.

A further withdrawal, with the loss of another edition, followed and finally the Newspaper Society decided that NGA members be suspended on their refusal to resume normal working. For a fortnight, publication of the Mercury and the weekly papers did not take place, with considerable loss to the men and to the company. The absence of news and the means of advertising had a noticeable effect on trade and social life throughout the circulation area. A one-page news-sheet was printed each day and displayed in newsagents' shops, libraries and other places, but this could in only a minimal way compensate for the paper's non-appearance.

The news poster apparently had an ancient precedent. Early newspapers were exhibited on walls in places which citizens frequented. In fact, the name Gazette originated from this practice. An Italian coin called a gazetta is said to have been the charge made for a peep at those news posters and the final 'a' was later replaced by an 'e' for the title of many popular journals, of which the British Gazette is the most famous.

A price increase announced before the dispute had to be confirmed to meet escalating costs. Leaders of Leicestershire's local authorities were quoted as saying they had missed the Mercury. They tended to regard it as a useful barometer of public opinion. Leicestershire police missed the public response they receive from crime stories. Voluntary bodies lacked an avenue of advertising on which they were so dependent. Sales, recruitment and communication had also been the commercial casualties during the paper's absence.

The journalist behind Mr Leicester and Page 4 for the previous 13 years, Mr Ralph Lowings, retired in June 1980, after half a century in journalism. He came to the Loughborough Monitor in 1936 after serving his apprenticeship with the Newark-on-Trent Advertiser and then working at Peterborough, Ely and Wisbech. He edited the Monitor between 1949 and 1959. He published his own life story in Fleet Street Never Beckoned, which was published by Witmeha Press based in Wymondham in 1987.

January 1981 saw the start of a Memory Lane series of supplements, entitled As It Happened, which could be kept in a special folder. The first one covered 1937, but the front page was supposed to be a picture of the 1937 Coronation – what appeared was a picture of the 1953 Coronation. This was due to an error by the agency supplying the picture and an apology appeared on January 29, 1981.

Two days later, the price of the Mercury was increased to 10p, due to 'ever-increasing costs.' In February, Mr Roy Harris, Director and Advertisement Manager-in-Chief, was appointed Group Advertisement Director of Northcliffe Newspapers Group Ltd. He retained his seat on the Leicester Mercury Board. Mr Barry Wootten, display advertisement sales manager since 1980, succeeded Mr Harris as Advertisement Manager-in-Chief. He joined the display advertising department in 1974.

LAST NEWS

Leicester Mercury

Established 1874 — FRIDAY, MARCH 14, 1980 — 8p

LEICESTER SAYS IT WITH FLOWERS

Mrs. Jackie Mobsby, area organiser for the Northamptonshire and Leicestershire WRVS shop at the Leicester Royal Infirmary is pictured presenting the Queen with an Easter Egg for Princess Anne's son, Peter.

THE QUEEN and the Duke of Edinburgh will probably remember their first visit to Leicester for 22 years as one in which they were in danger of being buried in flowers. Everywhere she went people — officials and the public — besieged her with bouquets, garlands and simple bunches of flowers.

It was as if the tens of thousands of watchers had determined to offset the unexpectedly grey, chilly day and warm it with the riches of the county countryside. Her Lady-in-Waiting, policewomen and everyone in the entourage which accompanied the royal party seemed at one stage to be carrying the lovingly prepared gifts.

There was a carnival cosmopolitan atmosphere to match with thousands of children everywhere as the Queen opened the new extension at the Leicester Royal Infirmary, visited the Town Hall, and did a Gallowtree Gate walkabout before going on to County Hall for lunch

There was massive security. The route and vantage points had been searched and searched again before the royal arrival.

Ranks of uniformed police and massive numbers of plainclothed officers could be seen among the crowds, and scanning from prepared roofs and windows.

The 10-coach royal train arrived at the red carpeted platform four of Leicester station precisely on schedule.

Hundreds of children waved home-made flags from a little way down the platform.

The royal couple were greeted by the Lord Lieutenant of Leicestershire, Colonel Andrew Martin, who presented his wife and other county leaders.

Still in the throes of reconstruction, the station was brightened with banks of spring flowers and evergreen sprays.

Thousands more children

★ Continued on page 29

Warm splash of colour

THE QUEEN, resplendent in scarlet and black, was greeted with a gasp of admiration and a jubilant cheer at the station, writes Joan Stephens.

Her bright red coat provided a warm splash of colour.

The close-fitting coat, with top-stitched pleats falling from hip level, was worn over a matching round-necked dress.

The colour was echoed in the ribbon bow at the right of the Queen's black velvet beret-style hat

Nalgo black rates work in city and Charnwood area

THE Leicester City branch of the National Association of Local Government Officers last night voted overwhelmingly to "black" the production of rate demand notes and working with outside contractors or agencies. Similar action is being taken by Charnwood borough local government officers.

Leyland lose £122 million

BRITISH Leyland made a loss before tax of £122.2 million last year against a profit of £1.7 million in 1978, chairman Sir Michael Edwardes said today.

BL cars had a loss of £46 million last year compared with a profit of £63 million in 1978?.

Sir Michael said he would stay with BL at least until the end of 1981.

He said BL Cars would make a loss again in 1980.

Job security would depend on readiness of workforce and unions to move away from unproductive practices, he said.

This is in line with the action called for by their headquarters in support of the union's wage claims and against the employers' refusal to implement the findings of a comparability study.

The Leicester branch voted by 349 to 26 in favour of taking the industrial action, which will mean that for the time being at least, no rate demands will be issued in Leicester.

The decision should, however, resolve a controversy which has arisen over the new city rate, agreed last night. Labour Group leader, the Rev. Kenneth Middleton had planned to send out a letter with the demand notes explaining the reasons for the new rate figure and the council's policies. Tories claimed that

letter was loaded with party political points and blatantly anti-Government.

Only exceptions to the ban on work with outside agencies are computer maintenance and the catering company who provide the meals for the New Walk Centre. This is so Nalgo members can get both paid and fed.

In Charnwood area, 300 Nalgo members are joining in the national action, and the dispute could spread to East Midlands Airport over the Easter holiday weekend, when air traffic controllers may strike.

Members of the union at the airport are to be balloted on industrial action over Easter, and a union official has predicted that members there would strike.

FANFARE AT COUNTY HALL

THE huge crowd at Glenfield erupted as the royal cavalcade came into view from the County Hall campus.

There was a tremendous cheer and flurry of flags as the black limousine swept up the drive to the main entrance.

Buglers from Glenfield scout band struck up a fanfare as the Queen stepped out to the flagstaff where the Royal Standard was hoisted.

Then came the big moment for eight-year-old Pauline Cooper, a foster child, who stepped forward, curtsied and presented a nosegay to Her Majesty.

WEATHER

Leicester and East Midlands: Rather cloudy, outbreaks of rain dying out. Wind fresh to strong. Cold, max 6 to 7C (43 to 45F).

Outlook: Mostly dry with sunny intervals

Light-up: 6.39 p.m.—5.54 a.m.

Above: The Leicester Mercury marks a visit to the city by the Queen on Friday March 14, 1980.

Above: Tuesday February 24, 1981 saw a big expansion of royal stories throughout the media, with the announcement of the engagement of Prince Charles to Lady Diana Spencer.

Right: The Leicester Mercury for Wednesday February 25 finds a strong local angle with Diana's sister, Lady Sarah McCorquodale, whose home was 'on the Leicester Border', at Stoke Rochford.

Mr Douglas Goodlad, doyen of film reviewers and editor of the former Leicester Chronicle for 31 years, retired from full-time journalism after a career spanning 49 years. He began his career in 1932 as a cub reporter on the South Yorkshire Times in Mexborough. In 1979, he was awarded the Rank Organisation's Showmanship Star to mark 40 years of film criticism, a role he was to continue in his retirement.

In May 14, 1981's edition, a new service was begun for local investors and industry. Leading local share prices were supplied by Hill Osborne and Company as part of the already comprehensive stock prices report. On the same day, a special late edition was produced to enable readers to read of a sad event – an attempt on the life of Pope John Paul as he entered St Peter's Square for a general audience.

Another initiative from Editor Mr Neville Stack for a special edition was on Sunday, July 12, 1981. Contingency plans were made anticipating riot trouble in the city and a special Sunday edition appeared. It sold 30,000 copies at 10p with free copies being given to policemen on riot duty. It carried picture and story coverage on front, back and centre spread, the rest of the special being bulked out with pages from the normal Saturday Mercury. The special came off the stone at dawn and the editor praised all his staff for their efforts. The Mercury's normal free Sunday Extra had already been printed before the riots reached their peak. Two Mercury reporters found themselves facing a police baton charge during the riots. Nick Atkins and Richard Wallace were trapped with the rioters. As the police charged, they escaped unhurt.

Mr Leslie Milliard, chief executive of Leicester and County Chamber of Commerce, strongly attacked the involvement of Leicestershire County Council in producing a new business guide. He said the Chamber had not been consulted and their own directory and the Leicester Mercury's comprehensive Citizen's Guide already provided adequate information.

July 1981 saw the Royal Wedding of Prince Charles and Lady Diana Spencer. Each edition on July 29 had updated pictures right up to the Royal Couple's departure on their honeymoon. July 30 and 31 had souvenirs of street parties held in the city and county and the edition of Saturday, August 1, was a Royal Round-up Golden Edition, setting the seal on a week everyone would remember.

The Mercury's Hinckley office moved to 9 Edward Centre, Regent Street, on August 17, 1981.

An industrial dispute involving the National Graphical Association caused the non-appearance of the Mercury on days in September, 1981. In an attempt to 'fill the gap,' news posters were again produced and displayed in news agents' windows. The paper re-appeared again on September 26.

Another new service for readers began on October 13, 1981. The Mercury began to reprint the bingo numbers from the national daily and Sunday newspapers.

A public inquiry held into a controversial proposal for a supermarket next to County Hall at Glenfield praised the Mercury for its 'helpful intervention when feelings were running high over the Gynsills. It took the helpful intervention of the local newspaper to achieve at least the beginning of a rapprochement.' On the afternoon of October 2, 1981, the Deputy Editor Lawrie Simpkin and news editor Roger De Bank met with property developer Mr Derek Penman, his solicitor and architect. After the intervention, Mr Penman towed a double decker bus off the site; took down some

94: The Overnight Riot Special, brought out on Sunday morning, July 12, 1981.

Overleaf: The Leicester Mercury celebrates the royal wedding on its front page, Wednesday July 29, 1981.

104

ROYAL WEDDING DAY

Leicester Mercury

Established 1874   WEDNESDAY, JULY 29, 1981   Ten pence

Princess Charming

LADY DIANA became Princess of Wales today in a ceremony that was at once a family occasion and an event of stupendous pageantry.

London was crammed with jubilant well-wishers, and her appearance, in a wedding dress of ivory silk taffeta and gold lace, brought a tumult of delight.

The splendour of the wedding in St. Paul's Cathedral was televised throughout the world, and the joy that erupted in the streets of the capital was in jubilant counterpoint to the solemnity of the marriage ceremony.

And all over the country — particularly in Leicestershire — street parties, family gatherings and celebrations of all kinds reflected the public goodwill for the Wedding of the Century.

Full story of the Royal Wedding
— Pages 17 and 20
Picture Special
— Pages 18 and 19

notices; arranged to complete other work on the site, including the repainting to a 'more pleasant colour' of a caravan and the removal of old farm implements.

A director of F Hewitt & Son (1927) Ltd for 18 years, Mr Gerald Sanger, died in October 1981, aged 83. He joined the Board in 1954 and resigned in 1972. In 1954 he was awarded the CBE for political and public services.

Mr A W Peake, a non-executive director of the Leicester Mercury since he retired as Chairman and Managing Director in 1970, retired from the Board in December 1981. He ended a period of 59 years with the newspaper. Mr J S Wallwork, Chairman of the company, said: 'Mr Peake is one of the great figures of our industry. His contribution over so many years has been of the utmost value.' In 1972-73, he had the high distinction of being President of the Newspaper Society.

A carriage clock was presented by the managing director Mr Robert Tyldesley to Mr Reg Sands in December 1981 when he retired as head of building maintenance after more than 24 years service. His son Stewart worked in the composing room.

Constantly increasing costs forced the price of the newspaper up to 12p early in 1982. The paper went to great lengths to explain that other neighbouring evening newspapers had been priced at 12p for some time; some were already costing 14p. It was considered that the Mercury was still excellent value for money. Where's The Ball and Climb the Clock Tower were two cash competitions running to entice people to buy.

Mr John Aldridge became general manager of F Hewitt & Son (1927) Ltd in February 1982. He succeeded Mr Robert Tyldesley, who transferred to Plymouth, where Mr Jeffrey Malton was retiring. (Mr Malton was general manager of the Leicester Evening Mail and his daughter was a police officer in Leicestershire). Mr Aldridge had been general manager of the South Wales Evening Post, Swansea, since 1974. He started his career in the advertising department of the Grimsby Evening Telegraph and became assistant general manager at The Citizen, Gloucester, before being appointed to the post at Swansea.

Mr David Welch, sports editor for the previous 8 years, married Miss Georgina Corah, whose father was Group Executive of the Leicester knitwear firm, Corah Ltd, in February 1982. Later in the month, Mr Alf Perkins retired as deputy sports editor after more than 50 years with the paper. He was president of the Leicester and District Mutual Football League and the 74 Sunday

IAN PARK
Chairman 1982-1991

Above: Mr Ian Park, Chairman.

Below: Mr John Aldridge, General Manager, then Chairman.

JOHN ALDRIDGE
Chairman 1991 - 1997

League. A founder member and past president of the Leicestershire Cyclists' Association, he campaigned vigorously for the creation of a world-class cycle track at Saffron Lane stadium.

Former editor, chairman and managing director of the Mercury, Mr John Fortune, retired in May 1982 as non-executive director after an association spanning 53 years. He joined the paper as a junior reporter in 1929 and became editor in 1948. He held the position for 22 years before becoming chairman and managing director until retirement in 1974. He was presented with a silver rose bowl by his fellow directors. On May 31, he married Mrs Elizabeth Matheson and went to live in Gourock, Scotland.

Right: Mr Ather Mirza.

Mr John Wallwork, who was chairman of the Mercury and managing director of Northcliffe Newspapers Group Ltd until he retired in March, was awarded with the CBE in June 1982.

Head reader Mr George Breward retired in August 1982 after 50 years' service. He was presented with a radio cassette player by composing room manager Mr William Green and a colleague Mr Peter Jackson.

One day less than 51 years of service to the Leicester Mercury were brought vividly back to life at a luncheon marking Mr F Brian Thompson's retirement from the Board in October 1982. Flowers and a silver coffee pot and tray were presented to Mr Thompson and his wife, Joan, by Mercury financial director Mr H N Chambers on behalf of fellow directors. Mr Thompson joined the Leicester Mercury in 1931, became company secretary in 1947 and a director in 1951. He was chairman from 1974 to 1978.

Mr Neville Stack, Editor, was appointed a director of F Hewitt & Son (1927) Ltd in November 1982. At the time he was chairman of the East Midlands region of the Guild of British Newspaper Editors.

The Editor of the Leicester Advertiser from 1947 to 1961, Mr Harry Ledbrooke, died in November 1982, aged 81. He joined the Mercury in 1927 as a sub-editor and was later promoted to deputy chief sub-editor. Mr Stack said: 'Harry Ledbrooke was an editor in the great tradition of journalism, combining high skill with warm humanity. In a long and distinguished career in journalism, he made many friends and will long be remembered for his vigorous editorship and professional integrity.'

Mr Ather Mirza was appointed a journalist in 1982, one of the first Asian journalists to be taken on. Mr Geoff Ellis was reporting on community affairs, but eventually Ather introduced an Asian film review column in 1984, which opened the door for a wider coverage of Asian cultural events. He was instrumental in setting up the very first daily Asian paper in the UK, along with Malcolm Pheby and Alex Leys. This attracted much national media attention.

A former editor of the Mercury, Mr Brian West, was appointed director of the Association of Independent Radio Contractors in December 1982. For the previous eight years he had been group public relations adviser to the Littlewoods Organisation. The association is jointly funded by the companies who have contracts from the Independent Broadcasting Authority to provide a local radio service.

The arrival on the scene of a second radio station for Leicester in 1981, the commercial Centre Radio with news bulletins every half hour and the extension of news and current affairs programmes on television, may have had some effect on the Mercury's daily total sales of 156,000 in 1982. But it can have been only small for neither the breadth of news coverage nor the number of listeners could in any way compare. For speed of dissemination of the most important news and sport in particular the broadcasting media of course had an advantage.

Mr Phil Pledger, the editor of the Oadby and Wigston News, was appointed editor of the Sunday Extra in February 1983. He began his career on a weekly paper in Lancashire and joined the Mercury as a district reporter at Market Harborough in 1974. Mr Jim Matthews became the new editor of the Oadby and Wigston News. He joined as a reporter in 1975 from the Coalville Times. Mr Roger Wolens had left the editorship of the Sunday Extra to become assistant editor of the Lincolnshire Echo. He had previously been the editor of five weekly papers in Northamptonshire and of the Island Sun, the Channel Islands' Sunday newspaper.

The installation of computerised setting lent itself to editionising and earlier printing. Furthermore, by now initial information fed into the computer served advertising, circulation and accounting purposes as well. The Mercury was, in fact, the first newspaper in the country to use this integrated approach. By early 1983 publishing had been brought forward by stages to provide a 1pm sale on Leicester's streets.

Dwindling sales and loss of advertising forced a substantial change of formula on the Leicester Advertiser in 1982. Unlike its sister-weeklies, a few years earlier, it was not replaced by an entirely free newspaper, but reached its readers by three different methods. Some 42,000 copies were included as a free supplement in the Mercury circulating in the county, nearly 2,000 were posted free to farmers and there were also copies for sale within the Greater Leicester area and to non-Mercury readers elsewhere. This attracted more advertising at a higher rate and the paper became profitable again. Furthermore, a much-respected 139-year-old newspaper was saved, for the time being at least. It was a newspaper to which that prolific writer of children's books, Enid Blyton, had contributed right at the beginning of her career.

The retirement in February 1983 of Mr Ken Wiltshire from the composing room after 36 years ended a family link of 120 years' service. His father worked in the production department for 54 years, while his grandfather was on the advertising side for 30 years.

A man who became known to thousands of people through his work for 13 years as commissionaire at the Mercury, Sergeant Arthur Heath, died in March 1983, aged 68.

The Mercury staged its first ever race meeting at Leicester Racecourse on June 11, 1983 and was billed as an evening no racing fan will want to miss with a host of sporting celebrities expected to attend.

April 1, 1983, saw Leicester's Morning Mercury published with 52 pages of international, national, local news, sport and features plus a free to enter £400 holiday competition, a special story on Sue Ellen of Dallas, a talk with Maggie Philbin and Keith Chegwin, crosswords and puzzles. Fleet Street was on Easter holiday and the Mercury filled the gap. It sold more than 65,000 copies and was considered an excellent sales figure. The exercise was repeated with equal success in the following two years until Fleet Street woke up to the threat from the provinces and began Good Friday publication.

Mr Arthur Peake, former chairman and managing director and one of the key men in the newspaper's post-war development, died in April 1983. Chairman Mr Ian Park said: 'He was one of the outstanding figures of our industry. His dedication both to the welfare of the Leicester Mercury and to the freedom of the provincial press in general were revered by us all. Arthur Peak's career demonstrated that it was possible to be an outstanding businessman and publisher, yet at the same time be punctiliously courteous

to his colleagues and readers in the community his newspaper served. He will be greatly missed.' His colleague for many years, Mr F Brian Thompson, said: 'Arthur Peake virtually dedicated his life to the Leicester Mercury. Many of his friends would say, with permissible exaggeration, that he could talk of little else. When, after almost 60 years, he severed his final link with the newspaper in 1981, he felt his main interest in life had gone. He had a remarkable ability to sum up a situation and express his conclusions clearly. He would have made a good Judge! And once a course of action had been decided upon, nothing could deflect him from it. The large and distinguished gathering which lunched in the Leicester Mercury building on the occasion of the opening by Princess Alexandra in 1967 will recall his masterly address to them, in which he spoke for some 20 minutes about the history of the newspaper, its role in the community, its exciting future and the mechanics of production which they were about to see. Not a note did he have, not a second's hesitation was there and not a word out of place.'

A retirement dinner in honour of Mr Jack Wallwork, former chairman of the Mercury and managing director of Northcliffe Newspapers, was held at the Rothley Court Hotel, Rothley, in April 1983. He was presented with an antique silver and mother of pearl snuff box by director and general manager, Mr John Aldridge.

A former Leicester Evening Mail reporter before the war, Mr Tom Henry, died in May 1983, aged 73. He joined the Manchester Evening News as a sports reporter in 1937 and became editor of the paper in 1946. On his retirement in 1969, he became deputy chairman of North News and Manchester Evening News. His son Kevin was a sub-editor on the Manchester Evening News.

A former Mercury employee, Mr Jack Kimberley, died in Timaru, New Zealand, in May, 1983, aged 80. He worked on the printing presses at the Leicester Evening Mail for 32 years and then worked for the Mercury until he retired in 1968. He had emigrated to New Zealand with his wife, Emmie, in 1974 to join their daughter Marjorie and their grandchildren.

Former chief sub-editor Mr Jack Atton, who had worked for the Mercury for 43 years, died in July 1983, aged 76. Deputy Editor Mr Lawrie Simpkin said: 'Jack was a wonderful colleague. He was unflappable and his meticulous attention to detail was ideal for his crucial role in the newspaper. But he was also a man of conviction and compassion, from his background in the church and he

108

1983

◆ Picture editor Mr Eric Taylor retired in September 1983 after 44 years' service with the Evening Mail and Mercury. He joined the Evening Mail photographic staff in 1939 and, after war service from 1940 to 1946, became a photographer and then picture editor. He was invited to become assistant picture editor with the Mercury when the Evening Mail closed and he became picture editor in 1978. To mark his retirement, colleagues presented him with a television set and a sandwich toaster. Mr Colin Axford was made his successor. He joined in 1949 and became a member of the photographic staff in 1950.

◆ Local Newspaper Week took place in October 1983 and the Mercury went to great lengths to outline every detail of its operation, revealing some interesting facts. Some 140 tonnes of newsprint was used in a week along with two and half tonnes of ink. Printing presses produced 36,000 copies an hour and a fleet of 80 vehicles covered one and a half million miles a year and used nearly 44,000 gallons of petrol to deliver the final product.

was never reluctant to put these fine personal qualities on display in his work.'

The certified nightly net sale of the Mercury in the six months from January to June 1983 was shown to be 158,275, compared with 158,104 for the same period in 1982, making the Mercury the fifth largest provincial evening newspaper in the country. The Editor said: These figures show that we are succeeding in the way that we are reaching out to our readers with an ethos that is entirely our own. This is proof that a policy of maximum coverage in a permanent and immediate form, of local news and sport, is what is wanted. Blend in general interest features, compelling pictures and coverage of the most significant national and international events and you have the complete newspaper: the world seen through a window in Leicester. Times have not been easy for the Mercury. Like every other newspaper, we have been hit by the recession and affected by social change. We certainly do not claim that everything we say pleases every reader. Far from it! We are always treading on somebody's sensitive toes. This newspaper is proud of its reputation for frank and fearless comment and nothing stops us saying what we believe to be in the public interest. We campaign vigorously for what we think is needed or should be stopped. We expose and attack as well as giving praise that is due. We back good causes and oppose bad ones. It would be a lifeless paper indeed that was not an active market place and our coverage of events is complemented by the diversity of advertisements for shopping, houses, cars, leisure and all other needs of a complex, modern society.'

October 1983 saw a 'new' newspaper in Leicester. The Leicester Mail replaced the Leicester Shopwindow, which was introduced in 1969 to defend the Mercury against the threat of competition from other free papers. Editor Barrie Holden said: 'We consider ourselves rather special – the first of a new generation. We will be filling a vital need. There is a desperate need for a bright newsy City weekly.' To mark the launch, the Mail was giving away a £2,200 free two-week cruise for two on the P and O cruise-ship the Canberra – heroine of the Falklands war.

Mr Harry Bourne, former picture editor, died in November 1983, aged 68. He maintained a great family tradition when he joined the Mercury in 1932 as a junior reporter. His father Mr Henry Bourne was a distinguished editor of the newspaper until his retirement in 1948. The Editor wrote:

'The news of Harry Bourne's death reached the Mercury during the morning editorial conference and his

friends and former colleagues at once expressed their shock and their sympathy for the family. I speak for all at the Mercury in paying tribute to a fine newspaperman and the best of colleagues. He led his staff with enthusiasm as well as wisdom and technical skill and many photographers and journalists owe much to his sage advice in their formative years. His example of craftsmanship, dedication and loyalty – coupled with modesty and good humour – was an inspiration to senior as well as junior colleagues.'

Former employees of the Evening Mail attended a reunion at the Grand Hotel on the occasion of the 20th anniversary of the paper's closure. Among those who attended were Mr Eric Taylor, picture editor, Mr Bernard Hobday, process manager, Mr Reg Lucy, chief photographer and Mr Ken Clapham, editor. Some had come a long way. Mr Frank Taylor of the Daily Telegraph came from Washington and Mr Brian Huggins came from Canada, where he had lived for 26 years. Former reporter Ken Thompson was then Cornwall's tourist chief and Roy Harris was then Northcliffe Newspapers group advertisement director.

A family association of more than 100 years ended with the retirement of process manager Mr Alec Gimson in November 1983. His career began 49 years previously when he joined from school as the junior in the process department in the Albion Street offices. He had followed in the footsteps of his father, William, an advertising representative and executive for 55 years.

Production manager Mr Eric Hollingworth was appointed a director of F Hewitt & Son (1927) Ltd in November 1983. He had joined as a composing room apprentice in 1943.

In the same month, deputy editor Mr Lawrie Simpkin was given a new title, that of Executive Editor. Editor Mr Neville Stack said: 'I wish him to have a title more descriptive of the sterling work he does for the paper.' Mr Simpkin had been appointed deputy editor in 1979.

After two troubled years, Centre Radio closed in October. Its losses had exceeded those anticipated by the Leicester and Leicestershire Radio Consortium.

It was found necessary to increase the price of the Mercury again to 14p in December 1983. Even so, it was still considered the lowest possible cost, with the Coventry Evening Telegraph and papers in Birmingham and Peterborough were selling at 15p and the Guardian at 23p.

The first woman agricultural writer to work for both the Leicester Advertiser and the Mercury died aged 59 in January 1984. Mrs Margaret McNeill came to Leicester from Norwich and spent 16 years with both papers. She was well respected in the farming community and won a national award for her writing in 1971.

Former deputy sports editor Mr Alf Perkins died in the same month, aged 66. His work for the paper spanned 50 years. Editor Mr Neville Stack wrote:

> Alf was not only a respected interpreter of the sporting scene – he was part of it. He was known by all who followed sport (especially his first loves of cycling and local soccer) as a man of complete integrity and never failing goodwill. His colleagues held him in the highest esteem also, for his technical ability was matched only by his imperturbable good nature. Even after his retirement he continued as a contributor to his beloved Leicester Mercury and maintained his involvement in local events and organisation. He has earned his place in the memory of all who share his devotion to the cause of sport. In every respect, a sporting gentleman.

The Mercury again 'bucked the trend' in newspaper circulation by increasing its sales. Nightly sales of the paper, from July to December 1983 were 153,713, a small, but significant increase over the 153,597 in the same period of 1982. It was the fifth largest regional evening publication in the country, headed only by the Manchester Evening News, The Birmingham Mail, the Wolverhampton Express and Star and the Liverpool Echo. Consistently high sales are of course important to advertisers and one of the reasons for the increase could be the increase in the promotional activity by the newspaper, with special theme weeks.

Sports editor Mr David Welch was appointed assistant sports editor with the Daily Telegraph in April 1984. Mr Alan Parr succeeded him. Alan had been with the Mercury sports desk for five years and had come from the Coventry Evening Telegraph, having started his career with the Leicester Evening Mail until its closure in 1963. He had also worked in Staffordshire and Yorkshire. He had instigated the successful Leicester Mercury Race Night at Oadby in 1983. He had briefly left the sports desk to launch the Sunday Extra.

The Independent Broadcasting Authority was to interview two groups who were bidding to operate the new commercial radio franchise in Leicester in April 1984. The newspaper was in a position to make an investment in a new radio station, to which it was entitled by law. General Manager Mr John Aldridge explained: 'We believe that local commercial radio has a role to play in the community and that Leicester Sound, one of the two groups, have got it right in terms of finance, programme ideas and expertise.' There was no clash of interest between the newspaper and the radio station who would be regarded by the paper as 'opposition' and not as part of the paper's operation. There would be no links between the editorial functions.

Talking of radio broadcasting, BBC's Irish superstar Terry Wogan had been having a go at the fair city of Leicester, claiming that no-one could find their way here. The Leicester Mercury was quick to take up the gauntlet and was locked in a friendly 'battle of blarney' with Mr Wogan. To his credit, he always acknowledged our defence, but so far had not taken up our invitation to come and visit us in the (legendary) 'lost city.'

By May 1984, there were fifty thousand Asians living in Leicester – one fifth of its population. The Mercury responded by appointing reporter Geoff Ellis as a communities correspondent. He outlined his duties in an article in Newstime in May 1984.

After 23 years of editing the Leicestershire Advertiser, Mr Leslie Wilkes took early retirement in July, 1984. Mr Wilkes left Manchester 30 years previously to join the Leicester Mercury where he became features editor and later motoring correspondent. During his time he launched the Oadby and Wigston Advertiser. He was chairman of the East Midlands group of the Guild of British Newspaper Editors in 1984. Mr Peter Gilbey was appointed to succeed Mr Wilkes. Mr Gilbey had been assistant editor since 1978.

In July 1984, the Press Council ruled against a Mercury headline. A series of articles about textile sweatshops was useful campaigning journalism, but the story which led to it was seriously flawed by a misleading headline, it had judged. The Council upheld a complaint by the Leicester and District Trades Council, but said it was satisfied that the fault was an unfortunate lapse and not an intentional piece of provocation. A front page lead story was headlined: 'Action urged on city Asian sweatshops.' The story said Mr Alec Kilsby, secretary of the Leicester East district of the National Union of Hosiery and Knitwear Workers, was disturbed by reports of what he believed to be up to 100 small firms in the city mostly run by Asians who he

1985

◆ Good Friday, April 5, 1985, saw the publication of the Leicester Morning Mercury, an enterprising venture, as no national papers had been published.

◆ The County Show in May, 1985, had a star attraction in the oldest Leicester Mercury van. It had been towed in to the garage at St George Street looking all of its 58 years of age and in a very sorry state. But a team of workshop mechanics led by workshop manager Mr Graham Clydesdale set to work and literally undid every nut and bolt and completely overhauled it. The rare 1927 Morris Cowley light van was exactly the same model as those used by the company to deliver newspapers in the 1920s. It was bought from Mr William Cooke, of Chestnuts Farm, Saddington, who specialised in collecting vintage cars and motorcycles. The Wigston pattern-makers and engineering firm Cooke's, of West Avenue, completely rebuilt the body using an authentic wooden frame and eventually it was valued at £10,000 plus.

believed were contravening the Health and Safety Act and other legislation. Mr Kilsby was quoted as saying there were many good Asian employers. The report added that the factories involved in disgusting abuses were run by people of more racial and cultural backgrounds than Asian. Mr Paul Gosling, Trades Council secretary, complained to the Press Council that the newspaper improperly published a prominent headline misleadingly implying that only Asians were responsible for textile sweatshops in Leicester city and in such a way to encourage racial prejudice against Asians.

Deputy transport manager Mr Bill Stretton retired in August 1984 after 50 years service with the company. During his time he was a paper boy, publishing foreman, deputy circulation manager and then distribution manager in the garage.

During 1984, the newspaper sales department sought new outlets in a bid to maintain circulation. Soon 5,000 copies a day were being sold from supermarkets, off-licences, garages and even public houses. Many thousands more were distributed by the newspaper's own Direct Delivery agents.

Financial director Mr Brett Chambers was promoted to take on additional responsibilities in November 1984. He became group project manager responsible for the implementation of commercial computers throughout the Northcliffe Group. Mr Kerrel Wills, data processing manager of the Leicester Mercury Group, was to assist Mr Chambers by serving on an implementation group which Mr Chambers was to chair. The appointments had recognised the knowledge and experience of both in commercial computing and the quality of the Leicester Mercury computer system.

Harking back to Mr Terry Wogan. He did find Leicester in November 1984, when he attended a Publicity Association of Leicester luncheon at the Moat House in Oadby. Hosiery manufacturer Mr Paul Marshall had some socks made for him with a special Terry Wogan motif and shamrock.

Deputy features editor Mr Frank Vasey retired in February 1985. He had come to the Mercury from Northampton in 1959 as a general news sub editor and was appointed deputy features editor in 1973.

In a new drive for more readers, the Newspaper Sales Department introduced the Mercury's first scratchcard game, Zodiac, with cash prizes, a holiday and the top prize of a car for the winners. More than half a million cards were distributed through the circulation area in March 1985 with the result

that after 15 publishing days the average daily sale had risen by 4,500 copies.

A dispute over new technology hit production of the Mercury's issues in May 1985 and resulted in the non-appearance of a Saturday edition. Members of the print union, the National Graphical Association, had been holding mandatory chapel meetings as part of their aim of securing guarantees over the introduction of single-keying. Single-keying was the computerised direct input of editorial and advertising material into the newspaper. This function was carried out by members of the NGA. Both management and union agreed that the cause of the dispute was national rather than local. The dispute had been brought to a head some weeks previous when the Wolverhampton Express and Star locked out and dismissed 150 NGA members and brought in single keyboarding technology overnight in spite of repeated assurances that this would never happen without negotiation.

May 1 saw the introduction of Value Added Tax at 15 per cent on newspaper advertising. It largely affected the private advertiser and proved to have little long-term effect on advertising volumes.

Two new appointments were made in June 1985. Mr Derek Foster became production manager and Mr Mark Johnston assistant circulation manager. Mr Foster was born in Plymouth and was formerly with the Evening Sentinel, Hanley, Stoke-on-Trent. Mr Johnston was formerly field sales manager with the Scunthorpe Evening Telegraph.

The cover price of the Mercury was increased to 16p on July 22, 1985, due to the continued increase in the cost of materials, particularly newsprint.

Mr Philip Brewin was appointed manager of the free weekly publications in August, 1985. He had been involved in the newspaper industry for nearly 24 years and was previously advertisement manager at The Citizen, Gloucester.

Celebrations of the 500th anniversary of the Battle of Bosworth in August were marked with the publication of a special addition with a 1485 front page with the headline The King Is Slain.

In January, 1986, Mr John Aldridge, director and general manager from 1982, was redesignated managing director. At the time he was chairman of the Press and Public Affairs Committee of the Newspaper Society and was responsible for organising events to mark the society's 150th anniversary in 1986.

The Leicester Mail celebrated 600 editions on March 13, 1986, by introducing full colour pictures in a bumper edition.

The Mercury had been campaigning for 14 paintings, part of the late Leicestershire art collector Mrs Anne Kessler's £4 million bequest, to come to Leicester from the Tate Gallery on indefinite loan. Success was registered in May 1986 after a hitch encountered with insurance cover and a projected date of November 1986 was given as a possible opening date at the New Walk Museum and Art Gallery. Mrs Kessler's daughter, Mrs Anne Haywood of Gunthorpe, was delighted.

Mercury photographer Mr Glen Tillyard found himself on the other side of the lens in June 1986, when he married Miss Angela Mackness at Holy Apostles Church on Fosse Road South in the city.

To commemorate the occasion of the 150th anniversary of the Newspaper Society, the Mercury produced a booklet, entitled Newspapers – Past, Present and Future in July, 1986.

Mr Wilf Toone, who was the man in charge of the Mercury's printing presses, retired in August, 1986, after 50 years' service with the paper. He was 14 when he started work in the publishing room in 1936. One of his first jobs was to paste up news posters announcing the death of King George V.

Sales figures for the Mercury continued to 'stagger the provincial newspaper industry.' The paper was winning the fight to retain its position as the fifth largest circulation provincial newspaper. Sales were higher than in other cities with a bigger population. The figures for July to December 1985 were 150,375 – more than those for Leeds, Newcastle and Sheffield. The audited average figure for the whole of 1985 was 151,602 daily.

After 59 years in journalism, Mr Mac Cherry retired in September, 1986 – for the second time. As a reporter, Mr Cherry was Coalville's Mr News for 31 years until his 65th birthday in 1977. Since then he had worked as a freelance. The editor, Mr Neville Stack, held a farewell reception for Mr Cherry and for Mrs Vida Cherry, a village correspondent in north Leicestershire for 15 years. He received a barbecue set from his colleagues.

Assistant editor Mr Michael Shuttlewood retired in the same month, after 45 years in local journalism. An Old Wyggestonian, he was the son of Mr A E Shuttlewood, headmaster of St Andrew's School, Countesthorpe and his wife, Violette, for many years headmistress at Willoughby Waterleys. He had been responsible for some large-scale projects, notably Climb the Clock Tower, a competition of his own devising which attracted some 30,000 entries, The Lollipop Lady of the Year contest and the Images of Industry competition.

Mr Shuttlewood was succeeded as assistant editor by Mr Terry Dwyer, an Old Newtonian, who had been chief sub-editor for the previous seven years. Mr Stuart Williamson replaced him as chief sub-editor.

Further dwindling advertising brought about the demise of the Leicestershire Advertiser. It had been included as a free supplement in the Mercury since 1982. The last edition was on September 25, nearly 145 years since its birth as Payne's Leicester and Midland Counties Advertiser, an auctioneer's sheet. It had served Leicestershire well. The coverage of rural interests was to be maintained through a weekly Country Matters supplement of three or four pages in the Mercury.

The 1986 president of the Young Newspaperman's Association, the junior part of the Newspaper Society, was the Mercury's data processing manager Mr Kerrel Wills. It was the first time an executive of the newspaper had been president.

Former Mercury advertisement manager Mr Roy Harris retired as advertisement director with Northcliffe Newspapers Group in December 1986. During his 40-year association with newspapers, Mr Harris had established himself as a popular and authoritative figure in the advertising industry. He had been appointed to the Mercury board in 1979 and became a London-based group director in 1981.

Mr Roger De Bank was appointed assistant editor (news) at the end of 1986. He was to continue to be responsible for local news acquisition and to take on extra responsibilities.

The installation of a new, hi-tech telephone system came early in 1987 and the Mercury's main number became 512512. Tele-ads, however, remained with 515151.

Mr Patrick Farrelly, circulation manager, was promoted in February, 1987. He was appointed general manager of Northcliffe Direct Marketing, a division of Northcliffe Newspapers Group, which is responsible for developing direct mail business at the group's weekly newspapers. Direct mail was proving to be the fastest growing advertising medium in the country. Mr Farrelly had been circulation manager at the Mercury since 1981. Mr Michael Geraghty joined the Mercury as newspaper sales manager from the Grimsby and Scunthorpe Evening Telegraph in April.

A consortium of six East Midlands newspapers was launched in May, 1987, to

1987

◆ At the beginning of December, the Mercury's tele-ads department started a new automatic telephone call distribution system, which aimed to reduce the length of time callers have to wait for a reply. Typewriters had also seen their day – now all advertisements are fed directly into a computer and early in 1988 came the introduction of direct input – at the touch of a button, information will be fed straight from tele-ad staff to the scrutineers where it will appear on screen for checking and then be out-putted in new technology's equivalent of type.

◆ Rising costs, especially of newsprint, forced the price of the paper up 1p to 18p in December, 1987. It was the first cover price rise since September, 1986.

Near right: Mr Barry Wootten.

Far right: Mr Alex Leys.

present a complete package to advertisers. The East Midlands Triangle could boast a total circulation of more than 925,083. A further four newspapers joined the scheme in October, 1987.

Assistant newspaper sales manager Ms Sarah Ramsden met the Duchess of York on May 12, 1987, to receive a national scholarship. The Duchess was handing out the first-ever Stationers and Newspapers Makers Guild scholarships for people under 25 in London. The £5,000 award was aimed at encouraging young people to develop their competitive skills. Ms Ramsden had decided to use hers visiting newspapers throughout the USA to research ways of improving circulation.

Top football writer Mr Denis Lowe, who began his journalistic career at the Mercury in August, 1946, died in June, 1987. He had joined the News Chronicle in Manchester in 1955. In 1969, he joined the northern staff of the Daily Telegraph.

London-born Mr Barry Wootten was appointed advertisement director of F Hewitt and Son (1927), publishers of the Mercury, in June 1987. He had joined the Mercury in 1974 as an advertisement representative and became display sales manager in 1980 and advertisement manager-in-chief in 1981.

Mr Neville Stack, Editor for 14 years, left on July 31, 1987, to become Press Fellow at Wolfson College, Cambridge. He had earned a national reputation as a campaigning editor. Since he took over in 1974, he had battled for a better Leicestershire. His long experience as a national paper news editor helped the success of his many campaigns for causes as diverse as more cash for the health service to safeguarding the wildlife in the

county. A reception was held in his honour at the City Rooms and many tributes were paid to him by colleagues past and present. Managing director Mr John Aldridge told the 200 guests: 'Neville has a great streak of compassion running through him and always responds swiftly to members of his staff who are in difficulties and one retired colleague described Neville as thoughtful, kind and caring.' Mr Stack also received a warm and heartfelt tribute from the city's Asian community when county councillor Mr Paul Sood said: 'Neville has sown the seeds for the growth of Leicestershire as a truly multicultural community. He leaves a good impression on the Asian community and in all the years I have dealt with him he has been very warm and kind-hearted.'

The Mercury's new Editor took over immediately. Mr Alex Leys was formerly editor of the Evening Telegraph in Derby and was the first double-holder of the Samuel Storey Award, made to the Provincial Newspaper Editor of the Year. He first won the award as editor of the Lincolnshire Echo in 1984 and the second, in 1986, was for his editorship of the Evening Telegraph.

The advertising administration manager of the Mercury, Mr Derek Robinson, died in August, 1987, aged 56. He had joined the company 23 years previously after starting his career with the former Fred Gilbert, turf accountants, in Belgrave Gate. He became involved in new technological developments in the advertisement section of newspapers in the Northcliffe Group.

The deputy manager of the composing room, Mr Denis York, retired in November, 1987, after 49 years in the industry. He had started his career with the Evening Mail and transferred to the Mercury when it closed in 1963.

Plans were being made for four-colour printing without investment in new offset presses. Two colour satellite units, using Civilox keyless inking, were built by Crabtree Vickers for installation into the top structures of the newspaper's two Goss Headliner presses. The first of the units arrived in November 1986 and was ready by February, 1987, the month which saw the arrival of the second unit. There were extensive trials before the Oadby and Wigston News became the first of the Mercury newspapers to use spot and multi-spot colour in July, 1987. It was not until Christmas Eve that the first spot colour was used in the Mercury. Colour became a regular feature of advertising. Some recognition of its effectiveness came when the Mercury was judged as winner in the display advertising multi-spot colour category at the Newspaper Society advertising conference in Blackpool.

The Oadby and Wigston Mail, as it was re-named at the beginning of 1988, also carried the first full-colour photograph in February. The pioneering picture was a page one study by Karsh of the Royal Family. A centre-spread line-up of Leicester Rugby Football Club was the first full-colour picture to appear in the Mercury – on April 25, 1988.

During his first year as editor, Mr Leys introduced the Mercury on Monday section, a lifestyle review. He also gave fresh zest and impetus to other regular weekly special interest sections --Business Tuesday, Driver Wednesday, Jobs Thursday, Time Out Friday and the Saturday Property Guide.

A new advertising initiative was the launch of Jobfinder in October 1987. With an average of around 40 pages, this weekly paper went on sale for 20p each Saturday throughout the East Midlands and was also posted to schools, colleges and libraries. It contained all the display advertising from the previous six days' Mercury publications and the trade display advertisements from Saturday.

Auto Extra made its appearance just a year later. Another tabloid, averaging 24 pages, it contained the display motoring advertisements from the week's Mercury publications. It was sold for 20p, but was carried free within the expanding Mail series.

Mr Barry Thompson was appointed financial director in January, 1988. He had joined the company two years previously as chief accountant and had come from Welcome Break, a motorway service area restaurant chain, whose headquarters were at

Leicester Forest East. He succeeds Mr Brett Chambers, who had retired from the post after 26 years with the company. Mr Chambers remained as a director, with responsibilities for the future developments of the company's computer system and expansion of the Fairfield News subsidiary of newsagents shops. He was to be also responsible for supporting commercial computer systems supplied by the Leicester Mercury at eight other Northcliffe Group offices.

A new church bell, in memory of top football writer Mr Denis Lowe and his mother Mrs Ida Lowe, was hallowed at St Peter's Church in Oadby in April, 1988. It was donated by the Lowe family, who were in church to hear the full peal of eight ring out.

After more than 20 years as one of the editorial managers of the Leicester Mercury, executive editor Mr Lawrie Simpkin left at the end of September, 1988, to set up his own press and public relations consultancy. He was to continue as a consultant to the newspaper. He had joined as chief football writer in 1960 and was appointed news editor in 1968. He was to continue representing the company on several local groups, including the City Council's Promotion Committee, where he had been appointed chairman of the Retail Promotion Committee. The managing director Mr John Aldridge paid tribute to Mr Simpkin by stating that he had established many links with the community and was held in respect by many in all walks of life. He had contributed much to the success of the newspaper.

Left: Mr Lawrie Simpkin.

1987

◆ The Mercury was only the second letterpress newspaper in Europe using satellite units to produce colour in its pages. It was beaten to the post just a few weeks before by the Dundee Courier, which had only one unit to develop.

◆ It has been recorded that, in 1923, 'there were now ladies on the staff.' By 1987, a considerable proportion of the 562 employees were women, but the appointment of three more on September 28 began what could be regarded as the start of a revolution – they joined what until then had been a traditionally all-male preserve, the composing room. Direct inputting allowed the introduction of a voluntary severance scheme for employees in the composing room and many accepted terms during the following months.

114

ROYAL PICTURES   City

Leicester Mercury

THURSDAY, JUNE 27, 1985   Fourteen Pence

Thousands welcome Charles and Diana

Royal fever sweeps the county

After a rapturous reception at Atherstone this morning the Prince and Princess of Wales moved into Leicestershire to stand on the historic Bosworth Field battlesite this afternoon.

Everywhere the royal couple went they were greeted by large crowds welcoming them at each stage of their prestigious tour of the two counties.

And the omens were good — at Atherstone the sun burst through for the first time as the Royal couple went on a ten-minute walkabout in Market Square.

The Princess wore a blue and white dress under a navy blue long coat, and a small white hat with a navy blue trim.

Retired plasterer, 78-year-old Mr. Solomon Cartwright of Grendon, near Atherstone, who shook the Prince's hand, said: "It made my life, never mind my day."

Thousands more were expected at Bosworth Field and Loughborough this afternoon as the popular royal couple continued their prestigious tour.

Prince Charles shakes hands with the High Sheriff of Warwickshire, Mr J L M Graham at Atherstone station.

After leaving the church this morning, they continued to Innage Park industrial estate where they saw hi-tech starter units. They then visited the Rowan Centre for the physically disabled.

Prince Charles and dazzling Princess Diana met delighted young children of Race Meadow First School and applauded a play on the Battle of Bosworth at Atherstone North Middle School.

After lunch at the Chapel House, Atherstone, the royal couple were due to travel by motorcade to the Quincentenary Celebrations at Bosworth Field.

They were to tour the award-winning visitor centre and the battlefield, where Richard III was killed 500 years ago by Henry Tudor's army, then watch mock jousting and hand-to-hand combat before a helicopter of the Queen's Flight was to whisk them back to the 20th century and off to Nanpantan.

There Prince Charles was due to attend a ceremony with the Men of the Trees, while Princess Diana planned to visit Dr Barnardo's shop in Market Street, Loughborough.

A local undertaker drove the royal couple past the thousands of cheering people in Atherstone.

Mr. David Evans, of Long Street, Atherstone — swore locally as Evans the Hearse — was chosen for the job because of his experience of driving at a snail's pace.

LEICESTERSHIRE'S ROYAL DAY

PAGES OF PICTURES in tomorrow's Souvenir Edition

£1,000 fines for soccer drinks

Tough new measures aimed at stamping out soccer hooliganism are spelt out in a Government Bill, published today, to control the sale and possession of alcohol at football matches.

Maximum fines of up to £1,000 are included in a measure which has all-party support and which should become law by the start of the next football season in August.

Mr. Leon Brittan, the Home Secretary, described the measures as "tough but fair" in a bid "to remove this stain from a great British game".

The Bill effectively bans the sale and possession of alcoholic drinks at football grounds, but special exemptions can be sought for hospitality suites.

However, magistrates will only be allowed to grant exemptions for a bar which is out of sight of the pitch. Even then, a uniformed policeman may order its closure on the spot.

WEATHER

Leicester, East Midlands and East Coast. Dull soon tomorrow. Showers. Near normal temps. max 17 to 18C (63 to 64F).

Outlook: Similar

Light up: 10.06 p.m. 4.15 a.m.

City ground safety: 'Very little to do'

Leicester City Football Club today gave an assurance that no serious alterations would have to be carried out on their Filbert Street ground, following the recent fire safety inspection.

The inspection was made in the wake of the Bradford City fire disaster.

Mr. Alan Bennett, Leicester City club secretary, said that a press conference would be held after the July fortnight, outlining the findings and the club's intentions.

He would only say: "Nothing serious has to be done, although there are a number of small things."

Veteran journalist Miss Monica Pearson, who began her career at the Mercury, died in June, 1988, aged 93. She and her sister May, who was the women's page writer for many years, were daughters of a Rothley vicar. Former deputy editor Mr Simeon Garner wrote: 'After Monica moved to Fleet Street (she worked on the Daily Express) she would occasionally call into the office in Albion Street to see her sister, who wrote under the name of Rita Wakefield. I remember on one occasion she turned up in a bright red open top MG car wearing a costume the same colour – she was a very lively character.'

Former Mercury farming writer Jonathan Wheeler was appointed press officer for the Royal Agricultural Society in June, 1988. He began his journalistic career in South Wales and had been a freelance journalist based in Leicestershire since 1985.

Former women's page editor, Glenn Barker, received the Freedom of the City of London in July, 1988. The honour came on the recommendation of a member of the Court of Common Council in the City and had been awarded because of her coverage of horticultural happenings in the City.

Composing room manager, Mr William Green, retired after more than 41 years with the company in August, 1988. He joined in 1937 as a reader's boy and spent nine years at the company before moving to the old Birmingham Gazette. He rejoined in 1956 as a Linotype operator and had been composing room manager since 1980. Mr Stan Clay, process department manager, retired in the same month after 38 years with the company. He had joined in 1950 as a photo engraver.

The Sports Mercury returned at the beginning of the 1988-89 football season after an absence of nine years. In 1981, a Sports Final edition, an amalgamation of the Saturday Mercury with 10 pages of sport has been launched, but the passing of the old Buff, a sports paper in its own right, was still mourned by many in the county. The decision to resurrect it was rewarded with a sale in excess of 9,000 copies.

Mr Norman Jones, advertisement manager, retired after nearly 46 years service in August, 1988. He had begun work as an office boy when he was 14 and then became the newspaper's only advertising representative in the early 1950s.

Former Midlands Journalist of the Year Mr Ian Amos was appointed editor of the Leicester Mail in August, 1988. He began his career in journalism 15 years before and served as editor of the Matlock Mercury before taking up an editorship in the Canary Islands.

More than 60 people gathered at Leicester's Grand Hotel in November, 1988, to mark the 25th anniversary of the closure of the Leicester Evening Mail. The former general manager, Mr Jeff Malton, who became Northcliffe Group general manager, paid tribute to a great team who worked hard.

Mr John Aldridge, managing director, was appointed to the main board of the parent Northcliffe Newspapers Group in December, 1988. He retained his responsibility as managing director of the Leicester Mercury Group and was to continue to be based at the St George Street offices. He played an active role in the Newspaper Society, being chairman of the advertising committee, a member of the society's council and a member of the general purposes committee.

Four new appointments were made in January, 1989. Mr Paul Kearney was the new assistant managing director. He moved from London, where he was Northcliffe group assistant advertising director. Miss Christine Ward came from Manchester to become advertisement manager (development). The new classified advertisement manager was Mr Nick Weston, who had worked at various newspapers within the Northcliffe group for four and a half years. Assistant publishing manager Mr Graham Macready became distribution manager. Graham used to run ten miles to work several times a week from his home in Quorn.

Following the tragic plane crash at Kegworth, the Mercury produced a 7am Special Edition. Reporters and photographers were praised by many for their words and pictures, which were presented without intrusion and sensationalisation.

1989

◆ Leicester Mail reporter Sarah Pilkington won the Young Journalist of the Year category in the Whitbread Regional Press Awards in January, 1989. She received £500 and a trophy. Sarah's work was praised by the judges as being 'of a consistently high standard, showing promise for the future and a maturity beyond her years.'

◆ The Christmas tree outside the Leicester Mercury offices in St George Street, Leicester, was deliberately left in place after Twelfth Night. The tree had been chosen by a pair of blackbirds to rear their family.

Left: Mr William Green.

1989

◆ One of Leicestershire's best known journalists, Mr Colin Vann, retired in May after 44 years, 33 of them spent reporting local politics. He was educated at Loughborough Grammar School and joined the newspaper at the age of 16. He had interviewed many famous people, including several prime ministers and The Beatles. An old friend, Sonny Monk, played at the retirement reception held at the Mercury offices.

◆ Fifty years had passed since the start of the Second World War and the Mercury marked the occasion with a special publication Leicestershire At War.

◆ A new superhero hit the streets of Leicester and astonished citizens with his inspiring powers. People were asking: Who is this blue and yellow caped figure? What can he do for us? 'My name is Captain Classified,' said the spaceman. 'I have the power to sell anything you want, fast, for cash, through the advertising pages of the Leicester Mercury. You earthlings come from the planet Earth in the Milky Way. But I come from the planet Mercury in St George's Way! May the force of Leicester Mercury classified advertising be with you!'

Former sports editor of the Mercury, Mr David Welch, was appointed sports editor of the Daily Telegraph. A racing specialist, he spent 15 years with the Mercury after taking a teacher training course at Loughborough college. Former Daily Telegraph sports editor Mr Ron O'Connor died in a car accident on Boxing Day.

Melton Mowbray's Mr Leicester Mercury, Mr John Newell, retired after a career spanning half a century, during which he had become one of the town's best-known characters. He was a familiar face to thousands of people in Melton, where he had worked at the paper's branch office since leaving school at 15.

The Mercury held its very first phone vote over two days in March, 1989. The Leicestershire Health Authority, on the casting vote of its chairman, Mr G Farnham, had said 'Yes' to the addition of fluoride in the water supply. The phone poll organisers were staggered by the level and intensity of the response. 24,181 people had taken the time, trouble and expense to vote. Only 1,566 said Yes to fluoride. Mr Farnham was urged by the editor, Mr Alex Leys, to back down from his decision. Mr Farnham stood by his decision and was backed by Mr G Cinderby, the District General Manager of the Health Authority in a letter to the paper. In the following April, Leicestershire's major news organisations joined in what was believed was a unique experiment in giving the people the right to vote in the fluoride debate. It was timed to enable members of the Health Authority to be aware of the current feeling before the met on May 10. The result was published on May 4. This time 66,215 people voted – only 4,394 voted in favour, which meant 93 per cent were against having fluoride in the water supply. Mr Farnham insisted telephone polls, although interesting, cannot be accepted as an assessment of democratic opinion. He knew of at least one person who does not even live in the county who recorded five votes. In February, 1990, Severn Trent Water told the authority that it would not add fluoride to Leicestershire's water supplies in the foreseeable future. The battle was won.

Miss Helen Clement, Mercury Newspapers in Education co-ordinator, won a £4,300 scholarship from the Worshipful Company of Stationers and Newspaper Makers in March, 1989, to study in the States for six weeks. She was hoping the trip would open up new horizons as to how schoolchildren can learn more about newspapers by using them in as many ways as possible in and out of the classroom. She

attended a special awards dinner in London in May and met the Duchess of York.

Features editor for the previous 15 years, Mr George Graham, retired in April, 1989. He began his career as a reporter and sub-editor on the Glasgow Herald in 1944. Nine years later he joined the Leicester Evening Mail and then from 1963 the Leicester Chronicle. He was presented with a hedge trimmer.

A former Mercury reporter, Mr Roger Kenyon, a former editor of the influential South African magazine The Drum, died aged 48 in May, 1989. Tributes sent to his wife, Christine, in Cape Town, included one from Archbishop Desmond Tutu, who knew him well.

Press room manager Mr Gordon Cooper retired in October 1989 after 30 years of ensuring the presses rolled smoothly. He had witnessed many changes to the paper since his appointment as a machine minder in 1959.

After examination of various editorial computer systems, the Mercury opted for GBT Mentor equipment which was delivered to St George Street on September 4. 44 sub-editor terminals and 37 reporter and inputter terminals were connected to the system and within two months, after in-house training, all editorial sections had discarded pen and paper and were working on screen.

Joan Stephens, in her column dated October 6, 1989, describes the working conditions current at the time:

> A few days ago a visitor to this office was greeted with the cheerful sound of dozens of typewriters all clattering away merrily as journalists committed their thoughts and reports to paper. Today the office is full of near noiseless concentration. We each have our own silent screen to hunch over, stare at and control. The trouble is that some of us, myself included, have a lurking suspicion that it is the infernal machine, not its operator, that actually does the controlling. Like my colleagues, I recently spent two days being converted to the new technology which now brings you your nightly Leicester Mercury. I was initiated into the mysteries of using a personal computer, tried to come to terms with a whole new vocabulary in which a cursor has nothing to do with swearing, a basket bears no relation to wickerwork and pressing a key marked alt does not cause the machine to sing to you in a high voice... Eventually, of course, my

VDU and I will establish a relationship of mutual tolerance, if not understanding. Meanwhile I search in vain for the missing key – the one option I need above all others – the panic button.'

Mr Alec Eves, who retired in 1975 as Industrial Correspondent, died in November, 1989, aged 78. His knowledge and enthusiasm made him a well-known and respected figure in companies throughout the city and county.

November 20, 1989, saw a new edition hit the streets of Leicester. A daily Asia Edition in English was targeted at the city's 77,000 Asians (27 per cent of the city's 285,000 population). It was the brainchild of the editor, Mr Alex Leys. It was like the 'mainstream' paper, except that five pages were devoted to news, features and sports from the Indian sub-continent. By December, circulation of the Asia Edition had jumped more than a third.

BBC Radio Leicester broadcast live from the Mercury offices on November 24. First Tony Wadsworth, then John Florance and Halyna Kozak followed the production process of the newspaper from the planning stage through to its delivery to newsagents. Before leaving the building, the visitors from the radio station were able to see photographs of themselves in the main edition of the newspaper.

Due again to rising costs, the price of the Mercury was increased to 22p in December, 1989. Newsprint cost upwards of £460 a tonne.

Archive Publications Ltd in association with the Leicester Mercury published Leicester in the Fifties in December, 1989. It had been prepared by Douglas Goodlad and the author, using photographs kept in the Mercury library. Although it contained one or two errors, it contained a feast of nostalgia for those who lived through the decade.

Mr John Fortune, who was appointed editor of the Mercury soon after the end of the Second World War and remained in the editorial chair for 22 years, died in hospital in Greenock, Strathclyde, at the age of 80, in December, 1989. He joined the paper as a junior reporter in 1929 and retired as chairman and managing director after the paper's centenary celebrations in 1974. He was survived by his third wife, Elizabeth, and an only daughter, Mrs Lindsay Taylor, of Groby Lane, Newtown Linford.

Fairfield News Shops continued to expand at a rapid rate and its shops numbered 38 by the end of the year. It contributed £7 million to a total 1989 turnover of £33,327,166.

Below: Fame on Radio Leicester!

Chapter 12

Looking to the Future
1990 – 1999

The beginning of the 1990s saw a major move forward in the technological revolution at the St George Street offices, an advance unequalled in the Group's long history.

The Mercury became one of the first daily papers in the country to be produced completely electronically and a £15 million investment in new offset presses, plate-making and inserting equipment resulted in full-colour reproduction and printing of the highest quality.

Direct input by the Advertisement and Editorial Departments, introduced in 1988 and 1989 respectively, was followed by full-page make-up on Apple Mac terminal screens. Pages until then consisted of bromides for pasting up on what was still known as the 'stone' (a hangover from the days of the heavy metal formes). By the end of 1992, pages were being transferred electronically direct from Apple Mac screens to negative. The bromides and the stone were no more.

Two new Goss HT 60 web offset presses were in action for the first time, replacing the two lines of Goss Headliner letterpress presses, which had served the Mercury and its allied papers so well for 25 years. Printing began on July 9, 1992, weeks earlier than had been planned because of a strike by haulage drivers in France. Plates for the old presses (supplied by a French firm because Mercury-sized plates could not be obtained in Britain) were stranded abroad. Advertising and Editorial page layouts were swiftly amended to fit the smaller offset format and the newly-trained press hall crews were alerted. That the premature launch was so successful was a tribute to the months of preparation and training by all departments involved.

The new presses, made by Rockwell Graphics Ltd of Preston, Lancashire, were

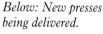

Below: New presses being delivered.

Above: The Goss HT 60 presses in situ.

Below: Press Hall staff.

each capable of printing 60,000 copies per hour, twice the speed of the letterpress lines. The new lithographic process allowed the scanning of pages electronically in order to pre-set the supply of ink to the presses, ensuring a crisp black type image and quality full-colour reproduction. The presses were linked to a Ferag inserting system and in January 1993 insertion of pre-printed supplements came on line.

The Multi-Media Promotions trophy was presented to the Leicester Mercury at the annual Newspaper Society conference in Harrogate for the promotion of the Asia Edition. The newspaper was praised for leading the field in target-marketing, for its point-of-sale promotion, merchandising, canvassing and after-sales care.

Reporting staff at the newspaper were shocked and saddened to hear of the death of

120

1990

◆ The Mercury launched a youth newspaper in September 1990, named the Merc. It was an instant hit with staff at the City Council. Ms Debra Reynolds, the press officer, rang within an hour of the paper hitting the streets to say young and older staff alike enjoyed the range of interviews, reviews and features in the first issue and were looking forward to the next one.

◆ Former Mercury cartoonist and music critic Mr Ralph Pugsley, died in October, 1990, aged 75. He retired to the Isle of Wight in 1977, then moved to his home county of Devon.

◆ Mercury Women's Page diarist from 1947 to 1967, Kaye Almey, retired in November, 1990. She became the highly successful researcher and writer of Inquiry Desk. She left Leicester to go and live in Essex.

◆ Mercury photographer Glen Tillyard was chosen as Midlands Press Photographer of the Year and colleague David White selected as Most Promising Newcomer in November, 1990. Mr Leys said: 'These awards are further proof, if it were needed, of this newspaper's continuing pursuit of excellence. I am very pleased for them.'

former journalist Graham Danter (24) in a swimming accident in Australia. He had spent more than two years as a reporter and sub-editor before fulfilling a long-standing ambition to head for Australia. He was working as a sub-editor with the Daily Mirror in Sydney. A fund was set up in his name to provide an annual travel award open to students at the Centre for Journalism Studies in Cardiff, where Graham learned his profession.

News editor Hugh Berlyn was appointed Deputy Editor of the Western Morning News in Plymouth in March, 1990. He had been at the Mercury for 15 months, but had lived in Leicester for seven years, having previously worked as news editor for BBC Radio Leicester.

Assistant editor Ms Anita Syvret was appointed the new editor of the Gloucestershire Echo in June, 1990. Her appointment meant she would be the only woman editing a regional daily newspaper in Britain. She had joined the Mercury in 1987 from the Derby Evening Telegraph where she was assistant news editor.

Press room manager Mr John Bosworth retired after 40 years and a day at the beginning of June, 1990. His very first job at the Mercury was the person responsible for sweeping up and collecting bits of waste paper in the press room. He was presented with a silver salver, a barometer – and six Mars Bars!

Deputy newspaper sales manager Mr Les Morgan left the company to become newspaper sales manager of the Torquay Herald Express in June, 1990.

The managing director of the Mercury, Mr John Aldridge, was appointed to the board of the Press Association in June, 1990. He was also senior vice-president of the Newspaper Society and a member of the main board of Northcliffe Newspapers Group.

The Mercury film critic for more than 50 years, Douglas Goodlad, died at the age of 74 in August 1990. He started work as a writer with the Illustrated Leicester Chronicle in the mid-1930s and became its editor soon after the war and continued until the paper's closure in October, 1980. He gained an increasing reputation as a broadcaster – a secondary career he pursued from the early 1950s – with Radio Leicester and his musical memories graced the airwaves for more than a decade.

London-based Mr Ted Glynn had joined the Board of Directors in December 1986 and, following the retirement of Mr Tony Dyer, Northcliffe Deputy Managing Director Mr Alec Davidson joined the Board in June 1989. In September 1990, two men,

who between them had clocked up more than 75 years with the paper, departed. They were former Director Mr Brett Chambers and Production Director Mr Eric Hollingworth.

Mr Hollingworth joined the Mercury in 1943 as an apprentice copy holder and compositor when 14 (popular rumour had it that he turned up for the interview in short trousers!) and he climbed the production ladder to become director in 1983.

Mr Chambers was the first accountant to be employed when he joined in 1961. It was his proud claim that since 1965, when he was appointed Company Secretary, he had not missed a single board meeting. He became a director of the company in 1982. One little known fact is that Mr Chambers was on the books of Leicester City Football Club both before and after his service in the Fleet Air Arm between 1944 and 1947. But cricket was his great love and had played for 50 years, including for the Newtown Linford's Over-40s Strollers side. He was given life membership of Leicestershire County Cricket Club and presented with a bat signed by the entire team at his retirement celebration.

Maybe, as a result of a phone vote in November, 1990, the old Lewis's tower still stands on Humberstone Gate in Leicester. 3,213 (78.3 per cent) were against demolition and only 893 for. A spokesman for the developers of Leicester Gates said; 'We would still urge the people of Leicester to weigh up the benefits of keeping an outdated, outmoded building against providing a European shopping centre that will last for years to come.' The Department of the Environment had refused to protect the store by listing it. Mr Peter Nottingham, who collected 1,800 signatures from people wanting the landmark saved, had conceded he had lost the battle to stop the developers knocking it down.

Mr Bob Russell retired in November, 1990. He first joined the Mercury as a 16-year-old copy holder in 1945 and his career included work as a reporter, sub-editor, Civics writer and editor, finally with the Loughborough Mail. He planned to spend more time in Norfolk, where he was brought up.

Mercury copytaker Mrs Joyce Parkin was a losing finalist in the BBC's Going for Gold quiz programme. She represented Scotland in the international contest. She was so close to winning the star holiday prize – in Kenya.

Health correspondent Mr Barry Nelson was presented with a framed certificate at the annual Private Patients Plan/Medical Journalists' Association Medical Journalism Advancement Awards in London. He was commended for Mercury articles during 1990, including the Lifebeat series.

The general manager of Mercury News Shops (formerly Fairfield News), Mr Gary Wells, left in December, 1990, to take over a chain of newsagents shops in Northamptonshire.

Mr William Kidd, who headed the paper's civics department from 1963 until he retired in 1972, died at the end of 1990. He began his career at the Leicester Evening Mail in 1930 and was appointed news editor. He was put in charge of the Mercury's civics department when the two papers merged. So successful was he at forging close links between the council and the newspaper that colleagues referred to him as 'Mr Civics.' Shortly after he retired, Mr Kidd was awarded the MBE. Former Leicester Lord Mayor Councillor Janet Setchfield described Mr Kidd as a much liked and well respected reporter. 'Mr Kidd was a familiar face at council meetings and epitomised the character of a local journalist. He was a larger than life figure who obviously enjoyed his work.' A park seat dedicated to the memory of Mr Kidd was sited close to the entrance of John's Lee Wood in Newtown Linford in March, 1992.

On January 22, 1991, the Mercury joined forces with the Royal Mail in a mission to airlift the paper to county troops in the battle-torn Gulf. Dozens of copies were to be flown out every night to keep our soldiers in touch with what was happening back home. As an extension to this, the Mercury played Cupid in the Gulf from January 28, giving readers the opportunity to tell our Gulf troops how much readers cared about them. A 30-strong team of volunteers manned telephones each day between 6pm and 8pm. Every day up to 50,000 letters were despatched to the British Forces sorting offices in London. The total eventually hit 70,000. Royal Mail Leicester communications manager Mr Graham Burdett described the response from Mercury readers as: 'phenomenal.' Leicester Mercury editor Mr Alex Leys said: 'It just shows how splendidly Leicestershire people respond at times of need.' The initiative even brought praise from the Foreign Secretary, Mr Douglas Hurd.

A senior internal promotion and three board appointments were announced at the beginning of February, 1991. Mr Barry Wootten, advertisement director, was appointed assistant to managing director Mr John Aldridge. Mr Bill Dinsmor joined the Mercury as technical director. He was in charge of production at the Thomson Regional Newspapers Scottish newspapers,

including The Scotsman. Mr Philip Brewin became advertisement director and Mr Michael Geraghty was appointed the paper's first circulation director. Mr Geraghty began his career with Thomson Regional Newspapers in 1973. An additional staff benefit was instituted at the beginning of February. An Alliance and Leicester cash machine was installed in the foyer of the Mercury building. It was the first machine the building society had placed in premises other than its own branches or the offices of an agent.

Mercury journalist Ather Mirza, who was in daily charge of the Asia Edition, won a prestigious travel scholarship to work in India. He was to spend a month at The Hindu newspaper after being awarded a Commonwealth Union scholarship.

Mr Colin Mullins was appointed the general manager, retail shops, of the Mercury Group. He had been running his own specialist retail news consultancy in Essex and previously held senior posts with the Martin retail group, where he was responsible for 150 shops in the south of England and then took up a purchasing post with them, as group news buying manager.

Mr John Aldridge became Chairman of the Leicester Mercury Group in May, 1991. He also became the new president of the Newspaper Society, which comprises more than 1,000 regional and local newspapers and publications in the United Kingdom – almost 95 per cent of the regional press. He was also a director of the Press Association, the Regional Daily Advertising Council and Associated Newspapers (Hungary) Ltd. The theme for his year of office was to be In Print In Mind. 'My basic concerns are that we must educate young people to use newspapers as a source of both information and entertainment and I shall be urging greater emphasis on Newspapers-in-Education. I also plan to work with the Department of Education and Science and the Adult Literacy Campaign. I believe the printed media must make a genuine commitment to the campaign and be prepared to put resources into it. If we do not, we could find ourselves in the future without a market as the electronic media assumes greater importance in people's lives.' Mr Aldridge became the fourth president of the Newspaper Society from the Mercury. He followed in the footsteps of Mr Francis Hewitt (1892-3), Mr Clement Barton (1957-8) and Mr Arthur Peake (1966-7).

Former Mercury news editor Mr Hugh Berlyn was appointed editor of the Gloucester Citizen newspaper in May 1991.

◆ Mercury political correspondent Mark D'Arcy was named Columnist of the Year in the UK Press Gazette British Regional Press Awards on April 17, 1991. The judges said he 'displayed measured, analytical and detailed approach to the events of the day.'

◆ It was up, up and away for the Mercury's newest recruit in April, 1991. The paper's hot air balloon took to the skies for her maiden flight and first to take flight were Mr John Aldridge, his wife June and Mercury publicity and promotions manager, Mrs Susan Hollins.

◆ The Saturday morning Sporting Green was launched in August, 1991 – almost 28 years since the former Leicester Evening Mail's 'Green 'Un' was last on sale on the city streets on Saturdays. Leicestershire became the only place in Britain to have three different coloured newspapers on sale on the same day. It had a special introductory price of 15p and 19,000 went out on the first day. Mr Cliff Ginetta, chairman of Leicester City Supporters' Club, said he was impressed. 'It's something completely different for Leicester. There's plenty to read.'

WAR EDITION

Leicester Mercury

Our thought: *May victory be ours* | THURSDAY, JANUARY 17, 1991 | Price: 25p

At 3.58am today Pentagon sources told waiting world:

SADDAM MAULED

RAF crews jubilant at spectacular success

> 'While the world waited, Saddam Hussein met every overture of peace with open contempt.

WAR exploded in the Gulf early today as President George Bush hurled the world's mightiest airforce against Iraq.

And after waves of allied fighter planes and bombers had struck at targets in Iraq and Kuwait, Pentagon sources reported that the Iraqi air force had been decimated.

The same sources were quoted as saying that much of President Saddam Hussein's elite Republican guard had been destroyed.

Jubilant RAF sources in the Gulf spoke of a 100 per cent successful operation by the Tornado crews.

"It is a spectacular example of a well-planned and well-executed operation," said one officer.

As eye-witness reports flooded in, the scale of the "surgical bombing" operation became apparent. Tomahawk cruise missiles and aircraft from the US, British, Saudi and Kuwaiti air forces were involved.

It was 2am GMT that President Bush told the world in a live television broadcast: "The battle has been joined."

He gave his address just hours after the order to attack was given.

Soon after that order, the clear, starry sky over Baghdad was illuminated by anti-aircraft tracer fire as bombs pounded the Iraqi capital.

Television reporters at the scene said explosions shook the ground and an oil refinery 10 miles away was in flames.

The attack signalled the end of Operation Desert Shield and the beginning of Operation Desert Storm.

In his address, President Bush said the US-led allied forces had "exhausted all reasonable efforts" to reach a peaceful diplomatic solution to the Gulf crisis sparked by Iraq's August 2 invasion of Kuwait.

Earlier, White House spokesman Marlin Fitzwater said: "The liberation of Kuwait has begun."

President Bush called [...] Major before the offensive [...]

In his address, the Pre[...] forces would crush Iraq's [...] weapons capability in t[...] Kuwait.

He blamed Iraqi leader [...] the conflict.

"This conflict started [...] dictator of Iraq invaded [...] neighbour."

The strike followed "m[...] virtually endless diplomati[...] of the UN, the US and ma[...] said.

As the President spoke [...] ment of Baghdad was rep[...] with waves of three or fou[...] 15 minutes to attack the cit[...]

Gulf war latest, pages 2,3 and back page; Weapons of wa[...]

Two of the main international news stories of 1991 are graphically illustrated by these front pages. The gulf war reached its climax on January 17, 1991, and a breakthrough was made for the hostages held in the Lebanon when, on Monday November 18, 1991 Terry Waite was finally freed after 1,763 days in captivity.

Leicester Mercury

Our thought: *Into the sunlight* | MONDAY, NOVEMBER 18, 1991 | Price [...]

FREEDOM

HOSTAGE Terry Waite, held hostage for 1,763 days in Lebanon, was freed this afternoon.

A Lebanese government source close to Syria said the 52-year-old Church of England envoy was released along with Scots-born American hostage Thomas Sutherland and both were on their way to Damascus.

The Syrian Foreign Ministry did not confirm the release. It said the two hostages were expected to be freed within the next few hours, that in Beirut Lebanese foreign minister Fares Bueiz said the two men had already been released.

The hostage-takers Islamic Jihad, a pro-Iranian Muslim group, said the move was connected to United Nations efforts to end the crisis.

As RAF VC-10 jet carrying Mr Waite's brother David, Foreign Office officials and representatives of Lambeth Palace, was on standby at Akrotiri, Cyprus, ready to bring the church envoys back to Britain.

The specially fitted-out plane left RAF Brize Norton, Oxfordshire, at 6am today at the request of the Foreign Office.

Mr Waite is reported to be flown to RAF Lyneham, Wilts, the scene of previous emotional homecomings for hostages John McCarthy and Jack Mann earlier this year.

FREEDOM for Mr Waite and Mr Sutherland brings to an end Britain's five and a half year hostage drama which began when schoolteacher Brian Keenan was bundled into a car by Muslim gunmen on April 11 1986.

Mr Waite disappeared on January 20, 1987, while on a mission for Lord Runcie, then Archbishop of Canterbury, to try to win freedom for Western hostages.

Islamic Jihad sent a brief typewritten statement to an international news agency in Beirut earlier today accompanied by an old black-and-white photograph of American hostage Terry Anderson.

The group said: "To complete what we have started with the Secretary-General of the United Nations (Javier) Perez de Cuellar, we announce today the release of 1) Terry Waite 2) Thomas Sutherland."

Continued on page 3

■ Day of drama: The release from captivity, Pages 3,4,5,14 and 23

Assistant financial director Miss Rosemary Kind won a three-week scholarship in the United States and Canada in May, 1991. The scheme, for young people in printing and allied trades, was organised by the Worshipful Company of Stationers and Newspaper Makers. She was to research the different approaches to producing a local newspaper.

Mercury Transport Manager Mr Peter Ganly retired in May, 1991, after 22 years' service. He took charge of the company's vehicles in 1969 when the paper had just six cars – in 1991 there were 107.

Internal auditor Mrs Jane Birch became the new chairman of the Midlands district branch of the Institute of Internal Auditors at the end of May, 1991. She said many businesses were looking for the institute's qualifications as they were 'more relevant than mainstream accountancy qualifications.'

At the beginning of June, 1991, Mr Paul Kearney was appointed deputy managing director of the Mercury. He joined the company as assistant managing director in 1988, having previously been in London as Northcliffe Newspapers group assistant advertising director. In April, 1992, Mr Kearney was declared winner of the East Midlands Young Manager of the Year Award. He received a free place on a British Institute of Management course and a trophy from NatWest.

After 39 years' service with the Mercury group, Mr Malcolm McIntosh retired at the end of July, 1991. He was assistant editor on the Illustrated Leicester Chronicle until its closure in 1979 and then worked on a number of other titles before moving to the Features Department in 1982 and became deputy features editor in 1987. He still writes the gardening column in the Saturday edition of the Mercury.

The next month saw three more retirements. Mr Peter Jackson had joined the Mercury in 1943 and was apprenticed in the composing room. He worked his way up and became deputy head reader. He had been a member of St John Ambulance for 40 years and was a member of the Leicestershire Council of the Order of St John and held the senior rank of Commander Brother of the Order. He had also been a magistrate for 13 years. Mr Derek Bonser had been at the Mercury for 41 years and retired as deputy manager of the plate-making department. One of the first tele-sales girls in 1963, Miss Marian Perry, retired in August. Previously she worked for the Evening Mail and her career had covered 38 years.

The Mercury commercial departments saw new senior appointments. Advertisement manager (classified), Mr Nick Weston, was made general manager Mail Group Newspapers. Advertisement manager (sales), Mr John Percy, became creative services manager. Miss Christine Ward, advertisement manager (development), was appointed display advertising sales manager and, joining the company from outside was Miss Alison Gordon, who became the new general classified manager. She was group sales development executive with Northcliffe in London.

To make more room for news in the early pages of the Mercury, the Letters and Mr Leicester page was moved from four to six on September 2, 1991. It gave the Mercury a busier new look.

They say things happen in threes! They certainly did for Mercury newsman David Harrison. His windscreen shattered when he opened issue one of The Sporting Green. A landlady alarmingly dropped a glass behind him when he opened issue two. When he opened issue three in his local ... nothing happened! Nothing at all! Convinced he had broken his run of shattering experiences, David went home to find ... yes, you've guessed it ... he had locked himself out! His comment? 'I was shattered!'

Mr John Murray, a member of the Board since 1970, retired in September, 1991.

At the beginning of December, 1991, county readers and shoppers gave a resounding thumbs down to Sunday shopping in a special Mercury telephone poll. An overwhelming 7,509 people called in on the controversial issue. The poll coincided with a move by supermarket chains across the country to open their doors to the public for the first time. But of those who called 61.3 per cent (4,603) said they were opposed to Sunday trading.

The first woman director in the 118-year history of the Mercury, Miss Marlen Roberts, took up her appointment as assistant to the managing director, responsible for newspaper sales, in January, 1992. She had spent 12 years on the Liverpool Daily Post before moving in 1988 to the Northcliffe Newspaper Group headquarters in London, where she was advertisement sales development director.

The Leicester Mercury's pioneering approach to Newspapers in Education was recognised with a major award. Miss Helen Clement, the paper's NiE co-ordinator, was an East Midlands regional winner of the Teacher Placement Service Award to Industry. She had also won the Newspaper Society NiE General Award, the Northcliffe

1992

◆ The Nuneaton Tribune closed at the beginning of 1992. Then a new paper hit the streets – the Nuneaton edition of the Mercury. A team of reporters and photographers were set up to capture the news as it happened in the town. They were Paul Webb, Marc Astley, James Hermon, Chris Hopkins, Ted Cottrell (formerly the Tribune's chief photographer), Trevor Moore and Coral Urquhart. Micky Payne joined the team in March, 1992. It was not long before the new edition changed its name ... to The Mercury. Towards the end of January, it was given an introductory price of 18p, the same price as the Tribune.

◆ April 1, 1992, saw the launch of the Mercury's new service bringing daily updates on the county's air quality. Weather experts said that in recent years the quality of the air we breathe had become of increasing concern to many people. As levels of pollution worsened, more people were being hit by breathing difficulties and lung complaints. Meteorological experts from the Warren Springs Laboratories in Stevenage, Hertfordshire, were to compile reports for Leicestershire.

Above: 'Leicestershire: Key changes 1930 to 1990', a publication from the Leicester Mercury Newspapers in Education

Right: Miss Claire Gillingwater

creator of popular journalism. Mr Paul Dacre took over as editor of the Daily Mail.

Terry Doughty, a statistics clerk at the Mercury, was a contestant on the television programme Countdown in July, 1992. He had promised to raise some £500 in sponsorship for the roof fund of St Paul's Church, Kirby Road, Leicester.

Deputy managing director Mr Paul Kearney was appointed managing director of Bristol United Press in July, 1992. He was to take up his new position in October, 1992.

Reader T R Chamberlain of Groby was praised by the editor in July for spotting that the newspaper's pictures had been very sharp and had a special quality about them. In fact the two new press lines were in action producing results that would be hard to better anywhere in the industry.

Regular Leicester Mercury writer Valeen Marriott, who had contributed features on practically every conceivable domestic and show business subject for the previous 35 years, died at her home in Southwold, Suffolk, aged 61, in August, 1992. She left a husband, Denis, former treasurer of Oadby Council before local government reorganisation and a popular cabaret pianist, who also produced many East Coast summer season shows, two daughters and a son.

Miss Claire Gillingwater, who was assistant news editor three and a half years previously and had been working in television, as a producer on TVam and Sky News, was appointed deputy editor in August, 1992, following the departure of Mr Malcolm Pheby, who left to become editor of

Newspapers in Education Enterprise Award and the Advertising Media Representative Agency Newspaper In Education Award.

The Herald and Post reported in June, 1992, that the Leicester Mercury was giving away its paper for a week in some areas 'in an attempt to turn-around its flagging sales.'

Mercury financial director Mr Barry Thompson was the new president of the Young Newspaper Executives' Association in July, 1992. His first task was to organise the annual conference, with speakers looking at ways of Navigating the Nineties. 'The recession has made it necessary to come up with new ideas, to be more creative and more competitive,' he said.

A new chairman was announced for Associated Newspapers, the group which owns the Leicester Mercury. Sir David English was editor of the Daily Mail for the previous 21 years and oversaw the transformation of the paper into a highly successful middle-market tabloid. He succeeded Lord Rothermere, whose great uncle was the first Lord Northcliffe, the

the Evening Star in Ipswich. Editor Mr Alex Leys said: 'Malcolm Pheby has had an enormous influence on all aspects of the newspaper, from the design perspective, the implementation of advanced editorial computer technology and, most important of all, the newspaper's content. His sheer professionalism, allied to immense hard work and unending enthusiasm were his hallmarks. He will be a hard act to follow.'

A new Mercury News Shop and newspaper branch office opened on the ground floor of Lewis's store in Humberstone Gate, Leicester, in November, 1992. It was further evidence of the still more exciting profile the newspaper was taking within the city centre.

'On This Day' first appeared on Mr Leicester's Diary page on November 30, 1992. It aimed to cover local and national events of 25 and 50 years ago and was compiled by the author from the microfilm files of the Mercury.

The television guide moved to page two on December 22, 1992.

UK News was created to supply Northcliffe group titles with national and international news. Titles from other groups also took the new service. Mr Leys became Managing and Editorial Director of the agency on June 15, 1993.

On leaving the Mercury, he said: 'Perhaps one of the greatest victories for the Mercury and its readers was our Woody Tree campaign, which brought the new National Forest to the county.'

Mr Leys was succeeded as Mercury editor by Mr Nick Carter, formerly editor of the South Wales Evening Post and before that deputy editor of the South Wales Echo in Cardiff.

Staff photographer Allie Day was an outright winner in the Kodak Regional Press Awards with an atmospheric picture, Black Widow, taken in Crete. She and photographic printer Jenny Schofield received £100 each for the entry.

Two new Swiss-made Ferag ETR-N inserting machines, costing more than £2 million, were first used in March, 1993. They slipped a separate section into the main body of every newspaper and doubled the amount of colour in each copy, at an incredible speed of up to 40,000 newspapers an hour.

Mr Roland Orton, one of the best known freelance journalists and broadcasters in Leicestershire, who worked for a short time as a paste-boy in the Mercury wire-room, died in May, 1993. His Leicester News Services agency was sold in 1987.

Mercury journalist Ather Mirza was appointed Assistant Registrar at the

Above: The last but one issue of the Leicester Mercury Citizens Guide, in September of 1992.

Left: Mr Nick Carter, Editor.

1994

◆ Former Mercury journalist and assistant news editor Anthony Abbott won the title of Most Romantic Man in Britain in February, 1994. He met his wife Karrie whilst in Leicester and, when the couple moved to Plymouth in 1990, Mr Abbott decided to make a proposition with a difference. He flashed the proposal on the electronic score board at a Plymouth Argyle football match. Karrie was so 'gobsmacked' that she could not give him an answer until half-time. They jetted off to Hong King and Bali on an all-expenses-paid two-week holiday as the prize.

◆ An astonishing 15,000 supporters turn up for the Family Night Football match against Manchester United Reserves in February, 1994. Leicester City Football Club had began running these special nights in association with the Leicester Mercury the previous month.

Right: Mr Simon Crane.

University of Leicester in June, 1993. He was to act as press and public relations officer in the University's external relations department.

Mercury News shops now totalled 43 and were able to offer facilities for placing classified advertisements.

The 17-year-old clock and temperature gauge on top of the Mercury building was replaced by a new improved model in July, 1993. It cost £14,600, had a dot matrix display and was radio-controlled from a transmitter in Rugby.

Former assistant editor, Mr Michael Shuttlewood, died aged 69 in August, 1993. He had enjoyed a 45-year career in journalism with the former Leicester Evening Mail and the Leicester Mercury.

One of the Mercury's longest-serving photographers retired after 44 years in September, 1993. Mr Colin Axford joined the company as an office junior in 1949 and had seen five editors come and go and a complete turn-around in staff.

The Hinckley edition took on a new look on September 7, 1993. It had a four-page pull-out named The Mercury in Hinckley and was packed with Hinckley news and information.

The cover price of the Mercury was increased to 26p in September, 1993, the first increase for three years.

The Newspaper in Education department launched a 'classroom in a newspaper' – a resource centre to offer newsroom and office facilities and act as a base for running fun practical learning activities using the newspaper.

A former Mercury chief telegraphist, Mr A J Fred Chandler, died in December, 1993, aged 92. He joined the company in 1921, when he helped install the Creed system of telegraphy, which revolutionised newspaper work.

Leicester City Football Club teamed up with the Mercury in December, 1993, to launch an innovative scheme to attract 5,000 new young fans. The new Fox Club was the figure-head of the 1994 community programme aimed at taking the club out into the county. The Mercury was set to play a key role in the enterprise by publishing a Fox Club page every Saturday from January 8.

Mercury News shops opened their 45th branch in the main concourse of the Glenfield Hospital in January, 1994. Two specially-designed trolleys made twice-daily rounds of the hospital's wards to deliver national and local newspapers.

Assistant editor Mr Terry Dwyer retired at the end of January, 1994, after 43 years'

service. He joined as a cub reporter in 1951, when he was 16.

Mercury sub-editor Deepa Pathi won the female newspaper journalist of the year award from the annual Asian Film Academy in March, 1994.

The Daily Mail and General Trust bought the Nottingham Evening Post, one of Britain's biggest evening newspapers, for £92.85 million in June, 1994.

Trail-blazing work by the Newspapers in Education team, headed by Ms Annemarie Shillito, won high praise from the Newspaper Society in June, 1994. The project came second out of nearly 500 other NiE schemes in the Society's award for excellence. The team earned the accolade for running regular tours of the Mercury offices for primary school children, working with the University of Leicester School of Education, helping schools produce their own newspapers and publishing special supplements on history and citizenship.

The Week entertainment supplement published on Fridays was launched on August 19, 1994. Mr Mike Polanyk was appointed to co-ordinate the project and the author was set the task of compiling events, music and theatre lists.

The deputy editor, Miss Claire Gillingwater, left in July, 1994, to take up the editorship of the Evening News in Norwich. She was the fourth deputy editor to move on in the previous five years. Her successor was Mr Simon Crane, who had been assistant editor for the previous 11 months. Prior to that, he was features editor and had worked in Cheltenham and Loughborough.

The cover price of the Mercury was increased by a further 1p on September 19, 1994, to 27p.

The Mercury finished ahead of a strong field in winning a prestigious contract in October, 1994, to print the Racing Post six days a week. Pages were to be transmitted by British Telecom's Integrated Services Digital Network (ISDN) for output by Mercury staff. This was one of the largest non-group contracts won by a Northcliffe Newspaper group centre. The contract, which was to begin on January, 23, 1995, was signed by directors of the Mercury and the Racing Post at a Leicester race meeting.

A £1.5 million contract with press suppliers Rockwell Graphic Systems in November, 1994, meant that there would be an increase in the newspaper's ability to print colour pages. All ten units would now be able to print full colour.

Northcliffe Newspapers' managing director, Mr Ian Park, retired from the post, early in 1995. His successor was to be deputy managing director Mr Alec Davidson, who was to take up the post on May 15. Northcliffe finance director Mr Micahel Pelosi became deputy managing director. Mr Park was to replace Lord Rothermere as chairman of Northcliffe Newspapers.

A former Mercury employee who had spent more than 50 years in the newspaper business, died in February, 1995, aged 82. Mr Jim Wheeler had played a major part in preparing the paper for the changeover to computerised production techniques.

Mercury business editor, Mr John Stone, took early retirement in September, 1995, after nearly 25 years with the company. He was previously press officer with Rolls-Royce in Derby.

The Mercury and the Charlotte pub in Leicester launched a showcase night for new musical talent in September, 1995. Free entry vouchers were to be published in The Week.

Mr Barry Thompson, financial director, left at the end of September, 1995, to become financial director at East Midlands Airport. His successor was Miss Rosemary Kind, who returned to the Mercury after three years with another Northcliffe company, the Herald Express in Torquay.

Images of Leicester, compiled by the author and Peter Hollins, was published in October, 1995 and became an instant success. Dillons, Market Street, Leicester, called both the compilers in for a book signing session in the same month. A signed copy was presented to the Lady Mayoress of Leicester.

Former Mercury photographer, Eddie Lakin, died in November, 1995. During his career, he took pictures of the Queen's Coronation and the funeral of George VI.

Mr Phillip Inman joined the staff in November 1995 as Classified Sales Manager.

He came from the Hull Daily Mail, where he was General Advertisement Manager.

January 27, 1996, saw the first early Saturday morning edition, with its distinctive 'sunrise' masthead. The same day saw the demise of the Nuneaton edition, which was to be replaced by the Hinckley edition.

Some important improvements were made to the appearance of the Mercury at the end of February, 1996. A daily, four-page television guide was positioned in the centre of the paper. A detailed index to Mercury content appeared on page two, which was to also feature an at-a-glance guide to prime-time television highlights. The rest of page two was to contain a round-up of important news items from the rest of the county. Overall, the size of the paper was to be reduced to bring it in line with other tabloid publications. This was prompted by rising newsprint costs and the difficulties of securing the previous, non-standard size.

Louisa Bayley was appointed business editor in April, 1996. She had been acting in the post for six months after John Stone's departure. From April 8, Business to Business classified advertising was accommodated on the daily business page instead at the back of the paper.

Behind the scenes, a company called New Solutions was carrying out a market research operation called Project Jupiter. They were looking at the particular needs of different sections of the readership and potential readership.

John Meehan was appointed editor of UK News. He was previously joint editor along with Ian Campbell, who had now joined Northcliffe Newspapers in its New Media Division. John left in January, 1997, to edit the Express and Echo in Exeter.

Northcliffe had decided that libraries in the group were to automate with an electronic archiving system named Phrasea, which was devised in France. It was the Leicester Mercury's turn to begin the system in April, 1996. At the start, staff were running the manual and the computer system side by side, in order to train them in the new system. It had its problems, but the enthusiasm of the library staff overcame them. Initially, we needed to print each page of the Mercury to the pages database before we began the task of linking parts of stories together and indexing them. The first part of the operation proved to be quite time-consuming – each page taking three to five minutes to print. The author took the tentative step of finishing with the scissors and paste manual system at Easter, knowing that, if both were to continue, the work would get seriously

1996

◆ The beginning of May saw a slight improvement in the Mercury's sales on the figures for the same week in 1995. An extra 129 copies were sold, representing a rise of 0.11%. The average daily sale for the week ending May 4 was 114,724. Figures for the week ending July 6 also saw a slight increase – 234 extra copies, representing an increase of 0.22%. Similarly, the week ending August 17 saw 210 more copies sold that the corresponding week in 1995, an increase of 0.19%.

behind. By May, it was decided, through a library, editorial and IT departments co-ordinating committee, to persuade IT to perform the printing of pages to the database task automatically in their department. So we started again, this time spending more valuable time linking and indexing.

Pictures became automated using Photogrid and Phrasea in July 1996. Now editorial staff could consult a browser in their own department to find the article or picture required.

It was announced in April, 1996, that the Chairman and Managing Director of the Leicester Mercury Group, Mr John Aldridge, planned to retire from that post on January 11, 1997. He was to continue for a further year as a Northcliffe Director, become non-executive chairman of the Leicester Mercury Group and to undertake various projects for Northcliffe. His replacement was to be Mr Tony Hill, who joined Northcliffe as managing Director of the Leicester Mercury Group. He had spent nearly all his life in the newspaper industry and joined from Thomson Regional Newspapers, where, for the previous seven years, he had been Managing Director of their Newcastle operation. Prior to this he had spent two years as Managing Director in the Teeside operation. Before his move to the North East in 1987, he spent six years with Thomsons at their South Wales base in Cardiff. Mr Hill received the OBE in the 1998 New Year Honours for services to the community in the North East.

Janet Rowlands, who had been co-ordinating training for the three centres, Nottingham, Derby and Leicester, was

officially appointed Regional Training Manager based in Leicester in May 1996.

Chief Cashier Mr Ron Smith retired at the end of October, 1996, after 43 and a half years' service. The sales ledger and cashier functions within the Finance Department were combined into a single section to be known as Financial Sevices, which was to be headed up by Gordon Robinson, who became Financial Services Supervisor.

Mr Cliff Frazher joined Mercury News Shops as Operations Director. He previously worked for Littlewood Stores, Martin Retail Group, Trust House Forte and Welcome Break. Mercury News Shops had grown to almost 60 outlets and was expanding into Nottinghamshire. As a consequence of the rapid growth, it was decided that, as from January 1, 1997, Mercury News Shops would cease to be a division of the Leicester Mercury Group and become part of Northcliffe Newspapers Group. And be known as Northcliffe Retail Ltd.

Deputy Newspaper Sales Manager, Karen Edwards, was appointed to Northcliffe's Newspaper sales operation in a training role relating to Telemarketing on January 6, 1997.

From January 16, 1997, the Thursday issue of the North West Leicestershire edition was to be sold for 10p, initially for a trial period of 13 weeks. The edition was to contain a significantly greater amount of local property, local jobs and local motors advertising in a pull-out supplement. At the same time, there was to be a local Postbag slot.

Print Manager Tracy Wright was appointed Operations Manager of Triangle Print (Derby) on February 3, 1997. His position at Leicester was filled by Mark Clayton, Tracy's deputy.

The Leicester Mercury Community Action programme was beginning to take shape at the beginning of 1997. Nicki Ward was building up a network of contacts with existing community groups and projects and was working to investigate new, undeveloped areas of opportunity. Research had indicated that the paper needed to develop much better contacts with communities and improve credibility as a newspaper which does care about helping people. The project went public in March, 1997, with the first weekly page dedicated to helping community projects by encouraging readers to get involved.

Mr Tony Hill sent out an open letter to staff in January, 1997. In it, he thanked everyone who made him feel so welcome during his first week. He warned of the new developments which could threaten the Mercury's future. Digital TV will transform

Right: Mr Tony Hill.

the broadcast media arena, mass, niche and specialist publications will continue to proliferate and divide every interest sector, while the internet, radio, poster and direct mail will further fragment the market. '1998 will become "the year of the Mercury" with a major drive and focus on every aspect of the newspaper. 1999 will see us celebrating the Mercury's 125th birthday – what a party we'll have! So, exciting and challenging times ahead. We must make sure we remain market focused and marketing driven, whilst also ensuring we have the right products and services, together with the right people in the right positions at the right time.'

Mr Paul Webb was promoted to the position of assistant editor on March 24, 1997. His prime responsibility was to be for the initial investigations into a new editorial system to replace GB, which would be affected by the 'Millennium bug.' Ian Croson was to replace him as chief sub-editor.

Week ending April 12, 1997, saw a dramatic 2.56% increase on sales the corresponding week in 1996, 2,848 more copies. Leicester City were due to appear at Wembley in the Coca-Cola Cup and this created extra interest. Football achievements also affected sales for the following week, resulting in a 1.23% increase, 1,418 more copies. In fact, the Cup Final contributed to nearly 160,000 extra sales overall. The special The Road to Wembley sold around 125,000 copies. The Sporting Blue sold more than 9,000 extras. Monday, April 7 (post Wembley edition) sold about 7,500 extra and Thursday, April 17 (post replay edition) sold nearly 15,500 extra. The officially audited sale figure (ABC) for the first four months of 1997 was just 26 short of being level with 1996.

The Mercury was highly commended in the Daily Newspaper of the Year category of the BT Midlands Press and Broadcasting Awards 1997.

Mr John Murray, Production Director with the Mercury from 1970 until his retirement in 1989, died in May, 1997. He had been with the paper for over 30 years. His funeral took place on May 9 at Gilroes Crematorium.

Christine Dooley was appointed Finance Director in July, 1997. She had held a senior role within the Finance Department of Northcliffe Newspapers, having joined Northcliffe in 1996 from Anderson's audit and management consultancy practice in the City.

It was announced in August, 1997, that presentations on how the business is going and the plans for the future would be made to all staff at two days in November at the Odeon Cinema, Freemans Park.

News editor, Simon Orrell, was seconded to the Loughborough office from September 1, 1997. Working with all concerned, his brief was to improve the product serving the area. The appointment was part of a continuing investigation into how the sales of district editions could be developed.

An early edition of the paper was published on Monday, September 1, 1997, to record the death of Diana, Princess of Wales. It was the biggest set-piece operation for several years and staff responded magnificently. On the day of her funeral, editions of the Saturday paper were updated on the progress of the events in London. A Special 32-page Commemorative edition was published on Sunday, September 7. All proceeds from the sale were donated to the Diana, Princess of Wales Memorial Fund. This special edition was printed overnight at Derby.

A grand total of £29,203.50 was raised from the sales and Michael Gibbons, treasurer of the Fund, received the cheque

Below: The Special Tribute edition for Diana, Princess of wales, on Sunday September 7, 1997.

from Mercury editor, Nick Carter, at Kensington Palace on February 3, 1998.

In honour of the paper achieving an ABC sales increase for the January-June 1997 period, all editorial and newspaper sales staff were invited to attend a three-course meal and disco at the Grand Hotel on Thursday, October 30, 1997.

In November, 1997, Mr Richard Karn was appointed to the position of Assistant Managing Director (Strategic Development) with the Leicester Mercury Group. In his new role, he was to assume responsibility for a number of key strategic issues of the business plan. He was to remain responsible for the Leicester Mail, Mercury Direct and Mercury Associated Products.

The audio-visual presentations to all staff took place on November 4 and 5 1997. Busses took them from the Mercury building to the Odeon cinema, where they were treated to popcorn and drink. After the welcome by Managing Director Mr Tony Hill, each director gave a presentation.

Mr Hill made comparisons between the cinema and newspaper industries. Performance measurement trends were very similar. He urged change to drive the business forward and upward. 'We must change the way we do things and become focused, marketing-led and customer-driven in order to achieve a turnaround to our newspaper sales performance. Across-the–business success has allowed us

to put together a focused three-year strategic plan for the company.'

Marketing manager Mr Nick Wales then made his presentation on the market place. He pointed out that market research had given us a real insight into who lived in the county and what their attitudes, lifestyles and behaviour were. As far as the future was concerned, Mr Wales predicted that competition would intensify.

Editor Mr Nick Carter stated that the Mercury was on the threshold of the most ambitious period of development. Since January 31, 1874, the newspaper has been bringing news and information to people in the county for five generations, but, during the last 30 years, there had been a slowly declining sale.

People were now working to stop the decline. 'The aim must be to produce a magnificent Mercury and be the first choice for information throughout the county. We must have stature – a paper you can count on as a dependable and experienced source of news. Through our developing community action programme, we aim to keep the Mercury at the heart of what is happening. We also aim to "make a difference" and help people to help themselves.'

Mr Neil Hadkiss, circulation director, then expounded the plans for the sales of the newspaper. He used the analogy of a 'hockey stick' to illustrate target sales growth, to be achieved with homerun and retail sales.

Mr Colin Mullins then spoke of retail outlets, including Mercury News Shops, followed by Mr Philip Brewin.

Mr Bewin set a target of £23.2 million advertising revenue for the current year, building on last year's success, by helping sales people to increase our customer count, revenue and market share.

Mr Richard Karn then described Mercury Associated Products, which aimed to broaden the base of our business over the next three years and build on what the Mercury brand name stands for in the community. He mentioned our involvement with community radio, an internet web site, Hype magazine, MRM (one of the largest advertising agencies in the county, now owned by the Mercury) and De Montfort University (a business-to-business publication) and Channel 4 Teletext.

To fight competition, he mentioned the introduction of a 'War Room,' which would be a focal point for strategic planning and product development.

Mr Barry Wootten affirmed that the company's biggest asset was the staff. He described the training available to all and the introduction of project teams.

He introduced Christine Dooley, Finance Director, who had been appointed Leader of the internal communications programme. A questionnaire was to be handed out after the session and the internal communications team would be collating ideas from staff.

Mr Brian Morris then proceeded with the plans to make our building a workplace for the 21st century. The inside would receive a complete overhaul and the outside a complete facelift. Improvements to the workplace were taking place as this book was being written and were set to continue well into 1999

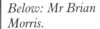

Left: Mr Barry Wootten.

Below: Mr Brian Morris.

Above and right: 'And Another Thing...', the first Staff Newsletter, in December 1997.

Below right: The Big Picture survey results.

The author was already on the Communications team and has since helped produce staff newsletters, named 'And Another Thing...' He is also on the Intranet team, the Millennium Champions team and the 125th Anniversary Exhibition team.

In December, Mr Stephen Lowe was appointed Newspaper Sales Manager. He joined the Leicester Mercury Group from the Sheffield Star, where he held the position of Newspaper Sales Manager for the previous two and a half years.

Week ending December 13, 1997, saw another slight improvement in the paper's sales figures. Around 500 extra copies were sold, representing an increase of 0.45%. This was followed the next week with a figure of 6,804 extra, an increase of 6.19% One reason for this was a number of sponsored copies.

Sub-editor Louise Benson was sent on a six-month secondment to the Budapest Sun – a Northcliffe-owned English language weekly. She would be subbing, writing and deputising for the editor. Her secondment was to take place between December 29 1997 and June 30, 1998.

Mel Atkinson took over from Kay Wright as chief Political Correspondent in January 1998. Owen Haynes became his No. 2.

The Mercury's Millennium coverage was launched on January 1, 1998. It had four main objectives: to establish the Leicester Mercury as the driving force for the Millennium by developing our role as the main source of information about Millennium matters in Leicester, Leicestershire and Rutland; to mobilise communities to come forward with projects that would provide a lasting benefit beyond the immediate celebrations of the Millennium; to mobilise businesses across

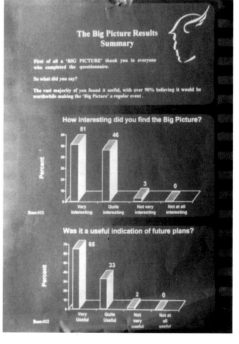

the area to volunteer their services to help make those projects happen and to bring communities and businesses together, thereby establishing the Mercury as facilitator and community champion. The regular flow of information on all aspects of the Millennium provided the ideal background for the drive to create a Mercury-led Millennium partnership involving businesses, local authorities and other bodies. This partnership has facilitated a bid for substantial Lottery funding to distribute to worthy projects.

Maureen Milgram started work as Millennium Champion on 1 January 1998, with 735 days to go to the year 2000.

She said: 'When I was invited to become the Mercury's Millennium Champion I realised it was an opportunity in a lifetime. A magnificent challenge! It's a job that only comes around once every one thousand years.'

It's all her husband's fault, of course. He is Alan Forrest, who writes the Your Century column every Monday in the Mercury. Since he was five years old he has been fascinated by the magic of the ending of the Century and the beginning of the new Millennium. For years he has been making notes on the outstanding events of the 20th Century and the people who made them happen. In 1997 he approached the Leicester Mercury with his proposal to use his years of research as a basis for a weekly column. The newspaper was interested and wanted to hear more. Meanwhile, he talked the idea over with Maureen, and she also became enthusiastic about the project. All her life she had been working on projects on three continents to make the future a better place. When Alan received a call to come to the Mercury to chat about his column idea, he asked if he could bring along his wife who had a number of useful suggestions to contribute to the discussion.

The rest, as they say, is history. They both were invited to become key players in the Mercury Team. Alan was employed to write his weekly column for the newspaper and Maureen was invited to become the Mercury's Millennium Champion, a first for the Northcliffe group.

Her role was to place the Mercury and consequently Leicester, Leicestershire and Rutland in the heart of the millennium. The strategy was 'partnership'. She had travelled around the county forming a unique partnership of media, local authority, business, faith, education, volunteers and landmark projects working effectively together. The Millennium partnership shared one logo and was attracting money and resources to our region. It was an exercise in developing pride.

At the same time as realising the opportunities this singular moment in time affords, the Mercury's Millennium Champion was also working on the organisation of the Mercury's 125th Anniversary celebrations. There was a skilled team of enthusiasts within the Mercury who were working with her. Many of the 125th Birthday celebrations were leading into millennium activities. The chief of these was the 125th Anniversary exhibition that would have a 20-week life at both the New Walk Museum in the City and at Snibston Discovery Park in the county. ·The multi-media exhibition would house a major historical look at the past 125 years of Leicester, Leicestershire and Rutland as seen

The Millennium Partnership objectives are:

◆ To leave Leicester, Leicestershire and Rutland with a lasting legacy, to make a difference.

◆ To work together to record the achievements of the past and present and look towards the future.

◆ To co-operate on a wide range of celebratory activities.

◆ To reflect and celebrate the diversity and multi-culturalism that is our society.

◆ To recognise concerns about the environment and ensure it's future sustainability.

◆ To break down artificial barriers and create better understanding.

◆ To foster life long learning.

◆ To develop community life in a safe and creative environment.

Above: Mr Jack Gresley, designer of the Exhibition, describes the layout to the senior management team.

through the eyes of the number one historical resource and communicator, the Leicester Mercury. The exhibition would feature, with the aid of the Mercury's partners a glimpse of the next 125 years. It was an interactive look at what we have been, are and will be segue into the millennium.

A local Leicester firm with work world-wide, Atkinson Associates, designed the exhibition. Other partners and contributors included the City of Leicester, Leicestershire County, Parish Councils (get right name), British Telecom, Canon UK, TTL and Owl Electronics and Cybermind. The interesting feature that the Mercury and all the partners had in common was that they were all located here in our area and had developed 'firsts' in their fields.

With the help of the Mercury, we were able to showcase the talents of Leicester, Leicestershire and Rutland in both our 125th Anniversary activities and our celebration and legacy initiatives into the 3rd millennium.

Week ending April 4, 1998, saw another slight improvement in sales. 580 copies extra were sold, representing an increase of 0.52%. A new promotion, bingo, may well have contributed to this.

A huge expansion of the Mercury's internet site Gateway to Leicestershire was launched as thisisleicestershire in April 1998. It was to feature on-line chat and a bulletin board and enable users from across the world to interact with each other through the

Mercury site. The new internet site was the most dramatic venture the Mercury had launched in its history. For 124 years, the Mercury had been words and pictures printed on paper. Now we could work in a medium that included sound and video as well as other elements, such as interactivity, push technology, bulletin boards and a chat site. It may all sound like a lot of techie jargon, but look at this way. Information of the Mercury PLUS noises, moving pictures, letters posted on a noticeboard, the ability for each reader to decide what kind of information is most important to them, instant communication with people around the world and a database of 27,000 businesses. Imagine a product that is not limited by van runs or the time the cornershop closes on Saturday night. There are six people dedicated to making sure the new site, at www.thisisleicestershire.co.uk, is busy, informative and attractive every day. These include Deborah Law and Lee Pilmore, both web editors who take information from the Mercury and publish it worldwide, Lakhvinder Rajput and Phil Kay who are introducing the internet to businesses through the county and broadening our client base and two designers. Mercury deputy editor Simon Crane, project champion, said: The latest reader research shows that internet use in Leicestershire has rocketed. This platform puts us in touch with a whole new area of people who perhaps have never read our newspaper. It is an

An early picture of the Mercury building at night.

opportunity for us to develop new markets and new skills as well as make better use of all the information we currently publish. The internet is no longer something that just involves people who know the difference between megabytes and megahertz'

The editorial system used by the reporters and sub-editors, GB, was found to contain the Millennium bug! To avoid the inevitable catastrophe, deputy editor Simon Crane and sub editor Roger De Bank travelled to Suffolk in April 1998 to look at a system called Tera. They also travelled to Aberdeen to see the system in action. Mark Clayton, features editor, and John Hodby, from the Mac page make-up desk, joined to be the supertrainers. Mike Polanyk and the author were among the first to be trained, to

help with future editions of The Week supplement, on September 28 and 29.

It was with some disappointment for the company that the licence application for a Community Radio in South East Leicestershire was turned down by the Radio Authority in the spring. Contact with The Big Dial Radio Company, however, continued and plans were being made to apply for a Restricted Service Licence for four weeks in May, 1999, to celebrate the Mercury's 125th anniversary.

The War Room was opened on May 29, 1998. The concept was introduced to the Mercury by Mr Tony Hill. As the market place becomes increasingly competitive, the company was making new technology available to every member of staff with the

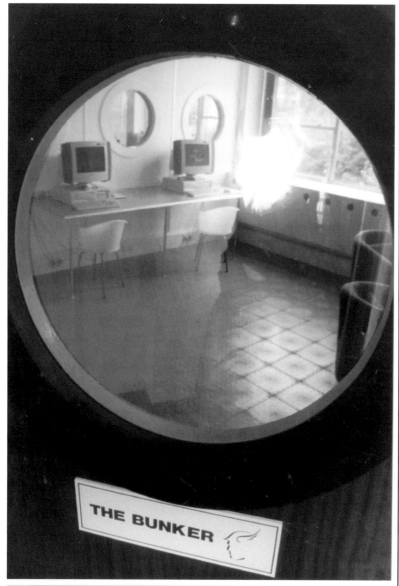

The Bunker, part of the Leicester Mercury's War Room.

open access room and was open to all Mercury employees. Facilities include Internet, CD ROMs, magazines, newspapers, books, satellite, cable, terrestrial television and videos. Mission Control was a bookable room seating 10 people. It was not intended to be used as a general meeting area, but for project development and brainstorming and the room had been designed to encourage this. It had internet access and an electronic whiteboard, which allowed staff to print out notes while brainstorming. A projector has been connected to a PC so that staff could present during brainstorming sessions straight on to the wall.

Mr Andrew MacKinnon-Ure joined the Leicester Mercury Group as circulation director in July 1998. He came from The Sentinel in Stoke on Trent, where he had developed the newspaper sales operation into an excellent unit during the previous eight years.

As mentioned in the 'Big Picture" presentations at the Odeon cinema, one of the most important long-term objectives of the company was to create a 'magnificent' Mercury. Staff needed to look at the overall design of the newspaper and the company hoped to commission one of the world's leading consultants to work with the staff on how the paper should look for the future. The editor, Mr Nick Carter, was to visit newspaper centres in Europe and America for six weeks, starting on August 17, to find out how they tackled similar design changes.

Lord Rothermere, chairman of the Daily Mail and General Trust plc, died at the beginning of September 1998. There was to be no change in the Harmsworth family's control of DMGT.

The Mercury scooped two prizes at the prestigious Newspaper Society Advertisement Awards in September, 1998. For the second year running, the paper won the Best Classified Section for Daily and Sunday newspapers award and also added the Best Multimedia Advertising Promotion to the trophy cabinet for its Workplace supplement. Judges also awarded certificates of merit to the Mercury in the Best Classified Motors Supplement and Best Stand Alone Display Publication categories. Classified advertising manager, Phil Inman, said: 'I think for us to win the Best Classified Section award twice is testimony to our emphasis on making the section so user-friendly from a reader's perspective. We devote a lot of space on a daily basis to ensure the section is easy to use and that was recognised by the judges who advised all the other regional newspapers to basically copy our classified section.'

desire that this will increase market awareness and enhance skills and expertise. Market intelligence wins wars! Sited on the second floor of the building, the War Room had two different rooms, called the Bunker and Mission Control. The Bunker was an

*Above: Mercury
Holiday Show at the
City Rooms in 1996.*

*Left: The Historic
Transport Pageant and
Vehicle Rally – tough
going for these cyclists.*

138

Leicester Mercury

CITY P.M. EDITION

Established 1874　　　THURSDAY, DECEMBER 17, 1998　　　Price 27p

 WIN A TRIP TO LONDON
To see a top TV show - Page 8

 WIN A LUXURY HAMPER
Magic of Christmas prize - Page 15

BRITISH FIGHTERS JOIN IRAQ ATTACK

DESTRUCTION: An Iraqi child stands amid the rubble left after a missile hit a residential area of southern Baghdad in the first wave of attacks last night.　Picture: Peter Dejong, Associated Press

'Saddam must not be allowed to threaten his neighbours with nuclear weapons, poison gas or biological weapons
Bill Clinton

by PA News Staff

British aircraft were due to go into action over Iraq for the first time today as the Allied pounding of Saddam Hussein's regime continues, Defence Secretary George Robertson confirmed.

He told a news conference that the 12 Tornado GR1 aircraft based in Kuwait would launch

Tornados to fly within hours

their first strikes in the coming hours.

Foreign Secretary Robin Cook said the RAF would make up one-fifth of all the manned bombing missions against Iraq. Last night's attacks were carried out using only sea-based American aircraft and cruise missiles.

No details have been released by British officials or ministers of the effects of last night's attacks.

Chief of the Defence Staff General Sir Charles Guthrie told a news conference this morning that it would be later today at the earliest, or more likely tomorrow, that details would be released.

Mr Robertson said Saddam had left Britain and America no alternative but to launch the strikes.

He also fiercely denied that US President Bill Clinton's domestic predicament had played any part in

the decision to attack.

The Defence Secretary told a news conference at the MoD in Whitehall that it would be "inconceivable that the President would hold back from doing what he knows to be right because of any domestic considerations".

He continued: "There was no alternative. The President has done the right thing. The President and the Prime Minister are doing the right thing for the world community and I don't believe domestic considerations have played any part in it at all."

Mr Robertson and Sir Charles stressed Britain had no quarrel with the Iraqi people - and said

■ Continued on Page 2

■ **MPs back air strikes - local reaction - Page 3**

■ **Russia and China condemn attack - Page 7**

■ **Targets and weapons - graphic - Page 3**

■ **Stealth planes are set for key role - Page 7**

The Mercury published a multi-faith 1999 Calendar with scenes from the county in October, 1998.

Much preparation had gone into the setting up of a 125ᵗʰ Anniversary Exhibition, 'A Passage Through Time,' at the Leicester Museum, which opened on January 11, 1999. Maureen Milgram, the Mercury's Millennium Champion, had enlisted the help of local businesses as Partners to create the design and to assist in the manufacture of multi-media exhibits. After a long stay at the Leicester Museum, the exhibition moved on to Snibston Discovery Centre in Coalville for five weeks and then, in a smaller mode, to other places, such as libraries.

Also planned was a multi-media CD-ROM for schools, which would include a history of the Mercury and a computer game. A 125 Supplement was published on January 25, 1999, which related the ways in which Leicestershire people have been touched by the Mercury. A service was held at the Leicester Cathedral with Chorale Matin on January 31, 1999, followed by an open house at the Guildhall. February 1ˢᵗ, 1999, saw a Souvenir Edition of the very first edition of 1874 published. Much more was planned, especially for the staff, at this momentous time, such as plates, thimbles, tankards, a 125 Ale and a 125 sports day gala.

There was much celebration at the time of the 125ᵗʰ Birthday of the Leicester Mercury around January 31, 1999. Staff were invited to a party at the Christmas Company marquee at Leicester Airport in Stoughton on January 2 and this book itself was published in recognition of the fact that Leicester's local newspaper had attained 125 years of service. The author hoped it was an enjoyable read, but what will be more enjoyable is the progress the Leicester Mercury as a company makes over the next 125 years. Will there still be a newspaper as we know it on January 31, 2124? Or will it be in another form as yet undiscovered? The only guess the author was prepared to make is a form something like a virtual reality headset, with which people will be able, not only to read the news, but actually see the events as they happen. Perhaps it will not be a headset at all, perhaps it will be a piece of equipment attached to your wrist, like a watch, or, more bizarrely, a computer chip implanted in the brain, which would pick up signals and alert people to the latest news items. However strange or improbable the method of delivering the news, we can be certain of one thing – the Leicester Mercury as an organisation will still be there to serve its communities – at the heart of everything.

Opposite page: A fresh crisis in Iraq hits the headlines on Thursday December 17, 1998.

Below: The Leicester Mercury building on St George Street.

LEICESTER MERCURY, TUESDAY, SEPTEMBER 22, 1998

A special **Leicester Mercury** publication

National Space Science Centre

The mission: To present the excitement and significance of space and planetary science, astronomy and technology in a way which captures and inspires the public's imagination.

To promote a wider understanding of the science of space and to demonstrate its significance to life on Earth in the 21st century.

This special supplement sets out the background and reports on the progress in developing the landmark Millennium project based in Leicester

Above: A Leicester Mercury Supplement from September 22, 1998, with an artists impression of the National Space Science Centre being planned in the city.

 as it more and more national. (Cheers.) The hour is ting late, and I shall have many opportunities before a day of election of exchanging ideas with you. (Cries "Go on.") Bearing in mind what Parliament has done under the great English leader, I ask you are they entitled to reproach? (Cries of no, no.) No reproach shall fall from my lips (Hear, hear.) They would have preferred to do their work more perfectly than it has been done, but the fact is that in this country nothing can be done without compromise. The first Act for any great Reform is never the last. The rough-hewn stone is not more unlike the finished work of the artist than is the Act which first enters the legislature like the finished work which comes forth at last. (Hear, hear.) And now as to the future. Does Mr. Gladstone promise us bad things? We should not be able to value the amendments of the law and the settlement of the question of Church and State if they were not accompanied by a skilful management of finance. (Hear, hear.) Then what was the best thing to do? To sweep away the odious income tax. (Cheers.) I don't mean to make it more obnoxious as incomes rise higher, but to do away with it entirely, because it never can be a just tax. (Hear, hear.) If you make it heavier so as to become a property tax, then it is confiscation. If you take it lower, so as to reach all classes in the community, it is oppressive and iniquitous. (Cheers.) You cannot draw a line with the income tax. This monstrous tax must be abolished altogether. (Cheers.) It was imposed purely as a war tax, and never ought to have been retained in time of peace. I hope it will never be imposed again in time of peace. (Cheers.) But Mr. Gladstone has not confined himself to that promise—he promises also an adjustment of other taxes—(hear, hear)—a promise pointing towards that desideratum for us all—a free breakfast table—(cheers)—and I will do all in my power to prevent such measures being shipwrecked by being taken out of the hands of our Premier into the hands of the opposite party. (Cheers.) I am sure you don't wish me to draw the opposite picture. We are not so tired of measures of progress and improvement that we wish to resist them and return again into the cycle of Tory misrule and misgovernment. (Cheers.) I do not think we have learnt our lesson so badly as to be inclined to do that. (Hear, hear.) I must make just one allusion to our personal position. The dissolution was sudden and unlooked for by everybody. It comes upon us when we are all more or less unprepared for it, and it will require all the more energy on our part between this and the day of election. As election after election had gone against the Government—generally from some local causes—the Government were, I think, justified in asking the country to say whether they desired a continuance of the present Government or not, and the answer will be favourable. (Cheers.) In each division of the county you will be able to vote for candidates who whose principles you agree Mr. Packe deserves our thanks for coming forward, and I hope he will have the support he deserves. (Cheers.) And in the borough you will, I doubt not, return a gentleman who has served you in the past, and I sincerely hope you will send his colleague too. (Hear, hear, and cheers.) The land question will have to be considered in the future, and it will require consideration in the kindest possible spirit to do justice to all. (Cheers.) If those friends who have known me so long think my judgment on the questions relating to the laws between landlord and tenant of any service in the settlement of the question—and if you think my voice or vote will be of service to you—they are yours to command. (Loud cheers.) I know the intricacies of this question, but I think something must be done to prevent our hearing so often, as we drive through the country, the remark that so much per acre could be produced from this or that land—so much more for the maintenance of man. And now, if there is any point upon which any gentleman would like to ask me a question—anything upon which I was satisfy anyone present—I shall be happy to hear the question, and it shall receive my most candid and explicit answer. (Cheers.) In the absence of such question, I have only to thank you for the great honour of this manifestation of your confidence in myself—a manifestation which I shall never forget. Whether our struggle be crowned with success, or as some others have ended, should end in defeat, our days of defeat are numbered. (Loud cheers.) I am quite sure that with the growing population of the country, the spread of industry, the increasing intelligence of the farming classes—together with a system of education spreading all around us—I am sure, I say, that you will not very long remain contented with the present state of your country representation. (Loud and long continued cheering, in the midst of which Mr. Paget resumed his seat.)

Mr. F. HEWITT moved a vote of thanks to the Chairman, Mr. R. Harris, for presiding on the present occasion. It had been his pleasure, he said, that day to talk to one of their staunch Liberal friends in an agricultural district of the county, and he was pleased to hear him say that in one village they should poll six more votes on their side than they had ever got before. The reason why there were not more was this—it was very difficult to convince the voters in the villages that they might vote perfectly free and independent under the Ballot. (Mr. Hewitt) had been interested ... say that any man could go fearlessly to the ... with the greatest freedom. The Ballot was so drawn ... that he would defy any one to pick out who was the man who had voted. To inform he hoped every man in the county would go to the poll and give a perfectly free and independent vote. If Mr. Paget went to Parliament for South Leicestershire, he would like to go by the free exercise of the votes of the electors. It was exceedingly desirable that they should plump for Mr. Paget. He (Mr. Hewitt) wished they had a second candidate, a tenant farmer, to go with him. The Conservative party had had the power in their hands too long, but the time was passing away when six gentlemen could meet at the Castle and decide who should sit for the northern and who for the southern division of the county. Mr. Paget was the best landlord the tenant farmers had in Leicestershire. One of his tenants, a Conservative, told him that if other landlords were like him there would be in the county thousands and thousands more employed upon the land, and the land would yield to the country a great deal larger production of human food, because, as was said, he never turned a widow off his farm or put a gamekeeper in. (Applause.)

Mr. PAGET briefly seconded the vote of thanks to the Chairman.

Mr. LOVEDAY (Kibworth) said if all the landlords were like Mr. Paget there would be no necessity for such a thing as compensation for unexhausted improvements. He considered Mr. Paget the proper man to send to legislate on the subject. After remarking that it could not longer be permitted that a man residing in the town should have a vote, whereas a man living in the county was denied the privilege, Mr. Loveday said Mr. Paget sometimes thought he went too far, but he believed they both were on the same road. He would not trouble them with any further remarks. (Voices : Go on.) Let them "go on." It was all very well to say "go on" at public meetings, but let them "go on" at the poll. If they did their duty Mr. Paget was all right.

The motion was then put and carried unanimously. The CHAIRMAN briefly acknowledged the compliment, and the proceedings were brought to a close by three hearty cheers for Mr. Paget.

LIBERAL MEETING IN WEST ST. MARY'S.

Councillor Grimaley presided at a largely-attended meeting of the Liberal party in Oxford street schoolroom last night, in support of the candidature of Messrs. Taylor and McArthur. The Liberal candidates were accompanied to the platform by Mrs. Taylor, and Messrs. Macdonald, W. W. Preston, Wm. Collins, and H. Stroud.

Mr. P. A. TAYLOR, who was most cordially received, commented upon the main principles of the addresses of Mr. Gladstone and Mr. Disraeli, and intimated that he regarded the recent movements for the elevation of the agricultural classes as the most hopeful signs of the times. In regard to the game laws, he thought the temptations to trespass be greatly reduced if they were abolished, and the head of game reduced. He regarded wild animals as the property of the people. So far from having another trespass law, they should rather have the bond loosened. It was the common right of the people to wander in the fields, to gather the wild flowers, and enjoy the beautiful scenery. He would compel the roads farmers made round the fields to be made public, so that the people might enjoy them. He thought the two great parties were like huge sponges, out of which the public could, if they chose, squeeze a good deal. In regard to the Establishment question, they had not much to condemn after Mr. Gladstone. He thought the best way to condemn the man to disendow the Church of England this session, but if he did not, let them hope Mr. Disraeli would do it the next. If they were to be returned by a triumphant majority it must be by a spontaneous vote. The Conservatives hoped some geese would vote for him, and for Mr. McArthur, and others for Mr. McArthur and not for him, and that others would not vote at all ; but let them show by their votes that they were far mistaken.

Mr. McARTHUR, who was likewise warmly received, after referring to the improving condition of the agricultural labourer, said he thought the income tax was an evil injurious tax, which should form their opinion about, and but if it was removed there ought to be a corresponding reduction of the taxes which affected the great mass of the people. There should, he thought, also be a something like tenant-right, and if a farmer was compelled to leave a farm he should have compensation for the improvements he had made. It was not only an evil to the farmer, but also to the people, because there was not nearly the quantity of ...

ation were given. He saw no reason why land should not be sold as simply as shares or railway stock. He always liked to express his views honestly and fairly. He liked men who could form their opinion and stick to it, and be approved of open voting ; but at the same time there were men, placed in such circumstances as that they could not indulge in these manly sentiments. In regard to the Education Act, in London it had had the effect of taking 70,000 children off the streets and bringing them into the schools, and so far it had done good, but he hoped they would have a much more comprehensive scheme. With regard to the disestablishment question, he had so hated against any church, and he wished for perfect equality to all. He believed disestablishment would be for the benefit of the Church and the country at large. The Burial Bill was one which every Liberal should support. He thought it a pity when party feeling was carried so far that they could not find a common burying-place. Nonconformists had just as much right to have their own ministers at burials as other marriages and other ceremonies, and he wished for as those interferences with their liberties entirely removed. He thought they had too much good sense and appreciation of what Mr. Gladstone had done as a financier (and to deal with financial questions there was no one so well qualified as Mr. Gladstone), not to return candidates who would give him a consistent support. (Cheers.)

At the conclusion, on the motion of Mr. Preston, seconded by Mr. Moore, the meeting unanimously pledged itself to use all legitimate means to secure the return of Messrs. Taylor and McArthur.

CONSERVATIVE MEETINGS.

The supporters of Mr. J. H. B. Warner's candidature held three meetings last evening. The first took place at the Black Boy Inn, Albion-street, and secured a moderate attendance, Mr. Sarson presiding.

The CHAIRMAN, in opening the proceedings, held that Mr. Warner was just the candidate required for Leicester at the present moment, inasmuch as there was a decidedly growing feeling of Toryism amongst the working men, not only of Leicester, but throughout the country The Chairman then went on to remind them that their candidate was a member of one of the most eminent manufacturing firms in the kingdom—one that made up the best of material, paid every man the full value of his labour, and one that stood altogether A1.

Mr. J. H. B. WARNER, who was then introduced, began by referring to the suddenness of the dissolution, pointing out that it made such meetings the only means whereby he could become acquainted with the electors. Passing on to notice the causes of the crisis, the candidate reminded them that they were attributed to dissensions in the Cabinet—differences which existed, if not immediately before the dissolution, had been observed some time previously. Turning to the conduct of the Government, he held that there was plenty of room for reform, more especially in connection with the Army and Navy. With regard to the military force Mr. Warner held that Mr. Gladstone had prostituted the whole of the establishment, and trusted for its thorough re-organisation to the operation of a bad scheme of purchase, which had already cost the country £8,000,000 and was likely to entail a still greater expenditure in the future. Moreover the alterations in this respect could not but have the effect of changing for the worse the position of the officers, who had hitherto been wanting in times of emergency ; while the money would have to come out of the pockets of the tax-payers though it might have been applied to a far more useful purpose. However the most unconstitutional measure of all was that which Mr. Gladstone adopted immediately after the discussion in the House of Lords on the subject, when he secured a Royal Warrant. If he desired to adopt such an instrument of effecting his purpose it ought to have been adopted before the discussion in the House of Lords which would thereby have been saved. Then with respect to the navy, the administration of the present Government had likewise been a decided failure, and the unprecedented conduct had given rise to great disasters. He deemed unseaworthy and allowing the coaling a vessel and 500 valuable lives had gone to the bottom ; while in the case of the Megæra, a vessel that had been deemed unseaworthy and allowing the coaling a vessel and 500 valuable lives had gone to the bottom of the list of transports, had been taken out, sent to Australia or some other far distant colony with troops, and very nearly went to the bottom likewise, and was only saved by an accident. The treatment of the dock-yard labourers was also characterised as a sample of Gladstonian management applied to almost every class. Mr. Warner reminded them, under the circumstances, that they ought to look zealously after their rights and privileges, and not allow the present Premier to continue his paternal style of government. Such a form of administration had, in olden times, its advantages, inasmuch as it was allied with religion, but now the grand object of the government was to prevent a man having any religion at all. Mr. Warner concluded by reminding them that the time forward to test the representation as a thorough Conservative, and that the great question at the general election, so far at ... Leicester was concerned, would be, not whether ... ... Government, but the ...

ner, referred to the treatment which the late Sheriff Bell, of Glasgow, had sustained at the hands of Mr. Lowe, and the manner in which, when he was suffering from cancer, and had been ordered three months' rest, he was not only refused his application, but at once called upon to resign.

Mr. BROOKES, in seconding the motion, characterized Mr. Warner as the young David who would, with the small stones of the electors, slay the great Republican Goliath, Mr. Peter Alfred Taylor, and reign in his stead.

The motion was carried by acclamation, and briefly acknowledged.

Several other gentlemen subsequently addressed the meeting, and the usual compliment to the chairman terminated the proceedings.

A meeting was also held at the Cattle Market Hotel, Aylestone-road, at which there was a good attendance. Mr. Lawrence Willmore occupied the chair.—The chairman, having made a few remarks, introduced Mr. Warner, who addressed the meeting, and was enthusiastically received.—Dr. Barclay moved a resolution pledging the meeting to use every legitimate means to secure the return of Mr. Warner.—Mr. Oliver seconded the motion.—A question was asked Mr. Warner respecting the criminal law, and answered by Mr. Warner. Another question in reference to the assimilation of the borough and county franchise, was also answered by Mr. Warner.—The resolution was carried unanimously.—Mr. Millis proposed a vote of thanks to Mr. Warner for coming forward to contest the borough on Conservative principles, which was seconded by Mr. Parkinson and carried.—The meeting shortly afterwards terminated with a vote of thanks to the chairman.

A third, and somewhat noisy meeting, was held at the Richmond Arms, King Richard's-road. Dr. Marriott occupied the chair, and there was a very large number of electors present ; so large that it was impossible for any thing like all to get in the room, and the chairman said that Mr. Warner would address them from the window. It was evident, from the frequent interruptions the various speakers met with, the expressions of feeling, and the confusion and disorder that reigned throughout, that the whole of those present were not in favour of Mr. Warner's candidature.—Mr. Warner (who was loudly cheered by his friends) very briefly addressed the meeting, experiencing frequent interruptions ; and at the close he asked a question respecting the compulsory vaccination laws, which Mr. Warner did not answer.—Mr. Fox addressed the meeting ; and Mr. Anne proposed a vote of confidence in Mr. Warner and a resolution pledging the meeting to do their best to return him.—Mr. Clarke, of London, a representative of the Sunday Observance Society, spoke at some length.—The resolution which had been proposed was not submitted, and the meeting rather abruptly terminated.

REPRESENTATION OF NORTH LEICESTERSHIRE.

Mr. Hussey Packe, the Liberal candidate for the representation of North Leicestershire, attended the market ordinary at the King's Head Hotel, Loughborough, on Thursday last. The chair was occupied by Mr. Sidney Wells, and there were also present, Rev. E. Smythies, and Messrs. H. Dease, S. Adcock, R. Burrows, Coole, Rumsby, J. Angrave, J. Burrows, G. Henson, Mullett, Bauson, R. Lacey, T. Gill, Red-T. and C. Agnave, H. Humphrey, &c.

In the course of the afternoon and evening, Mr. Packe addressed meetings at Hathern, Kegworth, Castle Donington, Diseworth, and Sheepshed.

An attempt has been made at Yeddo to assassinate a Japanese Minister, the Second President of the Council. The Minister, however, escaped with only slight wounds.

THE LABOUR REPRESENTATION LEAGUE.—An address has been issued by this body to the working-class voters of the United Kingdom in reference to the pending elections. There are, it says, at the present moment several "labour" candidates in the field, and it makes an earnest appeal to working men who have the vote, as they prize their rights as free citizens, to place them in favour of such candidates, so that they practically support the principle of direct lab ...

THE LONDON WEEKLY PAPERS.

MR. GLADSTONE AT BLACKHEATH.

THE LONDON WEEKLY PAPERS.

MR. GLADSTONE AT BLACKHEATH.

After commenting upon the various points in Mr. Gladstone's speech, the Spectator says :—"We will leave the subjects on which we can hardly ever agree with Mr. Gladstone, and pass to the admirable conclusion of his speech, in which he pointed out how impossible it was for him to remain the leader of the Liberal party, if he was not to lead it as a whole, but only one portion of it, against the determined and uncompromising resistance of another portion. Now that is simply good sense stamped with the full authority of the Prime Minister's personal resolve. The Nonconformists do not really wish to be the occasion of Mr. Gladstone's retirement from the lead of the Liberal party, and of the break-up of which they accuse the moderate Liberals towards themselves. On the whole, we are inclined to believe that Mr. Gladstone's appeal to Liberals to forbear with each other will be successful. The Nonconformists were, in fact, relenting before he spoke. They will probably be, not indeed as hearty as ever, but anxious to disown anything like a disaffected spirit, after it."

WHAT THE GOVERNMENT HAS ACCOMPLISHED.

On the whole, the Spectator maintains, no sincere Liberal will doubt that Mr. Gladstone's appeal to the people of England ought to meet with a grateful and cordial response. This Government has been distinguished above all other Liberal Governments for the honesty and earnestness with which it has redeemed the pledges, instead of using them mainly as baits to catch votes. It has been a steady and an upright and a Liberal Government, not a Conservative Government with a Liberal name, and has done more to gain for the people of the United Kingdom, some addition to that stock of human happiness which, as Mr. Gladstone as truly as pathetically says, is "never too abundant," than any Government of the present generation. The genuine Liberals who see its shortcomings best, will also see best its immeasurable superiority to anything likely to replace it. If fidelity, gratitude, and trust are not political virtues, as we are sometimes told, politics are no true field for the English character. If they are, as we believe they are, Liberals will not desert the Government, which has been laboriously faithful to their instructions, and which has now so long been the target for a steady artillery fire of contempt and insult in their cause.

SUDDENNESS OF THE DISSOLUTION.

If, says the Saturday Review, it is any gratification to a Prime Minister to strike a sudden stroke to bewilder friends and foes, and surprise a whole nation, Mr. Gladstone has enjoyed that gratification to the utmost. There is no excuse for a dissolution so sudden, and so unexpected, to be found in Mr. Gladstone's manifesto. Mr. Gladstone naturally appeals to the services rendered to the country in the last forty years by the Liberal party. He is quite entitled to do this, and no manifesto from his pen could be complete without such an appeal. The Liberal party has done great things in the last forty years, and some of the greatest have been done since Mr. Gladstone has been Prime Minister. But although we may honour statesmen for what they have done in the past, we are obliged to judge their present policy by its own special character, and it is difficult to see anything in this sudden dissolution, and in Mr. Gladstone's bargaining for the price of a financial secret, which raises the reputation of the Liberal party or adds to the benefits it has conferred on the country.

EFFECT OF THE INCOME TAX ABOLITION.

The Budget which is selfishly prematurely published is, the Saturday Review considers, of the most startling nature. Mr. Gladstone undertakes not only to misapply the surplus, but to convert it into a large deficiency, to be supplied by the taxation of the classes from whom he expects no political support. It follows that the void left by the Income Tax will be supplied by property taxes, probably of more than one kind. The taxes on consumption will be reduced as an equivalent to the relief nominally given to property ; and then the burden which has ostensibly been removed will be replaced, perhaps in a more oppressive form. The promise of a reduction of expenditure may be summarily dismissed as irrelevant to the apportionment, though not to the amount, of taxation. As a weapon against a possible Conservative Government there is always a chance that professions of frugality may be useful. Whether a great statesman consults his own permanent interest ... his future reputation by unscrupulous resort to ... tion for moralists and historians ... Mr. Gladstone ... he were capable of thinking that he has no ... perhaps find satisfaction in the thought that ... the leaders of the Opposition to repeat his own prodigal offers ; but the tendency of lax political principles to propagate themselves is not consolatory to those who happen to prefer the welfare of England to the personal aggrandisement of Mr. Disraeli and even of Mr. Gladstone.

ADVANCED LIBERAL VIEW OF DISSOLUTION.

Mr. Gladstone has made his appeal to the country, and, according to the Examiner, no one can conceive for what he is appealing. It cannot be on the mere question of confidence in the name of Gladstone. A man who has no confidence in himself is seldom presumptuous enough to solicit the confidence of others. It cannot be on any question of policy, for no single proposition or measure stands prominently forth from the Greenwich manifesto that is not quite as conservative in its tone as Liberal. It is true that the Premier's hands are full of gold. He offers a bribe all round with the lavish profusion of a man who is painfully aware that gold alone will never serve his turn. "Here," he says, "are five millions, a surplus which has accrued during my Chancellorship. With this I will diminish the burdens of the landowners, abolish the tax on the incomes of the rich and respectable, and—out of my hearty commiseration for the poor—take a penny in the pound from the price of sugar. Hark how the gold jingles in my bag! Send me back to the Treasury, and you shall all share alike in the property of your country." We fear it will need more than Codlin's own assurance to persuade us that Short could not do just as much for us. And even if we believed in Codlin, we should have but slight cause to be grateful for his friendship. With regard to the election, the Examiner says, one anxiety is to see a good working body of intelligent and unfettered Radicals returned to Parliament : a hundred and fifty men who will vote for disestablishment ; as many, or more, who will vote for the County Franchise, the reform of Land Tenure, the repeal of the Game Laws, the modification of the Trades Union and Conspiracy Laws ; fifty or sixty who will be instant in season and out of season in attacking fiscal and economic abuses, in reducing our military, naval, and Civil Service expenditure ; twenty, or thirty, who will be utterly fearless and irreconcilable in a sense which a week ago would apply to barely half a dozen of our representatives. The Examiner wants the Radical element in the House so strong that no Liberal Government can dispense with its co-operation.

FINANCE AND THE DISSOLUTION.

The Economist remarks, a greater surprise than even the Dissolution is the fact that just after a great extension of the suffrage to the poor—so great an extension, indeed, as to give the poor, if they choose to use it, absolute supremacy—the most popular measure for electioneering purposes should be the abolition of the Income Tax. Many things were prophesied of the new voters, but no one ever suggested that the most agreeable thing to them would be the removal of a tax which the rich pay and the poor do not. There can be no doubt that the Income Tax will now be taken off. But the Economist will see it go with regret. The arguments for retaining it seem much weightier than those for removing it. The most palpable fact in our financial history is that since the imposition of the Income Tax we have never been in financial difficulty, and that before we were always liable to be so. The Economist would say not that an "effort" should now be made to "get rid of" this tax, but, on the contrary, that we should be glad to pay it as now made by the best persons of all parties to retain it. Doubts have been raised as to whether Mr. Gladstone can perform the promises of his address ; but these are all needless. The promise is to provide for—Local taxation, say £900,000 ; sugar duties, £1,500,000 ; Income Tax (in the first year), £4,500,000 ; total, £6,900,000. And there is a surplus of £5,2,9,000. This will leave £1,280,000 without an approximate a financier as Mr. Gladstone will find without merit relief. The year 1875-6 will have to bear a further burden, because the whole loss of the Income Tax will then fall on the arrears of the old tax. But in the next year, that of 1875-6, those arrears are ... probably £1,000,00), will be gone. There is no ... from ... on it is account. The ...

ELECTION MOVEMENTS.

UNOPPOSED RETURNS.

Mr. Bright (L)	
Mr. Dixon (L)	BIRMINGHAM.
Mr. Muntz (L)	
	CALNE.
Lord E Fitzmaurice (L)	
	CIRENCESTER.
	Mr. Bathurst (C)
	EYE.
	Lord Barrington (C)
	HARWICH.
	Col. Jervis (C)
	HEREFORD.
	Mr. Arthur J. Balfour (C)
	HUNTINGDON.
	Mr J. Karslake (C)
	LEOMINSTER.
	Mr. R Arkwright (C)
	LUDLOW.
	Col. G. H. W. Clive (C)
	MALMESBURY.
	Mr. W. Powell (C)
	MARLBOROUGH.
Lord E. Bruce (L)	
	RIPON.
Earl Grey (L)	
	TYNEMOUTH.
Mr. T. E. Smith (L)	
	WHITEHAVEN.
	G. C. Bentinck (C)

LATEST NOMINATIONS.

The Mayor (W. Kempson, Esq.), attended at the Town Hall from 11 a.m. until 1 p.m. to-day to receive the nominations of candidates for the representation of the Borough.

The following were the only nominations handed in :—

PETER ALFRED TAYLOR, (L), 22 Ashley Place, Westminster, Esq., candidate ; Geo. Toller New-Walk, Leicester, solicitor, nominator ; George Baines, 53, Princess-street, Leicester, worsted spinner, seconder.

ALEXANDER McARTHUR (L), Raleigh Hall, Brexton Rise, Surrey, merchant, candidate ; Richard Harris, Knighton, merchant, nominator ; John Cooper, 19, Bedford-street, Leicester, locksmith, seconder.

JOHN HENRY BOYD WARNER, (C), Quorn Hall, Leicestershire, Esq., candidate ; Charles Richard Crossley, Granby-street, nominator ; George Woodward, Upper Conduit-street, elastic web weaver, Leicester, seconder.

Captain Wellesley (L)	ANDOVER.
	Hon. D. Fortescue (C)
Mr. B. Samuelson (L)	BANBURY.
	Colonel Wilkinson (C)
T. Cave (L)	BARNSTAPLE.
S. D. Waddy (L)	J. Fleming (C)
	Colonel Holt (C)
Captain Hayter (L)	BATH.
Lord F Hervey (L)	Lord Grey de Wilton (C)
	Major Bousfield (C)
Mr. G. Griffith (L)	BEWDLEY.
Mr. C. Harrison (L)	Mr. S. Leighton (C)
Mr. J. Samuelson (L)	BIRMINGHAM.
	Mr. John Laird (C)
Mr. W. G. Ingram (L)	BOSTON (2).
Mr. T. Parry (L)	Mr. W. J. Malcolm (C)
	Mr. T. Collins (C)
Mr. S. Morley (L)	BRISTOL.
Mr. K. D. Hodgson (L)	Mr. R. N. Hare (C)
	Mr. K. H. Chambers (C)
Mr. R. Shaw (L)	BURNLEY.
	Mr. W. A. Lindsay (C)
Mr. J. A. Hardcastle (L)	BURY ST. EDMUNDS.
	Mr. E. Greene (C)
	Lord F. Hervey (C)
W. Fowler (L)	CAMBRIDGE AND BOROUGH.
Sir R. Torrens (L)	Mr. A. G. Martin (C)
	Mr. P. R. Smollett (C)
A J. Otway (L)	CHATHAM (1).
	Admiral Elliott (C)
Handel Cossham (L)	CHIPPENHAM (1).
	Mr. G. Goldney (C)
Mr. C. Millward (L)	CHRISTCHURCH.
	Sir H. D. Wolff (C)
Mr. Kay (L)	CLITHEROE.
	Mr. R. Assheton (C)
Mr. J. Henderson (L)	DURHAM CITY.
Mr. J. C. Thompson (L)	Mr. J. L. Wharton (C)
Mr. E. A. Bowring (L)	EXETER (2).
Mr. Johnson (L)	
Mr. James (L)	GATESHEAD.
Mr. Arbuthnot (L)	
Mr. Gladstone	GUILDFORD.
Mr. B. Langley (L)	Mr. ....
Mr. G.J. H. Onslow (L)	HACKNEY.
Mr. C. Reed (L)	Lieut. G.H (?)
Mr. J. Holms (L)	HALIFAX.
Right Hon. J. Stansfeld (L)	Mr. H. C. McCrae (C)
Mr. J. Crossley (L)	HEREFORD.
Mr. (Clive (L)	Major Arbuthnot (C)
Mr. J. Pulley (L)	Mr. Patishall (C)
Mr. J. Whitwell (L)	KENDAL.
	Mr. W. F. Saunders (C)
Mr. T. Lea (L)	KIDDERMINSTER (1).
	Mr. A. Grant (C)
Mr. Drinkwater (L)	LAUNCESTON (1).
	Colonel Deakin (C)
Sir T. Fowell (L)	LINCOLN (1).
J. H. Palmer (L)	Colonel Chaplin (C)
Mr. V ffolkes (L)	LYNN REGIS.
Mr. E. Wodehouse (L)	Hon R. Bourke (C)
	Lord C J. Hamilton (C)
Sir J Lubbock (L)	MAIDSTONE.
Sir S. Waterlow (L)	Major Ross (C)'
	Hon. F Stanley (C)
Hon. C. W. Fitzwilliam (L)	MALTON.
Sir T. Hesketh (L)	Mr. R. H. Bower (C)
Sir T. Chambers (L)	Mr. W. Forsyth (C)
Mr. D. Grant (L)	MARYLEBONE.
Mr F. H. Bolckow (L)	MIDDLESBROUGH.
Mr. J. Kane (L)	Mr. Hopkins (C)
Mr. W. B. Wrightson (L)	NORTHALLERTON.
	Mr. G. W. Elliott (C)
Mr. G. H. Whalley (L)	NORTHAMPTON.
Mr. W. Wells (L)	Mr. H. T. Wrenfords (C)
Mr. Thomson Hankey (L)	PETERBOROUGH.
Mr. Marriott (L)	
Mr. R. M. Kerr (L)	POWTEFRACT.
Mr. C. Hope (L)	
Right Hon H. C. E. Child-	PONTEFRACT.
ers (L)	Major Waterhouse (C)
	Lord Pollington (C)
Mr Mottershead (L)	PRESTON.
	Mr. E. Hermon (C)
	Mr. J. Holker (C)
Sir F. H. Goldsmid (L)	READING (2).
Mr. J. G. Shaw Lefevre (L)	Mr. R. Attenborough (C)
	Mr. W. D. Mackenzie (C)
Hon C. J. Dundas (L)	RICHMOND.
Sir C. E. Brinsmead Cooke (L)	
W. P. Martin (L)	ROCHESTER.
Julian Goldsmid (L)	A. Smee (C)
	SANDWICH (2).
E. H. Knatchbull-Hugessen (L)	Captain Hallett (C)
H. A. Brassey (L)	Mr. B. Raillie (C)
Mr. H. D. Seymour (L)	SHAFTESBURY.
	V. F. V. Bennett Stanford (C)
Mr. Macdonald (L)	STAFFORD.
Mr. Pochin (L)	Capt. Macdonald (C)
	Captain Salt (C)
Mr. J. Dodds (L)	STOCKTON.
	Hon T. L. Barrington (C)
Sir R. Peel (L)	TAMWORTH.
Mr. C. P. Butt (L)	Mr. R. W. Hanbury (C)
Ald Hawkes (L)	
Mr. H. Massey (L)	TIVERTON (2).
Sir J. W. Walrond (C)	
Mr. Charles Forster (L)	WALSALL.
	Major W. W. Bell (C)
Mr. R. B. Mackie (L)	WAKEFIELD.
	Mr. E. Green (C)
Mr. P. Rylands (L)	WARRINGTON.
	Mr. W. Greenall (C)
Mr. A. Lusc'nn (L)	WINDSOR.
	Mr. R. Richardson-Gardner (C)
Mr. R. Eykyn (L)	WINDSOR.
	Mr. R. R. Gardner (C)
	Mr. ... Lowther (L)
	P. P. Huwar (C)

LATEST NEWS.

[REUTER'S TELEGRAMS.]

ITALY.

ROME, Wednesday.—General Delamarmora has produced the original documents, the authenticity of which was challenged by the German Gazette.

SPAIN.

BARCELONA, Tuesday.—The Carlist leader Laviellel has unsuccessfully attacked Colonna.

NEW SOUTH WALES.

SYDNEY, Tuesday.—The New South Wales Club won the match against the English Eleven by 8 wickets.

GERMANY.

BERLIN, Friday.—A meeting of men of all classes will be held here shortly as a manifestation of sympathy with the meeting in London, expressing sympathy with Germany in her struggle with the Pope.

BANK RATE.

The Bank rate of discount is unaltered.

THE CASE OF LUIE.

Luie was brought up at Bow-street to-day. Mr. Whalley stated he never saw the prisoner at Brussels, nor anywhere within the 7th July. He then mentioned the crooked finger.

THE TICHBORNE TRIAL.

THURSDAY.—The Lord Chief Justice commenced his charge to the jury to-day. He referred at length to the Stonyhurst episodes, pointing out that Roger was a lad of average intelligence, and severely censured the aspersions cast on the authorities there by the defendant's counsel, who characterised the teaching there as absolutely demoralising.

FRIDAY.—The Lord Chief Justice dwelt on the period of Roger's preparation for the army, as showing he was a different student

The Lord Chief Justice also referred to Roger's relation to the Doughty family, expressing an opinion that Lady Doughty played with him, and he observed in the matter of the Doughty estates that Roger manifested considerable intelligence. He also observed the good taste of Roger's letters, especially those relating to his cousin, and asked whether such letters on the subject nearest his heart were ever to be forgotten?

Latest Sporting.

GRAND NATIONAL.
100 to 6 on the Field (o)
GUINEAS.
7 to 1 agst Spectator (o)
DERBY.
500 to 74 agst Dukedom
LINCOLNSHIRE HANDICAP.
100 to 6 agst Aubrey | 20 to 1 agst Newry
1 — Curate | 20 — 1 — Hochstapler
100 30 — Infanta Cade | 40 — 1 — Wenlock (t)
1000 80 — Oxford Mixture †
WATERLOO CUP.
7 to 1 agst Hemming's | 11 to 1 agst Jardine's (t)
20 — 1 — Dunn's (o) | 33 — 1 — Lord Stairs (t)
500 — 15 — Cheashyre's

Latest Markets.

DONCASTER CATTLE MARKET, Jan. 31. Although our quarterly cattle fair is held on Monday, we have a fair supply of stock to-day, and trade is brisk at fully last week's quotations. We have also a fair supply of sheep, but there is little doing in these, and the pig trade continues good, and small ones maintain the lately advanced rates Stores are about the same. Pork 5s. per stone.

LONDON DEAD MEAT MARKET, Jan. 31. Good supply on view ; trade quiet, but steady at the following quotations :—Beef, 4s. 4d. to 6s. 4d. ; mutton, 5s. 8d. to 8s. 4d. ; veal, 4s. 8d. to 5s. 4d. ; large pork, 5s. 8d. to 6s. 8d. ; ditto, small, 4s. 10s. to 5s 4d.

LONDON STOCK EXCHANGE, Class 4, Jan. 31. Quiet demand for money, rates 8 to 8 per cent. Consols, 92⅜. French Rentes firm. Turks, 41. Eries firmer, and 454 on higher prices from New York. Railways flat. Canadian weaker. Telegraphs weaker.

DONCASTER CORN MARKET, Jan. 31. Our supply of wheat is much less than last week, d trade slow at former quotations. There is a good shew of and malsters not being anxious buyers. Fra ... checked. Oats dearer

LONDON STOCK EXC ... A quiet demand for mon ... with settlement ...
94½ firm ...
Nort ...

... to ... may, measures all present that if returned to Parliament, h would do his utmost to further the interests of the county. Mr. Packe was not only warmly received, but frequently applauded during the delivery of his speech. Mr. W. Barfoot, of Leicester, afterwards addressed the meeting, urging all present to support the candidature of Mr. Packe. The canvass on behalf of Mr. Packe is said to be highly satisfactory, and the votes promised are four times greater in number than was anticipated.

SOUTH LEICESTERSHIRE.

Between one and three o'clock to-day Mr. Paget visited the Corn Exchange, Leicester, where he was received by many of the agriculturists present in a manner which by tokened a feeling thoroughly friendly to his candidature. More than once the quiet and significant remark was made—"We have the Ballot, now, Mr. Paget." Mr. Pell and Mr. Heygate were also present. The feeling was evidently in favour of the popular candidate, whose own example as a landlord attests his qualification to be the true representative of the tenant farmers.

ELECTION MOVEMENTS.

UNOPPOSED RETURNS.

Sir Henry James (L)	TAUNTON.
Mr. Barclay (L)	
Mr S Holland (L)	MERIONETHSHIRE.
	WEST SURREY.
	Mr. Cubitt (C)
	Mr. Lee Steere (C)
	LINCOLNSHIRE, NORTH.
	Mr. Wynn (C)
	Mr. Astley (C)
	CHICHESTER.
	Lord Henry Lennox (C)
Mr. Holmes (L)	PAISLEY.
	OXFORD UNIVERSITY.
	Mr. Gathorne Hardy (C)
	Mr. Mowbray (C)
	NORFOLK, NORTH.
	Mr. Walpole (C)
	Mr. Lacon (C)
Dr. Lyon Playfair (L)	EDINBURGH UNIVERSITY.
	SOUTH SHIELDS.
Mr. S. Vernon (L)	
	STAFFORD (EAST).
	Mr. Allsopp (C)
Mr. Bass (L)	SUFFOLK (WEST).
	Mr. Hervey (C)
	Mr. Parker (C)

Contests are proceeding to-day at Andover, Barnstaple, Bewdley, Burnley, Chatham, Guildford, Kidderminster, King's Lynn, Maidstone, Rochester, and Tiverton.

CITY BETTING.

WATERLOO CUP.
7 to 1 agst Hemmings | 1000 to 20 Swinburne
11 to 1 — Jardines | 1000 to 20 Paterson
25 to 1 — Cheashyres | 500 to 10 Ingleston
25 to 1 — Dunns | 100 even on Pageants Boy
40 to 1 — Lawton's | winning two courses
40 to 1 — Brocklebanks (t)
LINCOLN HANDICAP.
100 to 6 — Aubrey | 25 to 1 Hoch
40 to 1 — Newry | 1000 to 2
25 to 1 — Curate | 100 to 8
30 to 1 — Oxford Mixture | 40 ...
... to 200 Even ...